C

Addison-Wesley Nitty Gritty

PROGRAMMING SERIES

C

Klaus Schröder

ADDISON-WESLEY

An imprint of Pearson Education

Boston • San Francisco • New York • Toronto • Montreal • London • Munich
Paris • Madrid • Cape Town • Sydney • Tokyo • Singapore • Mexico City

PEARSON EDUCATION LIMITED

Head Office
Edinburgh Gate, Harlow, Essex CM20 2JE
Tel: +44 (0)1279 623623 Fax: +44 (0)1279 431059

London Office
128 Long Acre, London WC2E 9AN
Tel: +44 (0)20 7447 2000 Fax: +44 (0)20 7240 5771
Websites:
www.it-minds.com   www.aw.com/cseng

First published in Great Britain 2002
© Pearson Education Limited 2002

First published in 2001 as *C Nitty-Gritty* by Addison-Wesley Verlag, Germany.

The rights of Klaus Schröder to be identified as Author of this Work have been asserted by him in accordance with the Copyright, Designs and Patents Act 1988.

Library of Congress Cataloguing Publication Data
Applied for.

British Library Cataloguing in Publication Data
A CIP catalogue record for this book can be obtained from the British Library.

ISBN 0-201-75878-4

10 9 8 7 6 5 4 3 2 1

Translated and typeset by Berlitz GlobalNET (UK) Ltd. of Luton, Bedfordshire.
Printed and bound in Great Britain by Biddles Ltd. of Guildford and King's Lynn.

The publishers' policy is to use paper manufactured from sustainable forests.

Contents

Part II – Take that!

Part III – Go ahead!

Preface

This book is a systematic introduction to C programming. It describes the ANSI standard language for C and introduces programming techniques typical of C.

Now that C has become *the* third generation programming language, the number of people interested in this language has grown accordingly. This book is designed for the following groups of readers:

1   Beginners to programming, who increasingly find themselves in the situation of having to learn C as their first programming language, during their professional training. From my own experience at work, I am very familiar with their problems and requirements and special attention will be paid to them in this book.

2   Programming freaks, who like the idea of a programming language with which you can do anything.

3   IT students, who are descending from the realms of finite automations and algorithms to the nitty-gritty of an actual programming language and want to quickly pick up the C programming language. (It is possible that they will be unable to suppress a slight yawn at the detail of the explanations in certain sections of this book.)

4   Professional programmers who know all the tricks of the trade, but have not yet really learnt C. These are the people who write programs in C by borrowing from similar-looking programs using copy and paste and are then amazed that their programs work (or not, as the case may be).

The latter, along with IT students, will mainly require the index or reference section of this book and should use this book for what it is: a practical reference work.

However, it is above all a systematically structured manual and the reader – especially the beginner to programming – is strongly recommended to work through it chapter by chapter. Having said that, you don't necessarily have to go through the whole book to get started with C programming. This is why the book is divided into three sections. The second section, which deals with advanced programming techniques, sometimes in great depth, could well be omitted on the first reading.

One of the aims of this book is to put the reader in a position to tackle the following more advanced subjects:

1   Object-oriented C++ programming
2   Windows programming
3   System programming
4   Generating Pro-C database applications

As well as providing lots of practical programming examples, at the end of almost every chapter there is a set of training exercises which the reader is recommended to work through.

The following icons are used in this book to emphasize particular points:

Tip To indicate tips and typical programming errors

Warning To indicate "Programming traps" or "Watch out!"

Obviously you cannot learn a programming language without having the opportunity to do actual programming on a computer. If you do not have a C compiler, the following advice may be useful:

→ Proud owners of the LINUX operating system automatically have the GNU C compiler (gcc).
→ The GNU C compiler is also available in a 32-bit version for MS/DOS at www.delorie.com/djgpp.
→ Borland also offers a 32-bit version of their C/C++ compiler (bcc55) for MS/DOS which can be downloaded free from www.borland.com.

Part I

Start up!

Getting started

1.1 C and the generations of programming languages

The C programming language is both a low-level and a high-level programming language (third generation language), although it is not problem-oriented.

This complex sentence requires some explanation.

The first computer programs were written in the machine language of the particular computer concerned (first generation programming language). Programs in machine language consist of sequences of instructions mostly comprising several hexadecimal digits (in the case of byte machines) or octal digits (in the case of some fixed-length computers), which can be understood directly by the computer's processor, and converted into actions.

The programmer then has to know the numeric codes for each individual operation, and the programs are difficult to read because of the cryptic columns of numbers. This difficulty created a demand for new programming languages with mnemonic instructions. These instructions have names that describe what the corresponding operation does. This gave rise to assembler languages (second generation programming languages).

This required a special conversion program, called an assembler, to convert the assembler constructions into the machine instructions for the particular computer concerned. (This conversion program itself of course first had to be written in machine language.)

It follows logically that each type of processor has to have its own assembler language, depending on the machine language of the processor concerned.

Several considerations gave rise to the need for third generation programming languages:

→ It became apparent that sequences of instructions had to be repeatedly programmed in several programs to solve a particular subtask. This gave rise to a requirement for single instructions summarizing several assembler instructions.

→ The instructions of the new languages were no longer designed to take account of the peculiarities of the particular type of processor, but to be the same for all computers. This meant that a conversion program or "compiler" had to be written for each type of processor (in the assembler language of the processor concerned, of course) to convert these universal instructions into the particular assembler language or machine language.

→ Programs were written for different domains, principally commercial and scientific/technical. The syntax and semantics of the new languages were accordingly designed to take account of a particular set of problems (problem-oriented languages).

FORTRAN and COBOL are examples of this, FORTRAN being the scientific/technical language, and COBOL being the commercially oriented language.

The two following sample instructions illustrate their problem orientation:

1 Calculating a quantum theory formula in FORTRAN:
    ```
    E=H/(2.*PI)*(0.5+1./(EXP(H*F/(K*T))-1.))
    ```

2 The following COBOL instructions speak for themselves:
    ```
    MOVE ZERO TO TOTAL
    ADD SALES TO TOTAL
    ```

The other generations of programming languages are mentioned below for the sake of completeness.

The fourth generation languages were also referred to as data-centered languages, and were principally database query languages such as SQL.

The fifth generation languages, the logical and functional languages, are used principally in the field of artificial intelligence (LISP, etc).

(Further information on the development of programming languages is to be found for example in Dworatschek [1].)

The C programming language does not fit readily into this classification. On the one hand it is a very low-level language. It enables main memory areas to be addressed at will, and permits bit manipulation of memory locations. Dworatschek [1] indicates that C permits efficient assembler programming.

On the other hand C provides all the functionality of a high-level language:

→ C is a structured language, i.e. it knows instructions that permit the construction of structured program elements such as loops and branches (see Chapter 4).

→ C is a procedural language. It strongly supports delegating parts of a problem to subroutines in the form of functions to which the arguments are passed and which then return an output value.

→ C is a modular language that permits and favors encapsulation of functions together with the data processed by the functions, in modules (program files).

(Some contemporaries go so far as to assert that all C model programs presented by Kernighan and Ritchie in their book [2] are in principle object-oriented, although the step to object-oriented programming was really only introduced with Bjarne Stroustrup's extension of the C++ language. But Axel T. Schreiner also proves in his book [3] that all the principles of OOP could already be achieved with ANSI C.)

C is not a problem-oriented language. C can be readily used for problems from the commercial or the scientific/technical world as well as for system programming. In general you could say that C can really do anything.

The historical development of C will not be repeated here. It can be found for example in Schreiner [4].

The key facts are:

→ C was invented by Dennis M. Ritchie (1973).

→ C was developed to implement the UNIX operating system on a Digital Equipment PDP-11 computer. As it developed further, C then became the in-house language of UNIX. Every UNIX version delivered will certainly contain a C compiler.

→ The C language was standardized by ISO and ANSI in 1990 (with an amendment in 1995). The representation here relates to the ANSI standard.

1.2 A first C program

This first chapter gives a non-systematic introduction to the C language, by introducing some instructions and other expressions. First comes the program with which Kernighan and Ritchie proudly introduced their baby to the world.

Here it is:

```
# include <stdio.h>
int main (void)
{
   printf ("Hello, world!\n");
   return 0;
}
```

This program displays on the screen the message: "Hello, world!". It does nothing else, which is why it is so short. (This may come as a surprise to readers familiar with COBOL!)

The commentary on these few lines takes up rather more space than the program.

The instruction: `# include <stdio.h>` is not even a C instruction! Any C compiler encountering this line would respond with error messages. The trick is that the compiler does not even get to see it. Because when the C compiler is called to compile a C program, it first calls the pre-processor to pre-process the program text. All the instructions starting with # are instructions for the pre-processor. The instruction `# include` ... links the file indicated (`stdio.h`) into the program text, and the instruction itself is eliminated. Since the `# include` instructions with which files can be included in a C program are usually located in the header of a program file, the included files are called header files. A set of header files including `stdio.h` are supplied with a C compiler, but programmers can also create their own header files. The file names are conventionally, but not necessarily, given the suffix .h.

What does `stdio.h` contain? Around 400 lines of text. Some of the lines of text are C instructions that may be of interest to the C compiler; others consist of additional pre-processor instructions. The latter may serve to replace certain expressions by other expressions. The pre-processor has no clue about the C programming language. It is a macro processor that works somewhat like a pure text processing program.

The role of the pre-processor will become increasingly important as we proceed, and Chapter 10 deals with the pre-processor in detail.

For present purposes, the file stdio.h contains important information for the compiler about `printf()`, the instruction we are proposing to use to output "Hello, world!" on the screen.

The instruction `# include <stdio.h>` is one of the most frequently used pre-processor instructions in C programs.

The expression

```
int main (void)
{
    . . . .
}
```

defines a program unit called a function in C. The term function has so far appeared as the typical C form of subroutine. As you will soon see, programming in C means writing functions.

Functions are identified by the () brackets after a function name. Function names can be chosen at will, but one function called main has to be defined in each C program. This function is not a subroutine, but the main program.

Our program contains just one function, the main() function. The expression void in the "main" brackets effectively means "empty". Instead of void, variables or "parameters", could have been defined between the brackets. Entering void in the function brackets thus means that this main() function has no parameters.

The { } brackets indicate a block, that can contain any number of C instructions. Our main() function consists of a function block of two C instructions. The first,

```
printf ("Hello, world!\n");
```

means calling a function with the name printf. The round brackets tell the compiler that a function is being called. Here a function is being called that has been defined elsewhere. More precisely, the manufacturer of the C compiler defined this and numerous other functions, and added them to the compiler as a library of standard functions. The important thing is that printf is not actually a C instruction, but an alien function whose program code has to be linked to our program.

The expression: "Hello, world!\n", in between the () brackets is passed to the printf() function as a current argument. printf() outputs to the screen the argument it receives literally, just as it is.

Our argument is enclosed in double quotes. This indicates a string constant. It is output without the quotes. The string \n represents a special expression for a character, namely the end-of-line character, moving the screen cursor down one line. Note the semicolon terminating the instruction. All instructions in C that are not followed by a { } block must be terminated by a semicolon.

The last instruction of the function block return 0; returns the integer value 0 to the caller of this main() function, and terminates execution of the function.

But who is the caller of the `main()` function, of the main program? The operating system from whose command line a user called this program.

When the program has run, it is possible to query at operating system level using `IF ERRORLEVEL` ... (in MS/DOS) or using the special expression : `$?` or other techniques (in the UNIX Bourne shell or Korn shell), which return code or exit code the program ended with. By convention, the value 0 indicates that the program run was satisfactorily. Other values greater than 0 are returned for various run-time errors. The various return codes 1, 2, 3, etc can be identified with various types of error.

0 is an integer, or in C terms an `int` constant.

Since this function returns an `int` value with `return`, the `main()` function must be defined as an int function. The compiler must already know when reading the function header which data type is returned at the end of the function, because it has to provide an area of memory for the return value.

One important point should be mentioned here. The C compiler is case sensitive. For example if you write `RETURN` instead of `return`, do not be surprised when you get error messages from the compiler.

1.3 The C compiler

Having discussed the components of the program, we now have to address the practical question of how to create such a source program made up of C instructions, to produce an executable program.

The program text must first be saved as an ASCII file using a normal text editor. Most C compilers require the file name to have the suffix .c.

The compiler must then be called indicating the source file(s). It then generates an executable program that can be called directly.

Two examples:

I. BORLAND C compiler in the MS/DOS operating system:

```
C:\> edit hello.c
      . . .
      . . .        (Create the source program and save)
      . . .
C:\> bcc hello.c
      . . .
      . . .        (C compiler run. Generates: hello.exe)
      . . .
C:\> hello    (Calls hello.exe)
Hello, world!
```

```
C:\>
```

II. C compiler in the UNIX operating system:

```
$ vi hello.c
      ...
      ...   (Create the source program and save)
      ...
$ cc hello.c
      ...
      ...   (C compiler run. Generates: a.out)
      ...
$ a.out    (Calls a.out)
Hello, world!
$
```

```
or:
```

```
$ cc hello.c -ohello
      ...
      ...   (C compiler run. Generates: hello)
      ...
$ hello    (Calls hello)
Hello, world!
$
```

(Modern C compilers such as those supplied by BORLAND or MICROSOFT also provide a graphic development environment in which a range of program development tools from the built-in program editor to the project management tool can be activated at the click of a mouse.)

Although the compiler run is fast, it includes calling a number of programs, as shown in Figure 1.1.

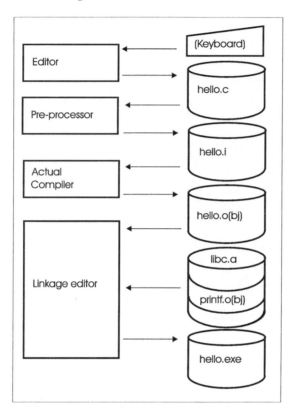

Figure 1.1 *Creating an executable program (libc.a is the name of the C standard library in UNIX)*

This is a simplified representation. Most C compilers first convert the C source code into assembler language. The assembler source program is often refined by an optimizer to make the program faster or more compact before it is passed to the assembler to generate the object file.

The linkage editor searches through the object code for unresolved references (function calls), looks for the corresponding functions in the object files presented, and if it does not find them there, it looks in the standard library or other referenced libraries. If it finds something in a library, it copies the object code of (only) this function, and links it to the object program.

After this practical excursion, let us turn to a second C program more worthy of the name program:

```c
# include <stdio.h>

int main (void)           /* sum.c */
{
    int s,                /* sum variable */
        i;                /* counter variable */
    s = 0;
    i = 1;
    while (i <= 100)      /* loop header */
    {
        s = s + i;
        i = i + 1;
    }
    printf ("sum of 1 to 100: %d\n", s);
    return 0;
}
```

Let us first concentrate on the language elements that we have not encountered before.

The expression `/* sum.c */` indicates a comment, which is ignored by the compiler. For documentation purposes you can insert comments into the program code, provided they are demarcated by `/*` and `*/`. The comments can be inserted at any point, and may run to several lines. For example the above comment could also have looked like this:

```
/* ----------------------------------- *
 *                sum.c                 *
 * ----------------------------------- */
```

The instruction: `int s, i;` defines two variables of the data type `int` (integers), one with the name s, the other with the name i. The instruction `s = 0;` ("s becomes 0"), the variable s is assigned the value 0. Likewise, the instruction `i = 1;` set i to the value 1.

Then follows a loop; this is one of three different types of loop available in C.

The loop header `while (i <= 100)` contains a comparison expression. If it is true (i.e. in this case, if the content of the variable i is less than or equal to 100) then the loop body

```
{
    s = s + i;
    i = i + 1;
}
```

is executed, shown here as a block. The first instruction s = s + i; first calculates the total of the contents of s and i, and then assigns the result of the calculation to the variable s. The effect of this is to increase the variable s by the contents of i. Likewise i = i + 1; increments the variable i by 1.

After the body of the loop has been processed, the condition in the loop header is checked again. The loop body is executed as long as i <= 100. After exactly 100 loop cycles, the variable i reaches the value 101; the loop condition is then no longer true, and the program continues with the next instruction after the loop. Accordingly, the variable s then contains the total of all the numbers from 1 to 100 (a total of 5050).

The printf() call that follows is also in a new guise; it now has two arguments: a string constant and the variable s separated by a comma.

The function printf() is a rarity amongst standard functions, permitting a variable number of arguments to be passed. This relates to an extension of the concept of a function that is not a matter of course, but is possible in C. This subject is dealt with on the website, because the technical process by which such a function is called is not at all self-evident.

First it looks as though printf() would output the string constant first, and then the content of the variable s. What actually appears on the screen is:

```
Sum of 1 to 100: 5050
```

The new line character (\n) contained in the string constant is output after the contents of s, not before; and the string %d does not appear to have been output at all. What has happened?

printf() outputs all the characters of the string constants just as they are, unless it finds the special character %. This character introduces a kind of placeholder, in this case %d, which is replaced by the next following argument (content of the variable s). Let us call this placeholder a format descriptor.

There are various printf() format descriptors for outputting a great variety of different types of data (see Chapter 2). %d (d for decimal) is used here to output an int number in decimal form.

The point to remember is that the printf() function must be passed at least one argument, and this first argument must always be a string. The string can contain several format descriptors, which are always preceded by %. For each format descriptor there has to be an additional argument that is output instead of the format descriptor.

The next example shows the same program, but in a different form:

```c
# include <stdio.h>

int sum (int, int); /*Declaration of the function: sum ()*/
                    /* In ANSI-C: called "Prototype" */

int main (void)       /* sum2.c */
{
    int s,
        i;
    s = 0;
    i = 1;
    while (i <= 100)
    {
        s = sum (s, i); /* call the function: sum () */
        i = i + 1;
    }
    printf ("sum of 1 to 100 : %d\n", s);
    return 0;
}

/* ---- Definition of the function: sum () ---- */
int sum (int sum, int inc)
{
    sum = sum + inc;
    return sum;
}
```

The instruction:

```c
int sum (int, int);
```

looks like the definition of a function with the name sum, but it is not.

If you compare this line with the definition header of the function main(), you notice some differences:

→ The function brackets are not empty (not: void).
→ Two int variables are evidently defined in the brackets, but no variable names have been assigned.
→ The whole instruction is terminated by a semicolon.

The last point is the most important. An instruction that looks like the definition header of a function, but is terminated by a semicolon, is "only" a declaration of a function `sum()`.

This declaration effectively tells the compiler that in the program a function is used that is called `sum`, is of the data type `int` (returns a value of type int), expects two arguments of the type `int` when it is called, and has to be defined somewhere.

The fact that the compiler needs to know the data type of the function was already mentioned in connection with `main()`. (It has to know what sort of memory area to reserve for the return value of the function.)

It is less evident why the compiler also needs information on the number and data type of the arguments. In fact this information was only required for a declaration when the ANSI standard for the C language was introduced. With the original standard formulated by Kernighan and Ritchie, the same declaration looked like this:

```
int sum ();      /* Declaration of the function: sum () */
                 /* after Kernighan & Ritchie          */
```

The old K&R C compiler was not interested in how many arguments the function had to be called with, or what data type the various arguments had to be. It was interested only in the data type of the return value of the function. It was therefore possible for the programmer to call functions with an incorrect number of arguments or with arguments of an incorrect data type, without the compiler noticing the error. You would only notice it when the program was run.

The ANSI C compiler therefore needs information on the arguments so it can check this function when it is called to see if the arguments received are consistent with the function definition header in terms of number and data type. An ANSI declaration, called special prototype, is nothing other than the definition header of the function, but terminated by a semicolon. It does not matter if you give the names of the arguments or not. So, the prototype of `sum` could have been:

```
int sum (int sum, int inc);
```

(Checking the arguments when a function is called arose from the much stricter security concepts of the C++ language that had already been in existence for several years when the ANSI C standard was defined.)

Another change to our program is in the loop body:

```
s = sum (s, i);     /* Call the function: sum () */
```

The function `sum()` has the task of calculating the sum of `s` and `i`: `sum()` is called, giving the variables `s` and `i` as current arguments. We can only hope that `sum()` will calculate the sum from the contents of `s` and `i`, and produce it as the return value. The return value of the function which is assigned to the expression: `sum (s, i)` is then assigned to the variable `s`.

The objection that delegating calculation of the total of two numbers to a special function is using a sledgehammer to crack a nut may well be justified. But the intention here is just to demonstrate the principle of using functions.

The actual definition of the function `sum()` follows immediately after the definition of `main()`. (Anyway, function definitions cannot be nested in C, unlike e.g. in PASCAL.)

In the definition header of the function

```
int sum (int sum, int inc)
```

the brackets have to contain variable names as well as the data types. `sum` and `inc` are the formal parameters of the function to which the current arguments `s` and `i` are passed when the function is called.

The way function parameters are passed is an important characteristic of the C language: when the function is called, two new variables `sum` and `inc` are defined, and initialized with the contents of the current arguments. In other words: `sum` or `inc` receive a copy of `s` or `i`. Whatever happens to `sum` and `inc` in the function, has no effect on the variables `s` and `i`. That is precisely why the result of the function has to be output as a return value.

This calling technique known as call by value also exists in an alternative form known as "call by reference", whose roots are in programming languages such as FORTRAN and COBOL. In that case the same variables `sum` and `inc` would just be references to `s` and `i`. Any changes made in the subroutine to `sum` and `inc` would also change `s` and `i`. (As we will see later, it is possible to construct in C something similar to call by reference (see Chapter 6).)

The function calculates the sum of `sum` and `inc` and allocates the result back to `sum`. The content of the variable `sum` is returned as the return value. The return value is the only thing left by the function after this function call (in a temporary area of memory). The variables `sum` and `inc` are created when the function is called, and cease to exist when the function terminates. But the return value is also very short lived. So it has to be assigned to a variable in the calling function (i.e. `main()`.) as soon as the function call returns. Otherwise the memory location provided for it will be used for other purposes.

To summarize the various forms in which we encounter the function `sum()`: The prototype (1) of the function has to be indicated before the first call (2) of the function. Then the definition (3) of the function can come at some later point. In principle it does not matter where the function `sum()` is defined. This is illustrated by the two following alternatives of the same program.

First alternative:

```
# include <stdio.h>

# define ENDZ 100 /* Preprocessor instructions */
# define START 1

/* ---- Definition of the function: sum () and
   also declaration!                          */

int sum (int sum, int inc)
{
   sum += inc;  /* increment operator */
   return sum;
}

int main (void)              /* sum3.c */
{
   int s,
       i;
   s = 0;

   for (i = START ; i <= ENDZ ; i++) /* for loop */
   {
      s = sum (s, i);
   }
   printf ("Sum of %d to %d : %d\n", START, ENDZ, s);
   return 0;
}
```

The main change is that the function sum() is now defined before the main()
function. The compiler does not mind what order the functions are defined in.
main() has no particular role in this either.

It is also striking that the prototype originally given for sum() has now disappe-
ared. Since sum() is defined before sum() is first called, the definition header
plays a double role, also serving to declare the function.

At the beginning of the program we encountered the new pre-processor instruction # define ENDZ 100.

This instruction defines the symbol ENDZ as the string 100. This instruction causes the pre-processor to replace the symbols ENDZ with 100 wherever they appear in the program text. When the C compiler receives the product of the pre-
processor, it finds no more ENDZ but just 100. START is likewise defined as 1.

The advantage of these symbolic define constants is evident. If you want to change the program to calculate the sum of the numbers from 43 to 298, you only need to make the following change to the text of the program:

```
# define ENDZ 298
# define START 43
```

So you do not need to look through the whole program to change the values of the start and end value of the calculation wherever they occur. You can leave that task to the pre-processor.

In the function block of sum() a new operator is used:

```
sum += inc;  /* Increment operator */
```

The effect of this operator += is the same as that of the instruction:

```
sum = sum + inc;
```

But it is executed faster, and is therefore preferable.

The situation is similar with the expression: i++ in the new for loop discussed below. In this context the expression is equivalent to : i = i + 1. (The increment operator ++ used here can also be tricky, as we will see in Chapter 3.)

This new expression is also clearly preferable to the old one. You can almost say that the instruction: i = i + 1; would be painful for a proper C programmer.

This new for loop:

```
for (i = START ; i <= ENDZ ; i++)
{
    s = sum (s, i);
}
```

could also have been written as a while loop:

```
i = START;
while (i <= ENDZ)
{
    s = sum (s, i);
    i++;
}
```

Knowing that both program extracts have exactly the same effect clarifies the action of the for loop. The for loop is described systematically in Chapter 4.

Second alternative:

```c
/* Module: sum.c */
/* ---- Definition of the function: sum ()          */

int sum (int sum, int inc)
{
    sum += inc;   /* Increment operator */
    return sum;
}



/* Module: sum4.c */
# include <stdio.h>

# define ENDZ 100 /* Preprocessor instructions */
# define START 1

/* ---- Prototype of the function: sum ()           */
int sum (int sum, int inc);

int main (void)              /* sum4.c */
{
    int s,
        i;
    s = 0;

    for (i = START ; i <= ENDZ ; i++) /* for loop */
    {
        s = sum (s, i);
    }
    printf ("Sum from %d to %d : %d\n", START, ENDZ, s);
    return 0;
}
```

Here we have distributed the definition of the functions sum() and main() to different program files (modules). Firstly this is possible in C, and secondly this facility makes modular programming possible. (There is more to this, as we will see in Chapter 8.)

For now, let us merely note that it does not matter to the C compiler over how many modules the functions of a program are distributed; the compiler only needs to know which program files constitute a program.

Here are the relevant compiler calls again:

I. BORLAND C compiler in the MS/DOS operating system:

```
C:\> bcc sum4.c sum.c
      ...
      ...        (C compiler run. Generates: sum4.exe)
      ...
C:\>
```

II. C compiler in the UNIX operating system:

```
$ cc sum4.c sum.c -osum4
      ...
      ...        (C compiler run. Generates: sum4)
      ...
$
```

One problem with modularization has to be mentioned. The actual compiler compiles each program file separately. When it compiles the file `sum4.c` it knows nothing about the contents of the file `sum.c`, and vice versa. That is why `sum4.c` again has to include a prototype of the function `sum()`, because that is where the function is called.

When the compiler has compiled all the source program files, each individually, it calls the linkage editor, passing it the object files it has generated, `sum4.o(bj)` and `sum.o(bj)`.. The linkage editor then links the object code of the functions from all the files (and the standard library if required) to make an executable program file.

So why does the file `sum4.c` contain the pre-processor instruction `# include <stdio.h>`? Because this file includes the prototypes for the standard function `printf()`, which is called in the `main()` function.

Why does this include instruction not have to appear in `sum.c`? Because `printf()` and other standard functions are not called there, or because nothing in `stdio.h` is used there.

1.5 Exercises

1 Write the program: `hello.c` discussed above. Find out about your C compiler's facilities for compiling and linking this program. Start the program. Savor the experience of reliving the birth of an inspired programming language!

2.a Change the program: `sum3.c` introduced earlier in this chapter, in such as way that the subtotals are output too. Compile and test this program.

2.b Call the pre-processor : `cpp sum3.c` and look in the results file: `sum3.i` to see what has happened to the define constants. (If the `cpp` call does not work, check in the compiler handbook for other ways of producing the result of the pre-processor run in the form of a file. (In UNIX for example, `cc -P ...`))

3 In the program file: `flist.c` create the `main()` function for a program to produce the following output to the screen:

```
Factorial calculation

  1! = 1
  2! = 2
  3! = 6
  4! = 24
   .   .   .
   .   .   .
   .   .   .
 12! = ......
```

The expression: n! ("n factorial") is a mathematical abbreviation for : 1 * 2 * 3 * ... * (n – 1) * n. The C operator "*" is used to multiply two numbers.

Select a long variable for the factorial, not an int variable. The data type `long` or `long int` means a double length int variable. A `long` constant is formulated in C as `12L` for the value 12.

`printf()` should be used for the output. `printf()` uses the format descriptor : `%ld` ("long decimal") for long data.

(If you wish, you can change the program to carry out the calculations up to 15. Are the results still correct?)

4 Write a program (program file: `fahr.c`) that calculates the °C(elsius) equivalents of all temperatures between 0°F(ahrenheit) to 300°F in steps of 20°F.

The conversion formula is:

`°C = 5.0 / 9.0 * (°F – 32.0)`

The C operator for dividing two numbers is : "/"!

Use symbolic names for the initial value (0°F), the final value (300°F) and the step increment (20°F), using a pre-processor instruction.

Example of the output:

```
    °Fahrenheit    °Celsius
    -------------------
        0           -17.8
       20            -6.7
        .             .
        .             .
        .             .
      280           137.8
      300           148.9
```

> **Tip** Note: For the variables, use the data type: `float`, because the results are not integers but decimal numbers with decimal places. Please note that they therefore use the constants 5.0 and 9.0, and not 5 and 9. (Further explanation in Chapter 2)

> **Tip** Note: When outputting the data lines with `printf()`, use the format descriptor: `%3.0f` for the Fahrenheit value, and `%5.1f` for the Celsius value. What could be the significance of the numbers 3 and 0 or 5 and 1?

If the output is not as shown above, try using the format descriptors : `%7.0f` and `%13.1f`. Is that better?

(This exercise relates to a model program in Kernighan and Ritchie's book [2]).

Data types and input/output

2.1 Variables, constants, and data types

In the instruction s = 0; s is a variable, and 0 is a constant.

A variable designates a location in the main memory where different values can be stored at different times during the program run. The above instruction saves the value 0 in the variable s. A subsequent instruction s = 13; would store the value 13 in the same variable.

Each variable has:

1   a name by which the program addresses it;

2   a defined length;

3   a defined internal format in which the value is stored.

The length and the internal format constitute what is called a data type.

All these three characteristics must be specified when defining a variable.

We defined the above variable s in the previous chapter with the instruction int s;. This specified that the variable had the name s, and the data type int (integer); this data type is automatically assigned a fixed length of 2 bytes in 16-bit operating systems and 4 bytes in 32-bit operating systems. The above declaration causes the C compiler to reserve a storage location of appropriate length for the variable s.

Constants on the other hand are constant values, as their name suggests. 0 remains 0 and 13 remains 13. The C compiler does not normally reserve a special area of memory for constants, but they are placed by the C compiler as "direct operands" in the machine instructions. One exception is string constants, which are dealt with below.

Constants also have a data type, and thus a fixed length within the machine instruction in which they occur. But they have no name.

All the data types known to the C compiler for constants and variables can basically be reduced to two forms:

1   Integer data types or fixed point numbers.

2   Decimal number data types, i.e. numbers with decimal places; also known as floating point numbers.

The following sections assume a knowledge of octal and hexadecimal number systems, and of the fundamental structure of fixed and floating point numbers. But this knowledge is only essential for understanding the bit manipulation operators in Chapter 3 and certain problems of system programming.

2.2 Constants in C

The C language has constants of the following data types:

int

These are integer constants. They comprise sequences of signed or unsigned digits.

```
13, -1094, 0
```

Their internal representation depends on the operating system, e.g. 2 bytes in MS/DOS, 4 bytes in UNIX.

The above examples use decimal digits, but you can also specify an int constant as an octal number. You then have to start with a leading 0, and can then use only the octal digits 0–7.

```
012 (= 10 decimal)
```

int constants can also be specified as hexadecimal numbers.

They have to be introduced with 0X or 0x, and may be followed by any hexadecimal digit 0-9 and A-F or a-f.

```
0xff (= 255 decimal)
```

long int or long

These are double length int constants; they differ from normal int constants in that the sequence of digits is terminated by an L or l.

```
13L, -1074l, 0L, -0x3FFFFF00L
```

Their internal representation usually consists of 4-byte fixed point numbers.

Character constants

These are really `int` constants, but are declared by a character in apostrophes rather than by a sequence of digits. Its numerical value is then equal to the ASCII code of the character indicated (or equal to the character code of another code table used by the computer concerned).

```
'A', 'm', '!'
```

An example of the internal representation of a character constant (in MS/DOS in ASCII code) is shown in Figure 2.1.

'A': | 00 | 41 | (Hexadecimal representation)

Figure 2.1 *Internal representation of character constants*

It is also possible to have character constants for characters that do not appear as keys on the keyboard.

For example, using the backslash \ followed by the octal ASCII code of the character to be represented:

```
'\7'  (beep)
'\14' (form feed character)
```

Or using backslash \x followed by the hexadecimal ASCII code of the character to be represented:

```
'\x7' (beep)
'\xC' (form feed character)
```

There are also special representations such as:

```
'\n'  (new-line character, synonymous with '\12')
'\f'  (form feed character, synonymous with '\14')
'\t'  (tabulator character, synonymous with '\11')
```

String constants

These are strings of characters appearing in quotation marks.

```
"Hieroglyphics"
```

Internal representation: each character in the string is represented in one byte by its ASCII code. A byte with the character `'\0'` (ASCII zero) is automatically appended to the end of the string (see Figure 2.2).

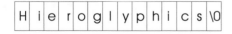

Figure 2.2 *Internal representation of a string constant*

Or in hexadecimal ASCII code representation as shown in Figure 2.3.

| 48 | 69 | 65 | 72 | 6F | 67 | 6C | 79 | 70 | 68 | 69 | 63 | 73 | 00 |

Figure 2.3 *Hexadecimal representation of a string constant*

The string constants are the only constants the compiler stores in a special area of memory known as the constants area of the data segment. In the context of a program, a string constant is represented by its starting address in the main memory, i.e. only the starting address appears after compilation by the C compiler as the operand in that machine command. The end of the string is indicated by the concluding '\0'.

All the backslash representations of the character constants can also be used in string constants:

```
"\7Error!\n"
```

The C compiler has a special syntax for dividing up long string constants into several parts. For example, if you write in a C program:

```
printf ("li"      "ne\s");
```

or:

```
printf ("li"
        "ne\s");
```

then the C compiler interprets this as:

```
printf ("line\s");
```

double

These are decimal number constants that may contain decimal places, using a decimal point (.) as separator. Powers of 10 can also be represented by the symbol E or e.

```
3.141592, 0. (= 0.0), .5, -2.7e23 (= -2.7 * 10^23),
1E5 (= 1.0 * 10^5)
```

Internal representation: usually 8-byte floating point numbers.

The following examples follow the IEEE standard, with a sign bit, and 11-bit exponent and a 52-bit mantissa:

```
3.141592:
0 10000000000
1001001000011111101011111100100010110000000001111010
```

```
-2.7e23:
1 10001001100
1100100101100101110101011010101000110101100001100110
```

float

These are usually 4-byte floating point numbers that differ in terms of syntax from `double` constants in their concluding F or f.

```
1.305f, -5.39e-12F
```

long double

These are distinguished in terms of syntax from `double` constants by a concluding L or l, and usually consist of 10-byte floating point numbers.

```
1.305L, -5.39e-12001
```

2.3 Variables in C, and their data types

The language C has variables of the following data types:

2.3.1   Integral data types (fixed point numbers)

For the length of the data types int, short, and long, the ANSI standard stipulates merely:

```
sizeof(short) = sizeof(int) < sizeof(long)
```

or:

```
sizeof(short) < sizeof(int) = sizeof(long)
```

Where `sizeof` is a C operator that determines the length (in bytes) (see Chapter 3). Thus for C compilers with the following operating systems:

operating system	sizeof(short)	sizeof(int)	sizeof(int)
16-bit (MS/DOS)	2	2	4
32-bit (UNIX)	2	4	4

Table 2.1   *The memory lengths of integer data types*

int

Signed integers

```
int value, sum = 0;
```

Internal representation as for `int` constants. The sign is stored in the most significant bit.

unsigned [int]:

unsigned int `attrib`;

The variable `attrib` can only store non-negative integers.

Internal representation as for int variables, but without a sign bit.

short [int]

Signed integers (usually 2 bytes).

unsigned short [int]

Unsigned short numbers.

long [int]

Signed integers (usually 4 bytes).

unsigned long [int]

Unsigned long numbers.

char

1-byte signed integers. These are usually used for storing single characters, but can also be used to store smaller numeric values.

```
char c = 'A';
```

or alternatively:

```
char c = 65;
```

unsigned char

Unsigned `char` variables.

Warning Both `char` and `unsigned char` are basically numeric data types that can also be used for calculation. There are no non-numeric data types in C.

```
char c = 'A';
putchar (c);          Output -----> A
c++;
putchar (c);          Output -----> B
```

(Note: `putchar (c)` outputs the content of the variable c as a character (see Section 2.5))

2.3.2 Floating point data types

float

Usually a 4-byte floating point number.

Internal representation: 1 sign bit + 8-bit exponent + 23-bit mantissa.

double

Doubles a precise floating point number, usually 8 bytes long.

Internal representation as for double constants.

long double

Usually a 10-byte floating point number with a 16-bit exponent and 63 bits for the mantissa.

To conclude this section, the characteristic dimension of the various data types are summarized in Table 2.2.

Data type	Size	Range of values
char	1 byte	-128 – +127
unsigned char		0 – 255
short [int]	2 byte	-32768 – +32767
unsigned short [int]		0 – 65535
int	2 or 4 bytes	as for short
unsigned int		or long
long [int]	4 byte	-2147483648 – +2147483647
unsigned long [int]		0 – +4294967295
float	4 byte	$3.4 * 10^{-38} - 3.4 * 10^{38}$
	8-bit exponent	
	23-bit mantissa	
double	8 byte	$1.7 * 10^{-308} - 1.7 * 10^{308}$
	11-bit exponent	
	52-bit mantissa	
long double	10 byte	$3.4 * 10^{-4932} - 1.1 * 10^{4932}$
	16-bit exponent	
	63-bit mantissa	

Table 2.2 *Sizes and value ranges of the C data types*

2.4 Input/output routines in C

To output the contents of variables of the various data types to the standard output (i.e. normally the screen), you can use the C standard function printf().

printf() is an unusual function in that you can pass it any number of arguments. The first argument must always be a string that is then output by printf().

But if this formatting string contains format descriptors, then the descriptors are replaced before output by a printable form of the next argument. To make the string printable, the argument must be converted from its internal representation into a format that can be displayed (see Figure 2.4).

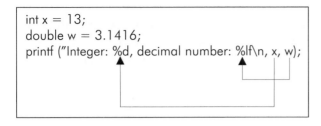

```
int x = 13;
double w = 3.1416;
printf ("Integer: %d, decimal number: %lf\n, x, w);
```

Figure 2.4 *printf(): allocation of arguments to format descriptors*

Output: `integer: 13, decimal number: 3.141600`

`printf()` starts to output its first argument, the string constant, character by character. When it reaches the format descriptor `%d`, the following occurs:

1 `printf()` accesses the next argument, the variable x;

2 interprets its contents as an int number (because of `%d`);

3 converts the fixed point number content of x to the sequence of decimal digits 13; and

4 outputs this sequence of digits instead of `%d`.

Then the following text ", `decimal number:` " is output. When the format descriptor `%lf` is reached (`lf` stands for "long float" and means "double"), `printf()` looks for the next supplementary argument, in this case the variable w. Steps 1 to 4 are repeated except that now the 8-byte floating point number content of w is converted into a sequence of digits (with a default of six decimal places).

Note that `printf()` always converts any internal data formats into strings. The content of the variable x is stored in the main memory in the form `000D` (in the case of 2-byte int numbers), whereas : 13 is displayed to the user. Everything displayed on the screen by `printf()` or other functions is a string.

The important factor when using `printf()` is that each format descriptor defines the interpretation of supplementary arguments in terms of data type. There is further information on the various format descriptors of the function `printf()` in Chapter 16.2.

In the converse operation of inputting data using the default input (normally the keyboard), the C standard library has the function `scanf()` available, a kind of twin sister of `printf()`.

Everything a user enters via the keyboard is a string.

If a numerical value is read into the int variable x, any string that is entered, e.g. "124", has to be converted into the internal fixed-point representation of x, namely 007C.

The syntax of scanf() is similar to that of printf(), with the key difference that the variables the data are to be read into have to have the operator &. The meaning of this address operator is explained in Chapter 6; at this stage you just need to know that when using scanf(), every variable to be read in has to have an &.

```
int x;
double z;
printf ("Enter an integer"
        "and a decimal number: ");
scanf ("%d%lf", &x, &z);
printf ("The following was entered: %d and %lf\n", x, z);
```

A program run could look like this:

```
Input an integer and a decimal number: 124 3.5
The following was entered: 124 and 3.500000
```

or alternatively:

```
Input an integer and a decimal number: 124
3.5
The following was entered: 124 and 3.500000
```

The user must always separate the information for the two numbers when entering them, either with a blank, a tab character, or a new line.

The function scanf() has its peculiarities. For example, a new line terminating an input is not always cleared from the keyboard buffer, which can disrupt subsequent input operations. We will therefore write some input functions in Chapter 5.

(Some C programmers take the precaution of preceding each scanf() call with the instruction fflush (stdin);, which removes any characters in the keyboard buffer.)

2.5 Input/output of single characters

The standard facility for this is getchar() and putchar(), which are usually implemented as pre-processor macros. They are also available in many UNIX C compilers as standard library function).

A getchar() call produces an input character as return value. At the end of the input (Ctrl + Z or F6 in MS/DOS, Ctrl + D in UNIX), getchar() returns EOF, which is defined as an int constant –1 in the C compilers with the pre-processor instruction # define.

In order to be compatible with this special int value, getchar() supplies all characters as int values, and not as char values, as one might expect.

putchar() accordingly also expects the output character to be an int value.

An example:

```
int c;
char ch;
c = getchar ();           <----- Input of A
if (c == EOF)
{
    printf ("End of input");
}
else
{
    ch = c;
    ch++;
    c = ch;
    putchar (c);          Output -----> B
}
```

The getchar() call delivers the input character (in this case: A) as a return value that is assigned to the int variable c. The query whether c then contains the value EOF (i.e. -1), is in this case not true, so the instructions of the else clause are executed. Assigning c to the char variable ch shortens the numerical value by the higher-order byte, but this consists only of 00. The character code of character A (namely 41) fits into the 1-byte char variable, so that no information is lost. When ch has been incremented by 1, the value 42 is stored there. That is assigned to the int variable c as 0042, and putchar() then interprets this value as character code, and outputs the corresponding character (namely B).

These operations are intended to show that the data type char is actually sufficient for inputting and outputting characters. Just the special getchar() return value EOF (the int number -1) forced getchar() to supply all the other characters as int values too. The question why we had to choose an int value as input terminator is answered in Chapter 8.

2.6 Exercises

I Create a main() function in the data file: datatype.c that displays the length of all data types. An output line could for example look like this:

```
Length of short: 2 bytes
```

Hint: use the operator: sizeof().

sizeof(datatype) or: sizeof(variable)

sizeof moreover delivers the length as unsigned int. Select the format descriptor %u for output using printf().

2 According to the theory of special relativity, a body does not have a fixed mass, but its mass grows with its speed relative to the observer. This phenomenon only becomes noticeable when the relative speed approaches the speed of light.

Calculate the "moving mass" m for a "rest mass" m0 of 1 kg at speeds close to the speed of light, and display the speed and moving mass.

The speed of light is: c = 3e8 [m/s].

Use the following sequence of speeds: 0.90 * c, 0.91 * c, 0.92 * c, ... 0.99 * c

The moving mass m is calculated from the rest mass m0 according to the formula:

m = m0 / sqrt (1 - (v / c) * (v / c))

Where v is the current speed.

The standard function: sqrt() calculates the square root. The header file : math.h must be included to use this function.

(program file: movmass.c)

A whole class of EDP problems can be solved by characterwise reading and processing. The C language provides the tools getchar() and putchar() for this purpose. (Which not every programming language can boast). The following tasks belong to this class of problem:

3 In the program file crypt.c create the main function for a program that reads in any number of characters from the standard input, and treats each character read in as follows:

1 If the character read (c) is a printable character, i.e. if the condition 32 < c < 127 is satisfied, the expression 159 - c is to be displayed on the default output as a character.

2 In any other case, the character is to be output in the same form it was read in.

This encrypts all the printable characters entered.

Test the program by inputting from the keyboard. Try entering a line of characters that has already been encoded. What happens then?

You can also arrange at operating system level for the standard input to be linked to a text file, so the program reads from a file instead of from the keyboard.

Call for a text file called letter (both MS/DOS and UNIX):

```
crypt <letter >letter.cry
```

and then:

```
type letter.cry    (MS/DOS)
```

or:

```
cat letter.cry    (UNIX)
```

What do you see if you then call: `crypt <letter.cry?`

`crypt` can also be used as a filter command – as can the following programs:

```
dir |crypt >dir.doc   (MS/DOS)
```

or:

```
ls |crypt >ls.doc    (UNIX)
```

(Tip: Make it your first job to encrypt the text file of all your love letters!)

4   Create a program (program file: `upper.c`) that reads in any number of characters from the standard input, and then displays them on the standard output, but with all lower case letters appearing in upper case.

Hint: There is a fixed distance in all code tables between lower case and upper case letters. In the ASCII code, this distance is 32.

To make the program code-independent, you can use the C expression from the following example:

```
int c = 'm';
c -= 'a' - 'A';
putchar (c);   -----> M
```

5   Create the program for the reverse process to 4. (program file: `lower.c`)

6   Create a program that reads any number of characters from the standard input and outputs the hexadecimal code for each character.

Each line should display not more than 16 character codes.

Use `printf()` for the output with the format descriptor: `%2.2X`.
(Program file: `hexdump.c`)

Test: `type letter |hexdump |more`

> **Tip** If an MS/DOS programmer thinks he or she can display a hexdump of a binary file with this program, he or she would be wrong. As soon as `getchar()` reads the character with the ASCII code 26 (of which there may be many in a binary file), it recognizes it as an end-of-input character, and terminates, although it has not finished reading the file. A solution to this problem is given in Chapter 14.

Seasoned UNIX users will never have encountered this type of problem. But they would prefer to use familiar commands such as `od -x` for such a task.

7 Create a `main()` function in the program file `cat.c`, that reads in any number of characters from the standard input (keyboard) using get-char(), and immediately outputs them using `putchar()`. The program must be terminated by entering Ctrl z or Ctrl d.

Please do not imagine this program is of no use. After all, you could use the call

`cat <ifile >ofile`

to copy the file `ifile` to the file `ofile`. DOS users could use

`cat >prn`

to start their typing machine.

The program was named after the UNIX command of the same name, which has many more capabilities than our `cat` program. We will elaborate on this cat command later, bringing it very close to the power of the UNIX command (in MS/DOS too).

8 Test the following program, and explore the effect of the various format descriptors (see Chapter 16.1).

```
# include <stdio.h>

int main (void)
{
    int l = 1234;
    printf (":%d:\n", l);
```

```
printf (":%5d:\n", 1);
printf (":%.3d:\n", 1);
printf (":%5.3d:\n", 1);
printf (":%-d:\n", 1);
printf (":%-5d:\n", 1);
printf (":%-.3d:\n", 1);
printf (":%-5.3d:\n", 1);
printf ("#%s#\n", "1234567890");
printf ("#%5s#\n", "1234567890");
printf ("#%5.5s#\n", "1234567890");
printf ("#%-5.5s#\n", "1234567890");
printf ("#%.5s#\n", "1234567890");
printf ("#%15.15s#\n", "1234567890");
printf ("#%-15.15s#\n", "1234567890");
printf ("#%.15s#\n", "1234567890");
return 0;
}
```

9 Create a program that calculates and outputs how many lottery rows have to be filled out to guarantee 6 correct numbers in one draw. The formula for this number is:

```
49! / (43! * 6!)
```

After expanding and simplifying all the numbers of the denominator, your are left with:

```
11 * 3 * 23 * 47 * 8 * 49
```

The main thing is to select the correct data type for these numbers, because the above produces an extremely large number, and the output has to be one hundred percent accurate.

Operators and expressions

3.1 Reserved words in C

The C language has very few instructions. The ANSI standard has 32:

auto	double	int	struct
break	else	long	switch
case	enum	register	typedef
char	extern	return	union
const	float	short	unsigned
continue	for	signed	void
default	goto	sizeof	volatile
do	if	static	while

sizeof is not really an instruction, but an operator. It is only included in this list because it is a reserved word in C, like the instructions.

A large number of the above instructions serve only to define variables or data types:

auto	double	int	struct
		long	
	enum	register	typedef
char	extern		union
const	float	short	unsigned
		signed	void
			volatile
		static	

This leaves the following instructions in the conventional sense:

```
break      else            switch
case

                return
           for
default    goto
do         if              while
```

The number of instructions becomes even smaller when you consider that words such as `switch`, `case`, `default` are only components of individual instructions.

Instructions are dealt with in Chapter 4.

You might think you can't program much with a language like that. Far from it!

Although C has so few instructions, it has a correspondingly large number of operators.

3.2 Operators

Table 3.1 lists all the operators in C.

Priority	Operator	Type	Grouping
1	() [] . ->	primary	from the left
2	+ - ~! * & ++ -- sizeof (type)	unary	from the right
3	* / %	binary	from the left
4	+ -	binary	from the left
5	<< >>	binary	from the left
6	< > <= >=	binary	from the left
7	==!=	binary	from the left
8	&	binary	from the left
9	^	binary	from the left
10	|	binary	from the left
11	&&	binary	from the left
12	||	binary	from the left
13	? :	ternary	from the right
14	= *= /= %= += -= <<= >>= &= ^= |=	binary	from the right
15	,	binary	from the left

Table 3.1 *Operators in C*

The priority level indicates the sequence in which operators are evaluated when an expression contains several operators.

`4 + 2 * 3` is synonymous with:

`4 + (2 * 3)` and is assigned the value:

`10`

The operator `*` (level 3) has priority over `+` (level 4).

The operator type:

→ primary: These operators have absolute priority over all others;
→ unary: These operators have only one operand;
→ binary: These operators have two operands;
→ ternary: This operator has three operands.

Some operator characters have two meanings, so they occur in two different places in Table 3.1.

`a - -b`

This expression is assigned the value:

`a - (-b)`

The unary operator: `-` in `(-b)` has only one operand, namely: `b` (minus sign, level 2). The binary operator: `-` in `a - (...)` has two operands, namely `a` and `(...)` (subtraction minus, level 4)

Grouping: indicates the sequence in which operators with the same priority level are evaluated within an expression.

In `7 * 3 % 5`, the operators `*` and `%` are both level 3, and are grouped from the left, hence: `(7 * 3) % 5`. `7 % 3 * 5` likewise becomes `(7 % 3) * 5`.

In `++*p`, the operators `++` and `*` are both level 2, and are grouped from the right, thus: `++(*p)`. `*++p` likewise becomes `*(++p)`.

Expressions in C are formed from operators and their operands.

All expressions (with the exception of untyped function calls) are assigned values when they have been evaluated. The expression `2 + 3`, for example, is assigned the value `5`.

Complicated expressions are assigned values according to the priority and grouping rules of the operators. The sequence of the individual value assignments can be changed using the parenthesis operator: `()`.

For example, `2 * 3 + 5` is assigned the value `(2 * 3) + 5` i.e. `11`, whilst `2 * (3 + 5)` returns the value: `16`.

The following example shows how far evaluation goes in C:

```
int a = 3;
a = 3 + 4;
```

```
1. Evaluation step:    (a) = (3) + (4);
   (Assigned:)           3    3    4
2. Evaluation step:    (a) = ((3) + (4));
   (Assigned:)                   7
3. Evaluation step:    (a) = ((3) + (4));
   (Assigned:)          7
4. Evaluation step:    ((a) = ((3) + (4)));
   (Assigned:)                     7
```

The fourth evaluation step means that the whole assignment expression is again assigned the value 7, even if this last evaluation value is no longer used (which it certainly could be in, e.g.:

`x = a = 3 + 4;` or in: `printf ("%d\n", a = 3 + 4);`.)

The operators (except for: `.`, `->`, `*`(unary), `&`(unary), that are introduced later) are dealt with systematically below.

3.2.1   Arithmetic operators

`*` multiplication, `/` division, `%` modulo operation (level 3)

`+` addition, `-` subtraction   (level 4)

The operands of these operators can be of any data type, with the following exceptions:

1   The modulo operator `%` must only be used for integral (integer) operands.

2   Only the operators `+` and `-` (with certain restrictions) are defined for the pointers (pointer variables) to be dealt with later.

The modulo operator `%` perhaps requires some explanation. A modulo value is the remainder from integer (!) division.

Remember your primary school lessons:

`13 / 5 = 2 remainder 3`

The remainder 3 is the modulo value. The C expression: `13 % 5` is therefore assigned the value 3.

A modulo value 0 is often of particular interest, e.g. in:

```
int year = 1997;
if (year % 4 == 0)
   printf ("%d: leap year\n", year);
else
   printf ("%d: not leap year\n", year);
```

The other four arithmetic operators correspond to the mathematical operators with the same name. It is worth mentioning here that the priority levels are consistent with the mathematical rules (multiplication before division).

A problem occurs where two operands are of different data types. For example, in: `3.5 * 2`, the type of the first operand is `double` and the type of the second operand is `int`.

In this case the int operand 2 is converted to type double: 2.0; the operation is carried out, and the result assigned the double value: 7.0.

The ANSI standard generally provides the following conversion rules where operands of different data types are to be used together:

1. Where the size differs, the smaller type is converted to the larger one.

2. An `unsigned` data type is deemed to be larger than the corresponding `signed` data type.

3. All `char` and `short` operands are always converted to `int`.

Some compiler manufacturers have their own implicit conversion rules.

Practice examples of arithmetic operators:

```
3 * 7 % 4 + 3.5     (Answer: 4.5)

3 + 2 * 4 + 2       (Answer: 13)

3 + 2 * (4 + 2)     (Answer: 15)
```

3.2.2   Relational operators

```
< (smaller)   > (greater)                              (level 6)

<= (smaller than or equal to)   >= (greater than or equal to)

== (equal to) != (not equal to)                        (level 7)
```

When comparing two operands with one of these operators, different data types may coincide. The same implicit type conversion rules apply as for the arithmetic operators.

The value assigned to such an expression is always one of the two int values:

1 (logically true)

0 (logically false)

```
3 <= 4        (assigned the value: 1 (logically true))
3 >= 4        (assigned the value: 0 (logically false))
int x;
x = 7 % 5 > 3;
printf ("%d\n", x);          Output: 0
```

Comparison expressions are generally used in branches or in loops.

```
if (7 % 5 > 3)   (evaluation: 0, logically false)
    printf ("O.K.\n");
else
    printf ("Not O.K.\n");   Output: Not O.K.
```

A common programming error is illustrated in the following program extract:

Warning
```
int x = 7;
if (x = 3)
    x = 1;
else
    x = 17;
printf ("%d\n", x);      Output: 1!!!
```

The programmer meant

```
int x = 7;
if (x == 3)
    x = 1;
else
    x = 17;
printf ("%d\n", x);      Output: 17!!!
```

Did you spot the difference? (The effect of if (x = 3) is explained in greater detail in Chapter 4).

3.2.3   Assignment operators

++ (increment) -- (decrement)   (level 2)

= (assignment)   (level 14)

+=   -=   *=   /=   %=   (assignment combinations)

<<=   >>=   &=   ^= |=

All operators in this group share the characteristic of being grouped from the right.

In the simple assignment: x = 7;, two things happen:

1   The constant 7 is assigned to the variable x, better represented as : x <-
    -- 7 (the equal sign as an assignment operator is thus unidirectional,
    and is therefore not to be confused with the mathematical equals sign.)

2   The whole expression: x = 7 evaluates to the assigned value, i.e. 7.

The characteristic indicated in point 2 enables multiple assignments, e.g.:

```
int x, y;
y = x = 5;
```

1   Evaluation step: x <--- 5
2   Evaluation step: (x = 5) is assigned the value 5
3   Evaluation step: (y <--- (x = 5), i.e. 5
4   Evaluation step: (y = 5) is assigned the value 5

The general rule is:

→ There must be a variable to the left of an =.
→ There can be any expression to the right of =.

The variable to the left of = is also referred to as an Lvalue. Now it appears that an Lvalue is just a synonym for a variable. But the key point is that an Lvalue refers to a memory location to which a value can be assigned.

So it is evident that 7 = y cannot be a valid C expression, since the contents of the variable y cannot be assigned to the constant 7. In other words, 7 is not an Lvalue. Likewise a + 3 = 7; is not valid, since a + 3 is not an Lvalue.

When we look at pointers (Chapter 6), we will meet expressions that are Lvalues. Then the true significance of the concept will become clear.

In the general expression: variable = expression variable and expression can have different data types. In contrast to expressions with arithmetic operators, the implicit type conversion rule applies here and is described below.

Whatever the data type of the value assigned to `expression`, the value is always converted to the data type of `variable` when it is assigned to `variable`.

```
double x = 3.5;
int z;
z = 3 * x;
printf ("%d\n", z);          ---> 10
printf ("%lf\n", 3 * x); ---> 10.5
x = z;
printf ("%lf\n", x);         ---> 10.0
```

Apart from the simple assignment operators, there are combinations of arithmetic and assignment operators. For example consider the operator +=:

```
int z = 3;
z += 5;                     is synonymous with: z = z + 5;
printf ("%d\n", z); output: 8
```

The variable z is thus incremented by the second operand (5).

The other operators also have a corresponding meaning:

```
z -= 5;    means: z = z - 5;
z *= 5;    means: z = z * 5;
z /= 5;    means: z = z / 5;
z %= 5;    means: z = z % 5;

z <<= 5;   means: z = z << 5;
z >>= 5;   means: z = z >> 5;
z &= 5;    means: z = z & 5;
z ^= 5;    means: z = z ^ 5;
z |= 5;    means: z = z | 5;
```

(The last group of five assignment operators contains a combination with the bit manipulation operators, which are discussed later.)

The rules given for simple assignment apply to all combined assignment operators:

I   Multiple assignments are processed from right to left, e.g.:
```
int z = 3,
y = 8;
z += y -= 2;
printf ("%d : %d\n", y, z); ---> 6 : 9
```

2   The rule is that for each assignment operator in a complex expression there must be an Lvalue (i.e. a variable) to the left of the assignment operator. The following expression is therefore invalid: z += 2 -= y;

3   Each assignment expression is linked to, one, an assignment operation and, two, an evaluation of the whole assignment expression.

The increment and decrement operator

The distinction between the operation caused by an operator, and the value assigned to the expression becomes extremely important in the case of the increment operator ++ and the decrement operator -- discussed below.

Things are quite simple to start with. In the following program extract:

```
int x = 3;
x++;
printf ("%d\n", x);      output: 4
++x;
printf ("%d\n", x);      output: 5
```

the expression: x++ means the same as x += 1. The same also applies to the expression : ++x. The increment expression therefore always increments the value by 1.

You might ask why there are two notations, x++ (postfix notation) and ++x (prefix notation). This is precisely the crux of the matter. Although the expression causes the same operation in both notations (increment by 1), these notations differ in the value assigned to the expression concerned.

The following example illustrates this:

```
int x = 3,
    z;
z = ++x;
printf ("%d - %d\n", x, z);      ---> 4 - 4
z = x++;
printf ("%d - %d\n", x, z);      ---> 5 - 4
```

This example shows that in the expression ++x:

  1 x is incremented by 1, then

  2 the expression is assigned the value of x.

In the expression x++:

  1 the expression is assigned the value of x, then

  2 x is incremented by 1.

In other words, in the postfix notation, the expression x++ is assigned the value of x before x is incremented by 1.

The same situation applies with the decrement operator -- except that the operation underlying --x or x-- consists of x -=1. The evaluation value is again distinguished in exactly the same way as with the increment operator – depending on the postfix or prefix notation.

Increment and decrement operators have an internal advantage over the operators +=1 and -=1. They are faster, which can make a significant difference to the run time of a program.

The use of the increment operator is demonstrated in the following example:

```
int x = 1;
while (x <= 5)
    printf ("%d ", x++);
printf ("\n");
output: 1 2 3 4 5
```

As popular as these two operators may be with C programmers, they do suffer from some unfortunate side effects.

What value is output by the following program extract?

```
int x = 3,
    z;
z = x++ + ++x;
printf ("%d\n", z);
```

The answer 7 can be just as right or wrong as the answer 8.

The problem is that x++ is assigned the value 3, and then it increments x to 4. But what do we mean by then? Is x already 4, when a value is assigned to the expression ++x, or does ++x have to start from the old x value 3?

The C compiler can answer this question in quite different ways. The ANSI standard sets no guideline for this question.

The practical conclusion to avoid these side-effects is the following programming rule:

Tip If a postfix operator occurs for a variable in a complex expression, this variable must not occur twice in this expression.

This prevents side-effects in the above example:

```
int x = 3,
    z;
z = x++;
```

```
z += ++x;
printf ("%d\n", z);
```

So now the output is 8.

Another important comment: x naturally has to be an Lvalue in the expression ++x or x++, since it is based on the assignment operation x=x+1. But the expression ++x or x++ is not itself a Lvalue.

The following expressions are therefore invalid:

```
x++ = 5;
++x +=3;
++x++;
```

3.2.4   Logical operators

The logical operators && (logical AND, level 11) and || (logical OR, level 12) are binary operators that assign a true value to their operands if they are not equal to 0, and a false value if they are equal to 0.

The logical operator ! (logical negation, level 2) is unary. It too assigns values to its operands using the same procedure as && and ||.

The output value of a logical operation with one of these operators is given in the following truth table (Table 3.2).

op1	op2	op1 && op2	op1 || op2	! op1
true	true	true	true	false
true	false	false	true	false
false	true	false	true	true
false	false	false	false	true

Table 3.2 *Truth table of the logical operators*

(op1 stands for operand 1, similarly op2. Both operands stand for expressions that are interpreted according to the above rule as true when a value not equal to 0 is assigned, and as false when a value equal to 0 is assigned.)

The output value is always 1, if true or 0, if false.

Although these operators are used most frequently in branches (if) or loops (while, for), they can also occur in an expression.

```
int x = 19;
printf ("%d\n", x);        output: 19
printf ("%d\n",! x);      output: 0
printf ("%d\n",!! x);     output: 1
                         (double negation)
```

(In the last instruction, please note that ! is a level 2 operator, and is therefore grouped from the right. The expression: !!x is therefore assigned the value !(!x) .)

```
int x = 19;
int y;
y = x && x < 10;   true && false: false, that is 0
printf ("%d\n", y);              output: 0
if (y)
    printf ("O.K.\n");
else
    printf ("Not O.K.\n");        output: not O.K.
int j = 1997;
while ((j % 4 || j % 100 == 0) && j % 400)
    j++;
printf ("%d: a leap year!\n", j);
                Output: 2000: A leap year!
```

> **Warning** Note that in complex logical expressions the sub-expressions are only assigned values until the complete logical result has been established. Some sub-expressions may therefore not have values assigned.

```
int x = 4,
    y = 17,
    z;
z = x > 5 && (y = 8);
printf ("%d : %d : %d\n", x, y, z);
        Output: 4 : 17 : 0
```

Note that the condition x > 5 is false (equal to 0). Since it is followed by a logical AND (&&), the overall result – false – is already known. The second sub-expression (y = 8) is therefore not evaluated, i.e. the assignment (y = 8) is not carried out, and y retains the value 17.

```
int x = 4,
    y = 17,
    z;
z = x < 5 && (y = 8);
printf ("%d : %d : %d\n", x, y, z);
        Output: 4 : 8 : 1
```

Here the condition x < 5 is true, so the && operator goes on to evaluate the second expression *(y = 8)*, since it could be false, making the whole expression false.

```
int x = 4,
    y = 17,
    z;
z = x > 5 || (y = 8);
printf ("%d : %d : %d\n", x, y, z);
        Output: 4 : 8 : 1
```

Here x > 5 is false, but the final result is still not known, because the logical OR still depends on the second expression. The valuation of the assignment yields the result 8 (true) and the expression as a whole is therefore 1 because of the operator ||.

3.2.5   Bit manipulation operators

C has operators that can access or manipulate individual bits in memory areas of an integral data type.

According to the logical operators there is the bitwise AND (&, level 8) and the bitwise OR (|, level 10).

The bitwise XOR (^, level 9) also an exclusive OR operation on individual bits, and the bit complement (~, level 2) permits inversion of all bits.

The operators shift-right (>>) and shift-left (<<, both level 5), furthermore permit whole bit patterns to be moved a particular number of bit positions right or left.

For all these operators (except for the bit complement) there are also the corresponding combinations with the assignment operator, thus:

&=, ^=, |=, >>= and <<= (level 14, grouping from the right).

In order to clarify the effect of bit operators, you have to imagine the operands of an expression consisting of memory areas of several bits, e.g. long variables consisting of 32 bits, and unsigned char variables consisting of 8 bits.

Using the old IBM convention, the individual bits are numbered from the right starting from 0, as shown for example in Figure 3.1.

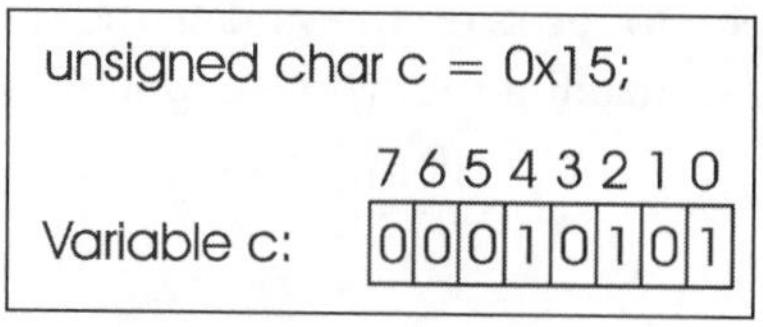

```
unsigned char c = 0x15;

                        7 6 5 4 3 2 1 0
Variable c:            |0|0|0|1|0|1|0|1|
```

Figure 3.1 *Bit numbering using the IBM convention*

The bit operators now link all the bits of both operands together in pairs; in a unary operator ~, each bit is manipulated individually.

The effect of the first four bit operators is again demonstrated in a truth table (Table 3.3):

B1	B2	B1 & B2	B1 | B2	B1 ^ B2	~ B1
1	1	1	1	0	0
1	0	0	1	1	0
0	1	0	1	1	1
0	0	0	0	0	1

Table 3.3 *Truth table of bit operators*

(B1 and B2 stand for a bit of the 1st and 2nd operator respectively.)

```
unsigned char x = 0x37,
              y = 0x2A,
              z;
z = x & y;
printf ("%X : %d\n", z, z);    Output: 22 : 34
```

For demonstration purposes, Figure 3.2 shows the two bit patterns of x and y one above the other, and then linked in pairs:

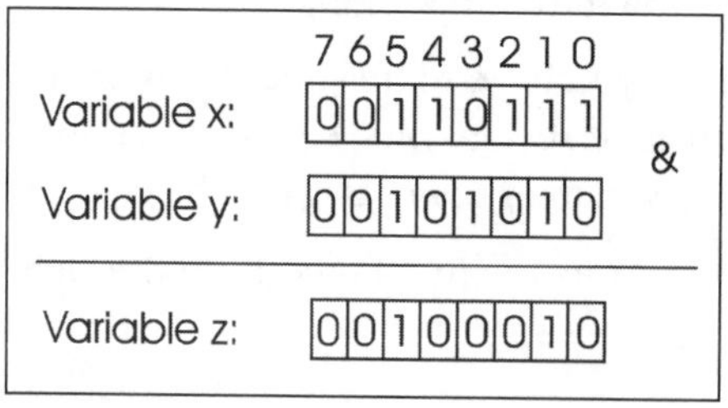

```
                     7 6 5 4 3 2 1 0
Variable x:         |0|0|1|1|0|1|1|1|
                                         &
Variable y:         |0|0|1|0|1|0|1|0|
                    ─────────────────
Variable z:         |0|0|1|0|0|0|1|0|
```

Figure 3.2 *bitwise AND (&)*

Now try verifying the following examples by recording the bit patterns:

```
unsigned char x = 0x37,
             y = 0x2A,
             z;
z = x | y;
printf ("%X : %d\n", z, z);    Output: 3F : 63


z = x ^ y;
printf ("%X : %d\n", z, z);    Output: 1D : 29


z = ~x;
printf ("%X : %d\n", z, z);    Output: C8 : 200
```

What practical application do the bit operators have?

In a word, they are used everywhere information is stored in individual bits. This occurs principally in system programming, some examples of which follow.

The simplest practical application of the bitwise operators is testing whether a particular bit is set. Bitwise AND is used for this.

In the MS/DOS operating system, there is a directory entry for each file. This entry includes the attribute byte that contains the attributes of the file bitwise coded. If the 2nd bit (or bit no. 1 using the IBM convention) is set (i.e. set to 1), then it is a hidden file.

The following example does not relate to accessing the attribute byte of a file, but testing whether it is a hidden file.

```
unsigned char attrib,
              mask = 0x2; /* Only 1 bit is set in mask   */
attrib = ...... ;         /* Here the attribute byte is */
                          /* acquired */


if (attrib & mask)
   printf ("Hidden file\s");
else
   printf ("Visible file\s");
```

If the hidden file bit is set, attrib & mask returns the value 2 – a value not equal to 0. The if condition is then true and hidden file is then output.

In the alternative case, attrib & mask returns the value 0 (false) and the output message is: Visible file.

The bit representation in Figure 3.3 relates to the case of a visible file.

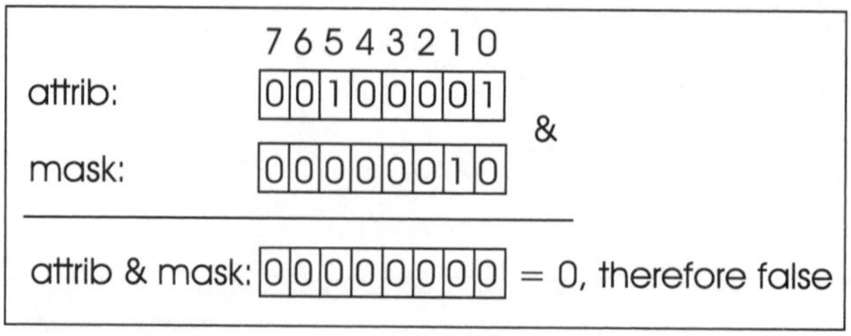

```
              7 6 5 4 3 2 1 0
attrib:      0 0 1 0 0 0 0 1
                               &
mask:        0 0 0 0 0 0 1 0
─────────────────────────────────
attrib & mask: 0 0 0 0 0 0 0 0  = 0, therefore false
```

Figure 3.3 *Test for "hidden file"*

Note: By changing the value of mask, all attributes of the file can be accessed in this way (see Table 3.4).

Mask	File attribute
0x1	Read only attribute
0x2	Hidden file
0x4	System file
0x8	Directory entry for label
0x10	Sub-directory
0x20	Archiving bit

Table 3.4 *Bit masks for MS/DOS file attributes*

The following applications use bit operators in combination with the assignment.

Clearing bits: operator &=

The read-only bit and the archiving bit in the attribute byte of an MS/DOS file are to be cleared (see Figure 3.4).

```
unsigned char attrib = 0x27,
              mask = 0xDE;
/* The bits to be cleared
   are set to 0 in this mask   */
attrib &= mask;
```

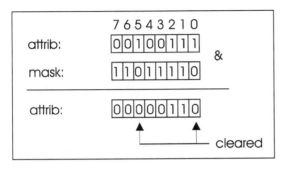

Figure 3.4 *Clearing bits*

Note that the following program extract would have achieved the same result:

```
unsigned char attrib = 0x27,
              mask = 0x21;   /* The bits to be cleared
                                are set to 1 in this mask */
attrib &= ~mask;
```

Setting bits: Operator | =

The read-only bit and the hidden bit are set in the attribute byte (see Figure 3.5).

```
unsigned char attrib = 0x20,
              mask = 0x3;
/* The bits to be set
   are set to 1 in this mask */
attrib |= mask;
```

```
              7 6 5 4 3 2 1 0
attrib:       0 0 1 0 0 0 0 0
                                 |
mask:         0 0 0 0 0 0 1 1
              _____
attrib:       0 0 1 0 0 0 1 1
                          ▲ ▲
                          └── set
```

Figure 3.5 *Setting bits*

Inverting bits: Operator ^=

The read-only bit and the hidden bit are to be cleared or set in the attribute byte, depending whether they were previously set or not (see Figure 3.6).

```
unsigned char attrib = 0x22,
               mask = 0x3;
/* The bits to be set
   are set to 1 in this mask */
attrib ^= mask;
```

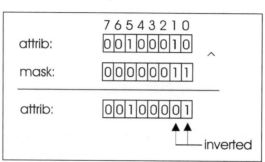

Figure 3.6 *Inverting bits*

The shift operators

In the expression: x >> n (shift right), the bit pattern of the integral variables is shifted n bit positions to the right.

If x is an unsigned data type, n zero bits are inserted from the left (logical shift); with the signed data type, n bits are inserted with the content of the signed bit (1 or 0 depending what was in the signed bit before) (arithmetic shift).

Tip With arithmetic shift right, the number's sign is retained. In both cases, the rightmost n bits are lost.

In the expression: x << n (shift left), the bit pattern of the integral variables are shifted n bit positions left.

n zeroes are inserted from the right; the n leftmost bits are lost.

x and n can be any integer expression (including a variable) whose value does not exceed the number of bits that make up x. For example:

```
short x = 0xFFA7,
      y;
unsigned short ux = 0xFFA7;
```

```
y = ux >> 4;              /* Operation 1 */
printf ("%X\n", y);       Output: OFFA


y = x >> 4;               /* Operation 2 */
printf ("%X\n", y);       Output: FFFA


x = 0x7FA7;
y = x << 8;               /* Operation 3 */
printf ("%X\n", y);       Output: A700
```

Figure 3.7 shows the bit pattern representation for operation 1 and Figure 3.8 shows the bit pattern representation for operation 2.

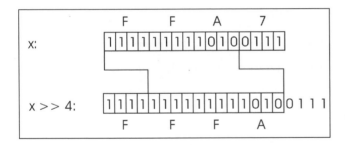

Figure 3.7 *"shift right" (unsigned)*

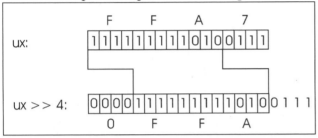

Figure 3.8 *"shift right" (signed)*

Tip In this example the sign bit contains a 1, so a 1 is inserted from the left four times.

Figure 3.9 shows operation 3:

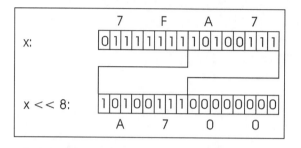

Figure 3.9 *"shift left"*

Tip The shift operation has the following mathematical meaning
→ $x >> n$ has the same effect as: x (integer)
divided by 2^n
→ $x << n$ has the same effect as: x multiplied by 2^n

3.2.6 The remaining operators

Arithmetic complement operator: – (sign minus, unary, level 2)

Can be applied to all signed data types. It reverses the sign.

```
int x = -7;              /* Application to an int
                            constant */
printf ("%d\n", -x); /* Application to an int
                            variable. Output: 7 */
```

ANSI C also introduced the operator + for a positive sign for reasons of completeness, but no one really uses it.

Conditional evaluation: (The only ternary operator, level 13)

```
condition ? expression1 : expression2
```

Effect: If the evaluation of `condition` returns logically true, then `expression1` is evaluated; otherwise `expression2`.

In a certain sense, a conditional evaluation is a short form for an (`if`/`else`) branch.

```
int x = 137,
    y;
y = x % 2 == 0 ? x / 2 : x / 2 + 1;
printf ("%d\n", y);        Output: 69

x % 2 == 0 ? (y = x / 2) : (y = x / 2 + 1);
printf ("%d\n", y);        Output: 69

printf ("%d\n", x % 2 == 0? x / 2 : x / 2 + 1);
                           Output: 69
```

Since 137 is not divisible by 2 without a remainder, the 2nd expression: x / 2 + 1 is evaluated.

Note the diversity of the application of this operator. In the first form it appears to the right of an assignment; in the second form it constitutes an instruction, containing an assignment in each of its two expressions.

In the third form the evaluated operator expression it is directly returned as an argument to the function `printf ()`!.

The brackets around the assignments in the second form are important.

The sizeof () Operator: (unary, level 2)

```
sizeof(expression)   or: sizeof expression
```

Effect: is evaluated with the memory requirement of expression in bytes (number of bytes as an unsigned int constant). expression can be any typed expression, or a data type.

The brackets can be omitted if the operand consists only of a token, and it not a data type.

```
int x = 137;
printf ("%u\n", sizeof x);          output: 2
printf ("%u\n", sizeof 15L);        output: 4
printf ("%u\n", sizeof(x * 1.5));   output: 8
printf ("%u\n", sizeof(int));       output: 2
```

(The output was in MS/DOS. In UNIX, the first and last output would have been 4).

The cast operator: (unary, level 2)

```
(type)expression
```

Effect: explicitly converts the value assigned to expression into the data type indicated by type.

```
double x = 3.5;
int y = 7,
    z;
z = (int)x * y;
printf ("%d\n", z);        output: 21
```

Note the high priority of the cast operator (level 2). First (int)x is evaluated with the int number 3. Only then is 3 multiplied by the int number 7.

```
double z = 3.26;
printf ("%.1lf\n", (double)(int)(10. *
            (z + 0.05)) / 10.);
Output: 3.3
```

Note that the cast operator that occurs here in the form of (double)(int) is grouped from the right (level 2). First:

```
(z + 0.05)                                  assigned the value
3.31, then
(10. * (z + 0.05))                          "       "  33.1   "
(int)(10. * (z + 0.05))                     "       "  33     "
(double)(int)(10. * (z + 0.05))             "       "  33.0   "
(double)(int)(10. * (z + 0.05)) / 10.       "       "  3.3
```

You may have noticed here that the expression used causes the number 3.26 to be rounded at the first decimal point. This expression also functions correctly according to the mathematical rules of rounding, e.g. in the case of the number 3.24.

(Also note that the format descriptor: %.1lf rounds itself on output. This makes the complicated rounding expression in this case superfluous. But this changes as soon as you want to save the rounded value in another double variable.)

The sequence operator: , (binary, level 15)

```
expression1, expression2
```

Effect: First expression1 is evaluated, then expression2. But the whole expression is evaluated as expression2.

In multiple applications expr 1, expr 2, ..., expr n, the whole expression is assigned the value of expr n.

It is essential to take account of this fact, especially because there are C programmers who prefer to use the sequences of expressions as a loop condition, as in the following example:

```
int x = 1,
    y = 2,
    z = 3;
while ((--x, --y, --z) > 0)
   printf ("%d, %d, %d\n", x, y, z);
printf ("After the loop: %d, %d, %d\n", x, y, z);

Output: 0, 1, 2
        -1, 0, 1
        After the loop: -2, -1, 0
```

Be aware that only the evaluation of `--z` plays any part in evaluating the loop condition.

The additional bracketing in the loop condition could even have been omitted, and the following loop header would have the same effect:

```
while (--x > 0, --y > 0, --z > 0)
```

The remaining operators: `[]`, `.`, `->`, `*`(unary) and `&`(unary) are discussed in Chapters 5 and 6.

3.3 Exercises

1 Create a `main()` function in the program file `leapy.c` that outputs all the leap years between 1900 and 2000.

> **Tip** According to the Gregorian calendar (introduced from 1583, and adopted throughout Europe in 1752) a year is a leap year if it is divisible by 4 but not by 100, or if it is divisible by 400.

2 What does the following program output?
```
int z = 12;
printf ("%d\n", z++);
printf ("%d\n", ++z);
printf ("%d\n", z++);
printf ("%d\n", z /= 5);
```

(a) First solve the problem theoretically.

(b) Is the following additional instruction valid?

```
printf ("%d\n", ++z /= 2);
```

If so, what is output? If not, why not?

(c) Make a complete `main()` function from the program extract, test the program and check your theoretical prediction.

3 Write the function `rotright()` in the program file `rotright.c`, which "rotates" a particular number of bits in a memory area, i.e. the bit pattern of the memory area is shifted right, and all the bits that are lost on the right are fed back in to the memory location from the left.

```
Arguments:   1. The memory location (unsigned int
                variable)
             2. Number of bits (int)
Return value:The shifted memory area (unsigned
int)
```

In the same program file, create a `main()` function that calls `rotright()` with sample data, and displays the results on the standard output (in hexadecimal form).

4 Create a `main()` function in the program file `numbers.c` that outputs the numbers from 1 to 100 in the following form:

```
 1   2   3   4   5   6   7   8   9  10
11  12  13  14  15  16  17  18  19  20
21  22  23  24  25  26  27  28  29  30
31  32  33  34  35  36  37  38  39  40
41  42  43  44  45  46  47  48  49  50
51  52  53  54  55  56  57  58  59  60
61  62  63  64  65  66  67  68  69  70
71  72  73  74  75  76  77  78  79  80
81  82  83  84  85  86  87  88  89  90
91  92  93  94  95  96  97  98  99 100
```

Each number should be followed either by a new-line character or by a blank, depending whether the number is divisible by 10 or not. Use conditional evaluation.

For each number use the format descriptor `%3d`.

Control instructions

Where a C program segment comprises several instructions, they are normally processed sequentially from the first to the last.

But since programming solutions often include repeating instructions (loops) or alternative execution of two or more blocks of instructions (branches), every programming language has instructions for the program to continue at another point.

The simplest instruction for changing a program run is the unconditional jump:

```
goto label
```

`label` is a jump address that forms an instruction somewhere in the program in the form of

```
label:
```

An example:

```
int i = 1,
    s = 0;
start:
if (i > 100)
    goto end
s += i++;
goto start
end:
printf ("Total: %d\n", s);
```

The program segment between the instructions `start:` and `end:` are executed one hundred times, since the instruction `goto start` continually returns the program to `start`. Only when `i > 100` does the program branch to the label `end:` and output the result.

(You will have noticed that this calculates the sum of the integers from 1 to 100.)

In the above program segment you will find a structured application of the goto instruction; the two goto instructions cause a particular section of instructions to be executed "cleanly" several times (known as a loop).

Unfortunately the goto instruction also permits wild jumps throughout the program – rightly deplored as spaghetti programming.

It would not be amiss to ignore the existence of the goto instruction in C, since there are structured alternatives discussed below. In other words, if a C programmer thinks he cannot avoid using goto, then he has written an unstructured program.

C has control instructions for all structure elements.

4.2 Control instructions in C

4.2.1 Loops

while (header controlled)

```
while (bed)
    instr
```

This syntax means:

bed: any expression to which a value can be assigned, whose value is interpreted as a logical value. (!= 0 means: true; == 0 means: false). The loop condition is a run condition.

instr: Instruction, can be:

1 void instruction (;)

2 an elemental C instruction (terminated by ;)

3 block of several instructions ({ ... })

An example of a loop with a void instruction:

```
int x = 4;
while (++x < 7)
    ;
printf ("%d\n", x);       Output: 7
```

An example of a loop with an elemental C instruction:

```
int x = 4;
while (x < 7)
    ++x;
printf ("%d\n", x);        Output: 7
```

An example of a loop with an instruction block:

```
int x = 4;
while (x < 7)
{
    ++x;
    printf ("%d:", x);       Output: 5:6:7:
}
```

An example of an endless loop::

```
while (1)
    printf ("Otto\n");
```

The program output is:

```
Otto
Otto
  . . .
```

The run condition is always 1 (true), so the program keeps on outputting Otto until you press an interrupt key.

do...while (tail controlled)

```
do
    instr
while (bed);
```

The above comment on `bed` and `instr` for the `while` loop also apply here.

Tip Be aware that the tail controlled loop in C requires a run condition, and not a termination condition like the corresponding structure chart element termination condition.

So, to implement the structure chart in Figure 4.1 in C, you have to write:

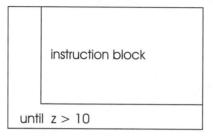

Figure 4.1 *Termination condition in a tail controlled loop*

```
do
{
    .
    . (instruction block)
    .
} while (! (z > 10) );
or:
do
{
    .
    . (instruction block)
    .
} while (z <= 10);
```

Be aware that a tail controlled do...while loop is executed at least once, whilst a header controlled while loop may not be executed at all, if the loop condition is false right from the start.

for
```
for ([init] ; [bed] ; [incr])
    instr
```

The above comment on bed and instr for the while loop also apply here.

→ init: initialization expression (any expression)
→ incr: incrementing expression (any expression)

All optional information in [] can be omitted.

Figure 4.2 shows the structure chart for this loop.

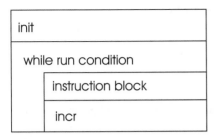

```
init
while run condition
    instruction block
    incr
```

Figure 4.2 *for loop in the structure chart*

This loop starts with a one-time evaluation of the initialization expression `init`. Then the run condition is evaluated. If it is true, the loop body is executed and the incrementing expression evaluated. Then the run condition is evaluated again, etc.

An example (a real counting loop):

```
int i;
for (i = 1 ; i <= 100 ; ++i)
    printf ("%d\n", i);
```

This loop outputs all the numbers from 1 to 100, one line each.

There are special instructions for counting loops in other programming languages as well (DO-LOOP in FORTRAN, PERFORM ... VARYING ... in COBOL).

The C variant differs in that it is not just a counting loop. Any expression is permissible for `init`, `bed`, and `incr`. The following example is by no means unusual, if inelegant:

```
int c,
    n;
for (n = 0, c = getchar () ; c!= EOF ; c = getchar ())
    n++;
printf ("%d characters read\n", n);
```

The first reading of a character from the standard input arises here in the initialization expression, as well as the assignment `n = 0`. The 2nd, 3rd, etc., character is then read in the incrementing expression. When input has been completed, the program leaves the loop and outputs how many characters have been read.

This universality of the `for` loop makes it the C programmer's favorite loop.

So the following example should come as no surprise:

```
int x = 4;
for ( ; ++x < 7 ; )
    ;
printf ("%d\n", x);        Output: 7
```

Of course, you could use a `while` loop for this, and it is indeed given as the first example in the section on `while` loops.

Not only initialization and incrementing expressions can be omitted, so can the run condition. Then the run condition is assumed to be the default value 1 (true).

The following example should also be familiar:

```
for ( ; ; )
    printf ("Otto\n");
```

4.2.2   Alternatives

if (branch)
```
 if (bed)
     instr 1
[else    ]
[   instr 2]
```

If the condition `bed` tests true, the instruction or instruction block `instr1` is executed, otherwise `instr2`.

If a jump has a void "no" branch, the `else` part can be omitted. But if the "yes" branch of a jump is void, then it must be given in the form of a void instruction, ";".

An `if-else` construct itself constitutes an instruction – as do all the other constructs described here.

`instr 1` or `instr 2` can thus each comprise a jump (or loop). This enables nested branching.

Tip A practical point based on experience: If `instr 1` or `instr 2` comprise several instructions, they must be inside braces { ... }.

The following example shows one of the commonest programming errors:

Warning
```
if (x > 0)
    y++;

    z--;

else      <--- Compiler error message
    z++;
```

The compiler error message is something like: else unexpected. What has happened? What the programmer really intended was:

```
if (x > 0)
{
    y++;
    z--;
}
else
    z++;
```

Since the braces were omitted, the compiler interpreted:

```
if (x > 0)
    y++;
```

as a jump without an else branch, since the following instruction is not else but z--;. The instruction z--; was executed after the jump, and independently of it, whether x > 0 or not. And then an else suddenly appears, but without an if.

This error is easy to spot, since the compiler identifies it. But you do not get a compiler message in the case of the following program:

```
if (x > 0)
    y++;
    z--;
printf ("%d:%d\n", y, z);
```

This is the same mistake, namely z--; does not belong to the if branch, but the compiler interprets it as an instruction coming after a conditional branch with no else clause. Indenting the instruction achieves nothing, since the compiler ignores all leading blanks. The only indication that there is something wrong with your program is that the output may be incorrect.

Can you imagine spending three days racking your brains to find the logical error in your program? You would not be the first!

We still have to deal with the problem remaining from Chapter 3. We had the following program with an error in it:

```
if (x = 3)
    x = 1;
else
    x = 17;
```

The error was the assignment: x = 3, which should have been: x == 3. The compiler might give a warning, but no error message. The instruction if (x = 3) is an entirely valid C instruction, which would be quite appropriate in certain circumstances.

What happens? First the value 3 is assigned to the variable x. The value 3 is also assigned to the expression x = 3. This evaluation value 3 is interpreted by the if instruction as logically true, because each value not equal to 0 is true for if. But in this context it means that it is always the if clause that is executed, never the else clause. If the programmer had really meant if (x = 3), then the whole branch would have been meaningless, and could quite adequately have been replaced by the instruction: x = 1;.

switch
```
switch (iexpr)
{
    case iconst 1:
        [instr]
            .
case iconst 2:
        [instr]
            .
case ....
            .
[ default:]
[      instr   ]
[      .      ]
}
```

iexpr is any integer, an expression to which a value can be assigned.

iconst1, iconst2, etc are integer constant expressions.

The effect of a switch starts with the evaluation of iexpr. The evaluation value of iexpr is then sequentially compared to see if it is equal to the case labels in-const 1, iconst 2, etc. If the comparison is true for a label, all the instructions from this label through to the end of the whole `switch` are executed. If none of the `case` labels are true, the instructions from the `default` label, if any, are executed; otherwise no instructions of the `switch` are executed. Any `default` label must come after all the `case` labels. There can be any number of instructions between two `case` labels, or none. An example:

```
int c;
c = getchar ();
switch (c)
{
    case 'A':
    case 'B':
    case 'C':
        c = c + 'a' -'A';
    default:
        putchar (c);
}
```

If a user enters the character B at a `getchar()` call, then case 'B': effectively becomes the entry label for all subsequent instructions:

1. `c = c + 'a' - 'A';` converts the character B into a lower case letter

2. `putchar (c);` outputs: b

The same thing happens when the user enters the character A or C. It is then output as: a or c respectively. But if he enters an M, only the `default` clause is executed, and M is output.

So a `switch` instruction only ever has one entry point, but it can be one of the various labels. But the exit point from the `switch` is always the end of the `switch` body, unless special instructions are used (see below).

As this last remark indicates, the `switch` instruction in this form is not quite the C equivalent of the case construct described above, because there only one case clause is executed, and not several in succession.

But you can very easily make the `switch` into a proper case construct. You just have to terminate each case clause with the instruction `break;`. In a `switch`, this instruction has the effect of jumping to after the end of the entire `switch` instruction.

switch as a genuine CASE construct

```
switch (iexpr)
{
    case iconst1:
      [instr]
```

```
            .
         break;
      case iconst2:
         [instr]

            .

         break;
      case ....

            .

            .

   [ default:]
   [     instr  ]
   [       .   ]
   [       .   ]
   }
```

For all C control structures (apart from `switch`) {} braces have to be used, if a clause or a loop body consists of more than one instruction.

When we looked at branches, we dealt in detail the source of errors that can arise from missing {} braces. The same source of errors exists with all loops. It often occurs when the number of instructions in a clause or loop body is subsequently increased from one to two, forgetting to add the {} braces that are then required.

Careful C programmers therefore enclose all clauses and loop bodies in {} braces even if they only contain one instruction. There is nothing wrong with this practice.

But if you prefer to minimize the use of {} braces, you may be interested in the following comment.

Each of the control structures shown above in turn represents just one instruction. Therefore, in the following example no {} braces are needed:

```
if (i % 2 == 0)
   for (k = 0 ; k < 10 ; ++k)
      s += k;
else
   if (i < 10)
      s = i;
   else
      do
         s += i--;
      while (i >= 10);
```

Thus, for example:

```
   for (k = 0 ; k < 10 ; ++k)
```

```
s += k;
```

represents an instruction constituting the "yes" clause of the outermost `if` instruction.

(Do not try and make sense of this program extract!)

4.3 Problems in turning structure charts into C programs

| We encountered the problem when considering tail-controlled loops: the termination condition in the structure chart has to be converted into run condition of the corresponding `do-while` loop by means of logical negation.

Suppose y, for example, is an int variable containing the number of a year. The condition for y being a leap year is then:

```
y % 4 == 0 && y % 100 || y % 400 == 0
```

But if the termination condition at the tail of a loop in the structure chart is:

```
until y is a leap year,
```

then the do-while loop must be formulated with the corresponding run condition:

```
do
{
  y++;
} while (! (y % 4 == 0 && y % 100 || y % 400 ==
0) );
```

Here the logical negation operator: `!` is used. But the inner brackets can also be removed by multiplying by `!`. But then the negation must be applied to all components of the brackets, especially to any comparison expression and any logical operator `!` `==` becomes `!=` with logical negation, `<` becomes `>=`, `<=` becomes `>`. Likewise, `&&` becomes `||`, `||` becomes `&&`, and a negation of `!` cancels itself out.

An initial conversion step could look that this:

```
do
{
  y++;
} while (! ((y % 4 == 0 && y % 100) || y % 400 ==
0) );
```

Here something else has been bracketed that did not really need to be, because && has priority over || anyway. But although this bracketing is already implied, it is necessary if && is turned into || by negation.

The second step then leads to:

```
do
{
   y++;
} while ( (y % 4!= 0 || y % 100 == 0) && y %
400!= 0 );
```

Or slightly more compactly:

```
do
{
   y++;
} while ( (y % 4 || y % 100 == 0) && y % 400 );
```

It does no harm to carry out a reality check of the condition in its final or penultimate form, after purely formal conversion.

It is best to carry out a desk test by entering, before the loop:

a) `int y = 1994;`

b) `int y = 1998;`

Do not forget that the program is to exit from the loop when y reaches a leap year, and that 1996 and 2000 are leap years.

2 A typical reading loop contains an initial read (preliminary read) before the loop, and a concluding read at the end of the loop body. Figure 4.3 shows a structure chart for characterwise reading.

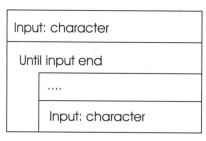

Figure 4.3 *Reading loop in the structure chart*

A corresponding C program might look like this:

```
int c;
```

```
c = getchar ();
while (c!= EOF)
{
    ...
    ...
    c = getchar ();
}
```

It is a 1:1 conversion of the structure chart. This solution is entirely correct, and there is no objection to it.

But you will find another solution in many C programs:

```
int c;
while ((c = getchar ())!= EOF)
{
    ...
    ...
}
```

Here there is only one reading point in the program. Be aware that the program runs in the same way as the first solution, but the preliminary reading and concluding reading coincide – in the loop header. That is possible in C because it permits any number of expressions to which values can be assigned to be included in the loop header in the most complex combination. But this is not possible in other conventional high-level languages such as FORTRAN or COBOL.

Be aware that the structure chart for this second solution looks exactly the same as the one above. You would not want to formulate something like Figure 4.4.

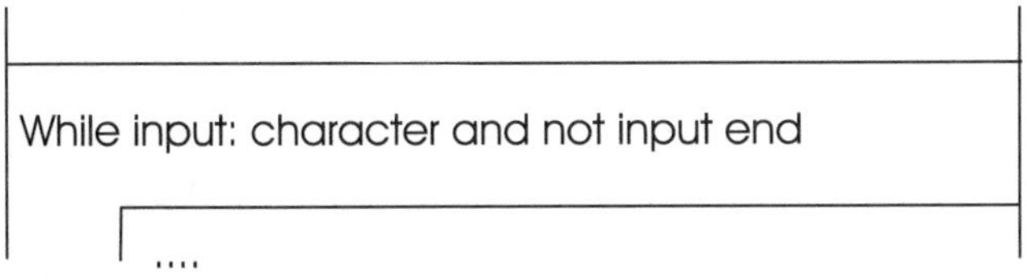

Figure 4.4 *Impossible loop condition in the structure chart*

It is not always possible for preliminary reading and concluding reading to coincide in the loop header, for example in the case of Exercise 2 in this chapter (p.79). Here the concluding reading occurs at different points in the loop body, and not always at the end. The preliminary reading therefore also has to take place before the loop.

3   In C programs you encounter many loops of the following type:

```
while (x < 100)
{
    ... (instr 1)
    if (z == 5)
        break;
    z++;
    ... (instr 2)
}
```

The instruction `break`, which was used before in the `switch`, can also be used within each of the three types of loop, and has the following effect. The loop is terminated and the program run continues immediately after the loop. A `break` instruction in an inner loop of several nested loops leaves only the inner one.

Whereas the `break` instruction in the case of the `switch` was used to construct a structured program element, namely a case construct, using `break` in a loop cannot really be called structured programming. You will not be able to draw a structure chart for the above program.

Structured programming demands that each structure element (loop / branch) has exactly one entry at the start of the element, and exactly one exit at the end of the element. But the loop shown above has two exits: one in the loop header (as it should be); and another in the branch, in the middle of the loop body.

You can try to convert it into a structured form:

```
while (z!= 5 && x < 100)
{
    ... (instr 1)
    z++;
    ... (instr 2)
}
```

The branch condition has now (in a negated form) been incorporated into the loop header. If this solution is to have the same effect as the first version, the variable z must not be changed in the remainder of the loop body (instr 1).

But let us assume precisely this case, e.g.:

```
while (x < 100)
{
    z /= 2;
    if (z == 5)
        break;
    z++;
    ... (instr 2)
}
```

then a structured solution becomes rather more complicated:

```
z /= 2;
while (z!= 5 && x < 100)
{
    z++;
    ... (instr 2)
    z /= 2;
}
```

Here not only does the loop condition become more complex, but an instruction (or in the worst case a whole group of instructions) has to be duplicated. But that was precisely the reason why Kernighan and Ritchie [2] introduced the break instruction and defended its legitimacy.

Of course it has to be said that if you develop a structured program (with a structure chart or some other structured tool) you would never use a loop with break.

But a program developed for example with pseudo code in which you find break instructions, should be treated with indulgence. A break in a loop by no means results in a spaghetti program. A break is by no means as unstructured as a goto instruction.

4   The above comments on the break instruction apply equally to the continue; instruction.

This instruction can only be used in loops. Its effect is to terminate the loop body and to start on the next iteration. For a for loop this means that as soon as the loop body has been terminated, first the incrementing expression is evaluated, and then the loop condition, etc. For example:

```
int i,
    s = 0;
for (i = 1 ; i <= 100 ; ++i)
{
```

```
    if (i % 2 == 0) /* if even ... */
        continue;      /* ... next iteration */
    s += i;
}
printf ("Sum of odd numbers: %d\n", s);
```

If the content of the variable i is even, the next iteration is initiated immediately with ++i and i <=100. So i is only summed if i is odd.

In this case (but not in every case) there is an easy transition to a fully structured solution:

```
int i,
    s = 0;
for (i = 1 ; i <= 100 ; ++i)
{
    if (i % 2)    /* if odd ... */
        s += i;   /* ... sum */
}
printf ("Sum of odd numbers: %d\n", s);
```

4.4 Exercises

1   Create a program (program file blankcut.c) that reads in any number of characters from the standard input, and then displays them on the standard output. All sequences of blanks should be output as just one blank.

Beware not to underestimate the logic of this program. Try a few sample inputs in paper, think about the procedure, and then create a structure chart.

Code the C program according to the structure chart.

2   Create a main() function in the program file morsen.c that reads in any number of characters, and outputs them in Morse code.

The only input characters, allowed are: upper-case letters, digits, blanks, tab characters, and new-line characters. The last three are to be output the same as they are input; the first two are to be output in Morse code followed by a blank.

The Morse code alphabet:

A	.-	J	.---	S	...	1	.----
B	-...	K	-.-	T	-	2	..---
C	-.-.	L	.-..	U	..-	3	...--
D	-..	M	--	V	...-	4	....-
E	.	N	-.	W	.--	5	.....
F	..-.	O	---	X	-..-	6	-....
G	--.	P	.--.	Y	-.--	7	--...
H	....	Q	--.-	Z	--..	8	---..
I	..	R	.-.	0	-----	9	----.

Use a `switch` for the individual characters.

Be aware that this is hard work. We will learn more elegant methods to create this program less laboriously (in Chapters 5 and 6).

3 What is the output from the following program extract?

```
int s,
    i;
for (i = 1, s = 0 ; i <= 10 ; ++i)
{
   if (i % 2)
      continue;
   s += i;
}
printf ("%d\n", s);
```

1 Carry out a desk test.

2 Convert the program extract into a strictly structured solution (omitting `continue`!).

Vectors/arrays 5

The exercises in Chapter 2 dealt with programs that process a stream of individual characters. A single variable was used just once to store the characters. That was possible because each character input was immediately processed (converted, output, etc.), and the variable was then immediately available for the next character.

Of course, problems arise where several values have to be stored simultaneously in different memory locations (variables). Consider, as an example, the task where a whole line of text is to be read, and then output in reverse order.

(This task could actually also be executed by defining just one int variable. See Chapter 9 on the problem of such a recursive solution).

One solution would be to define as many variables as there can be characters in a line of input, thus:

```
int c1,
    c2,
    ...
    ...;
if ((c1 = getchar ()) == '\n')
    goto end;
if ((c2 = getchar ()) == '\n')
    goto end;
    ...
end:
```

The longer a line of input can be, the more program code will be needed (apart from the ugly goto). But that is not all. At which variable does the reverse order character output start?

This problem could be solved too, but it would take at least as much space as the program part indicated above.

To solve this problem, C also provides vectors and arrays (also called tables or arrays), like other programming languages.

5.1 Vectors (one-dimensional arrays)

Vectors are data aggregates comprising several elements of one and the same data type. All the elements of the vector are associated in the memory, and each element can be addressed by an integer index, and then used like a normal variable (Lvalue).

An example of an int vector:

```
int z = 4;
int vec[5];               /* Definition with 5 int elements */
vec[0] = 13;      /* Assignment of 13 to the first element */
printf ("%d\n", vec[0]); /* Output: 13 */
vec[z] = 3;        /* Last element becomes 3   */
vec[z / 2] = vec[z] + 1; /* The third element becomes 4 */
```

The second instruction defines a vector of 5 int elements, whose elements can be addressed by integer indices, starting from 0.

Here the operator: [] (level 1) is used, which we have not yet considered.

The internal memory map then looks like Figure 5.1.

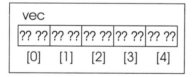

Figure 5.1 *Internal map of vec after definition*

Each element is as long an int variable. (A length of 2 bytes is assumed in the map, as is customary with C compilers in MS/DOS; in UNIX it would be 4.) The contents of the individual elements are initially undefined.

There is a simple reason why the consecutive index starts at 0 and not at 1 as in other programming languages: The index represents the distance of an element from the start of the vector, measured in int units. (This fact will play a major role in handling pointers (see Chapter 6))

In vec[0] = 13;, the value 13 is assigned to the element with a gap of 0 from the starting address of the vector, i.e. the first element. We now have the situation shown in Figure 5.2 (in hexadecimal notation).

vec

[0]	[1]	[2]	[3]	[4]
00 0D	?? ??	?? ??	?? ??	?? ??

Figure 5.2 ***Effect of vec[0] = 13;***

The contents of this element can also be output as:

```
printf ("%d\n", vec[0]);
```

Since the vector element type is `int`, the format descriptor `%d` is naturally used.

vec[z] = 3; gives the memory map shown in Figure 5.3.

vec

[0]	[1]	[2]	[3]	[4]
00 0D	?? ??	?? ??	?? ??	00 03

Figure 5.3 ***Effect of vec[z] = 3;***

This instruction demonstrates that when addressing a vector element as an index, a variable can also be used. (But this does not work with the definition instruction (see below)).

Accordingly a complex expression can be used as index:

```
vec[z / 2] = vec[z] + 1;
```

Figure 5.4 shows the value of the last element incremented by 1 being assigned to the third element.

vec

[0]	[1]	[2]	[3]	[4]
00 0D	?? ??	00 04	?? ??	00 03

Figure 5.4 ***Effect of vec[z/2]=vec[z]+1;***

This instruction again demonstrates that, wherever you can have a normal variable, a vector element can also be used.

The following instruction would also be possible (but not advisable) in C:

```
vec[5] = 24;
```

The memory map would then look like Figure 5.5.

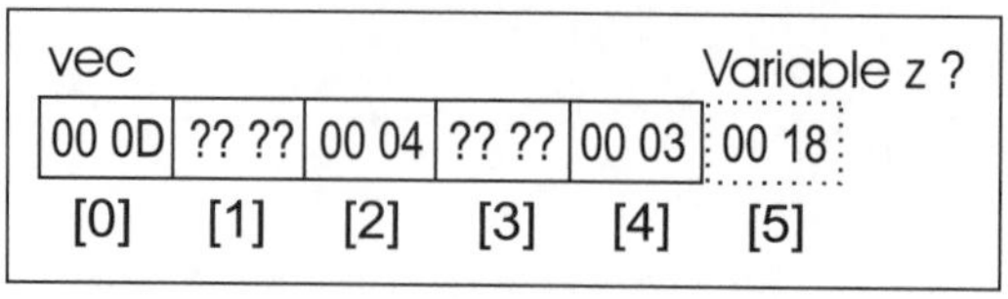

Figure 5.5 *Access to vec[5]*

This would access a memory location that does not belong to the area of memory reserved for the vector. (You would very probably overwrite the variable z, because most C compilers allocate memory for the variables in the order they are defined, from higher addresses to lower ones.)

In contrast to other programming languages in which such an impermissible access is treated as an error, in C, the programmer is responsible for staying within the limits of the defined vector.

The following unauthorized access is also possible in C:

```
vec[-1] = 11;
```

Here too (Figure 5.6), a location outside the defined memory area is accessed. (But an expression with a negative index can still be meaningful, as we will see when we discuss pointers later (Chapter 6)).

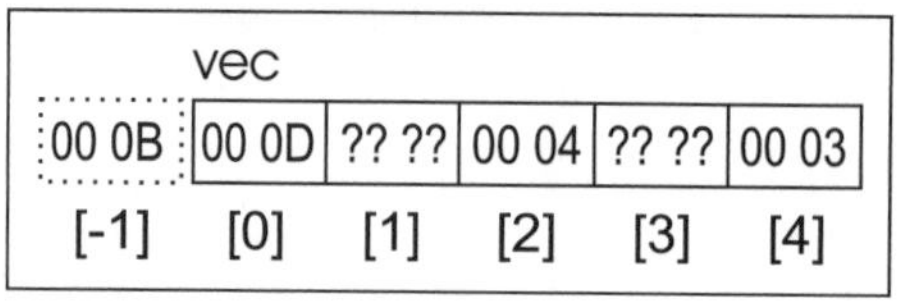

Figure 5.6 *Access to vec[-1]*

To summarize what we have learned so far about vectors:

1 A vector with the name vname and num elements of data type type is defined by:
   ```
   type vname[num];
   ```

Where:

1 vname is formed according to the C rules for variable names;

2 each elemental data type, and every self-defined data type (to be discussed later) is permitted for type;

3 the number of elements num may only consist of a positive, integer constant expression (!).

The following definition is therefore not permissible:

```
int num = 5;
int vec[num]; /* error! num must not be a variable */
```

But this is:

```
int vec[2 * 3 - 1]; /* pure constant expression */
```

  II An element of a vector defined in this way can then be used at any point in the program, in the form:
       vname[ind]

(And remember that an expression like this represents an Lvalue, i.e. it can be assigned a value).

The primary bracket operator [] is also used for this purpose, where ind is any integer expression, variable or other, but not negative.

It is precisely this last fact that now permits us to solve the problem at the beginning of this chapter, i.e. inputting a line of text and then outputting it in reverse order:

```
char line[80 + 1];
int i,
    c;
for (i = 0 ; i < 80 && (c = getchar ())!= '\n' && c!= EOF ;
++i)
    line[i] = c;
line[i] = '\0';
for (--i ; i >= 0 ; --i)
    putchar (line[i]);
putchar ('\n');
```

In this example we have a vector line of data type char, since one char element is sufficient to store one character. The fact that each character is first reach in to an int variable with getchar() is because the user could enter the end-of-input key combination and then be given EOF, the int number -1

The int variable i is used as an index to address the individual vector elements. In the first loop it runs from 0 to a maximum of 79.

The loop is terminated either when i reaches 80, or at a lower value of i if the user entered a new-line.

Each character read into c is successively stored in another element of line. A maximum of 80 characters can be read in this way and passed to the vector line.

This raises two questions:

→ What happens to the new-line character entered?

→ Why a maximum of 80 characters and not 81 (the size of the vector)?

As regards the first question, the new-line is read into c, but not stored in an element of the vector. That is useful if you want to store just the text in line, and not the end-of-line character (which is usually the case). The functions of the C standard library moreover behave differently in this question (the difference between gets() and fgets(), see p. 94).

As regards the second question, the first instruction after the loop line[i] = '\0'; assigns the string end marker '\0' to the first element after the last text character entered. We have met this character (ASCII zero) before under string constants (see Chapter 2), where it is automatically stored at the end of a string. Now that we have line with a variable length memory area, we have to mark the end of the string ourselves.

This leads to three conclusions:

I There is no data type for string variables in C . Instead, you define a sufficiently large char vector, and each character of the string is then saved in an element of this vector.

2 The beginning of the string is held in the first element of the vector (i.e. line[0]), and the end has to be marked by saving ASCII zero after the last character.

3 The size of a char vector will depend on the maximum number of characters to be stored, plus an element for the string end marker ('\0').
   (A maximum of 80 characters can thus be stored in our 81 character long vector line.)

Be aware that the string entered does not have to be 80 characters long, it can be shorter. But if the text entered is longer than 80 characters, only 80 characters will be read and stored, and the remaining characters will be held in the keyboard buffer, and can be read or discarded later.

If a user for example enters the string: "Otto", the memory profile of line looks like Figure 5.7.

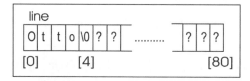

Figure 5.7 *Entering "Otto" into the vector line*

The second loop in our program outputs the individual characters starting with the last character before `'\0'`, then counts the index back down to 0 inclusive.

For the above example, this would produce the following text on the screen

```
ottO
```

The practical significance of the string end marker only really becomes clear when you output the string not in reverse order, but in its natural order. That is achieved by the following loop:

```
for (i = 0 ; line[i] != '\0' ; ++i)
   putchar (line[i]);
putchar ('\n');                     Output: Otto
```

Here, the query `'\0'` is used to output just the stored string, and not one character too many.

Note, incidentally, that `putchar()` enables a more compact form of loop:

```
for (i = 0 ; putchar (line[i]) != '\0' ; ++i)
   ;
putchar ('\n');
```

That is possible because `putchar()` not only outputs the character passed to it as an argument, but also returns it "as a return value". This formulation is not quite correct. It would be more correct to say the `putchar()` call is assigned the value of the character to be output because `putchar()` is not a function, but a macro (see Chapter 10).

But there is a difference between the two forms of loop. In the second form, `'\0'` is also output. That is inelegant at the most, but it is not really a problem, because outputting the symbol `'\0'` on the screen has no effect.

So we have seen how vectors are used in C to replace string variables. Wherever strings are processes, corresponding `char` vectors have to be defined. But do not forget that vectors are used in all possible types of problem, and so vectors can be defined in C before each data type.

Let us therefore consider a further example of sorting a `double` vector.

5.2 Sorting a vector

A simple algorithm will be used for sorting. Two neighboring numbers will be compared; if the first one is larger than the second, they will be exchanged.

To develop the program, let us write the sorting procedure for a small numerical example.

Numbers to be sorted (in the order they are stored in a vector):

	13.8	4.1	101.25	-8.9	27.4
1st Comparison:	4.1	13.8	101.25	-8.9	27.4
2nd Comparison:	4.1	13.8	101.25	-8.9	27.4
3rd Comparison:	4.1	13.8	-8.9	101.25	27.4
4th Comparison:	4.1	13.8	-8.9	27.4	|101.25

After this first sorting pass, it cannot be said that all the numbers were sorted. But it has successfully moved the largest number to the last element, where it belongs.

The second sorting pass only involves the first four elements:

	4.1	13.8	-8.9	27.4	|101.25
1st comparison:	4.1	13.8	-8.9	27.4	|101.25
2nd comparison:	4.1	-8.9	13.8	27.4	|101.25
3rd comparison:	4.1	-8.9	13.8	| 27.4	101.25

The largest of the four numbers, namely 27.4, is now in its correct place at the end, and can be excluded from subsequent sorting passes.

The third sorting pass is then:

	4.1	-8.9	13.8	| 27.4	101.25
1st comparison:	-8.9	4.1	13.8	| 27.4	101.25
2nd comparison:	-8.9	4.1	| 13.8	27.4	101.25

Now the numbers are actually correctly sorted, but only by chance, because of the numbers chosen. With another set of numbers, there would have to be a fourth sorting pass:

	-8.9	4.1	| 13.8	27.4	101.25
1st comparison:	-8.9	| 4.1	13.8	27.4	101.25

Now we have finished. All the numbers are sorted in ascending order. The result of this procedure can be recorded as follows:

```
We had 5 numbers to sort
This took 4 (= 5 - 1) sorting passes!
In the 1st sorting pass there were 4 (= 5 - 1) comparisons
In the 2nd sorting pass there were 3 (= 5 - 2) comparisons
In the 3rd sorting pass there were 2 (= 5 - 3) comparisons
In the 4th sorting pass there was 1 (= 5 - 4) comparison
```

This logic can be readily applied to n any number of numbers.

```
It takes n - 1 sorting passes to sort n elements. Sorting
pass k. includes n - k comparisons.
```

If you consider the above list of comparison operations, you notice that the whole program initially comprises one loop, namely the repetition of sorting passes.

Each sorting pass is in turn a loop, because it consists of a repetition of comparisons. The comparison itself is a branch. The structure chart for the program logic is therefore as shown in Figure 5.8.

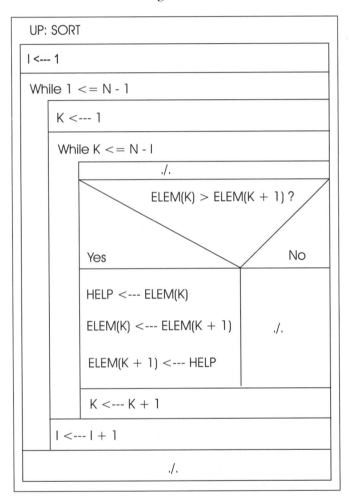

Figure 5.8 *Sorting in the structure chart*

The structure chart describes in the form of a subroutine just the pure sorting process. It could be written in C as an autonomous function called from a main program (`main()`).

ELEM(1) here designates the first vector element. When writing in C, you need to bear in mind that there it is called something like elem[0]. The loop conditions have to be adapted accordingly.

An initial version of the corresponding C program is given below, which starts by reading in any number of decimal numbers and then outputting them after sorting – extending beyond the structure chart:

```
# include <stdio.h>
# define MAX 100

int main (void)
{
   double elem[MAX]; /* numerical vector */
   double help;       /* Help variable for swapping */
   int i, /* counter for sorting passes */
       k, /* counter for comparisons */
       n; /* number of decimal numbers actually entered */
   /* -------------- Number input: -------------- */
   printf ("1st decimal number: ");
   for (i = 0 ; i < MAX && scanf ("%lf", &elem[i]) != EOF ;
++i)
       printf ("%d. decimal number: ", i + 2);

   n = i; /* save the number of numbers actually entered */
   /* ----------------- Sorting -----------------------
*/
   for (i = 0 ; i < n - 1 ; ++i) /* Sorting pass loop */
      for (k = 0 ; k < n - (i + 1) ; ++k) /* comparison loop
*/
         if (elem[k] > elem[k + 1])
         {
           help = elem[k];          /* three instructions for
*/
            elem[k] = elem[k + 1]; /* swap                  */
            elem[k + 1] = help;
         }
   /* -------------- Output of sorted numbers: ------ */
   for (i = 0 ; i < n ; ++i)
      printf ("%lf\n", elem[i]);
   return 0;
}
```

If you have difficulty with the conditions of the sorting pass loop and the comparison loop, it is advisable to carry out a dry run using this C program and the above sample data.

The sorting algorithm used here is called a "bubble sort" because each sorting pass brings the largest number to the top – like a bubble. There is a sophisticated theory of sorting algorithms, in which context the bubble sort is deemed something of a "lame duck", especially for large quantities of data. We do not need to detain ourselves here with all the various algorithms, but C provides the functions `qsort()` in its standard library enabling data to be sorted according to any criteria desired, using the quick sort algorithm, one of the fastest (see Chapter 9).

If you wish to pursue the subject of sorting algorithms, please refer to Wirth (1976) [5] and Sedgewick (1988) [6].

Two questions relating to the subject of vectors have still to be considered. How are vectors initialized with initial values, and how are vectors passed to functions as arguments?

5.3 Initializing vectors

Under the ANSI standard, any vector can be initialized with initial values when it is defined. Under the old Kernighan & Ritchie standard, that was only possible for global and static vectors (see Chapter 7).

```
int vec[5] = { 13, -4, 9 };
```

Here an `int` vector is defined with 5 elements, the first three elements of which are assigned the initial values: 13, -4 and 9. The last two elements are automatically initialized with 0. The internal memory profile is shown in Figure 5.9.

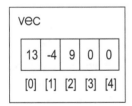

Figure 5.9 *Initializing vec*

It is not possible to initialize more elements than the vector possesses.

If all the elements of a vector are initialized, the number of elements can even be omitted from the definition. The instruction

```
int vec[] = { 13, -4, 9, 108, 25 };
```

is therefore synonymous with:

```
int vec[5] = { 13, -4, 9, 108, 25 };
```

This type of initialization, giving the initialization values enumeration in { } braces, exists for vectors of all data types. But it is only permitted in the definition itself. The following expression is therefore invalid:

```
int vec[5];
vec = { 13, -4, 9, 108, 25 };      /* invalid! */
```

If a vector is not initialized when it is defined, values can only be given by individual assignments to the individual elements of the vector:

```
int vec[5];
vec[0] = 13;
vec[1] = -4;
    . . . . .
```

An initialization for a char vector could look like this:

```
char line[] = { 'O', 't', 't', 'o', '\0' };
```

This vector contains five elements, because it is initialized with five characters. The string end marker '\0' must be specifically included.

Typing in such a definition instruction is tedious, especially if the text is fairly long. There is therefore an alternative notation in C (but only for char vectors) in which the initialization values can be specified in the form of a string constant.

The above instruction is identical to:

```
char line[] = "Otto";
```

Here too a vector is defined with five elements; the terminating '\0' is implicit in the string constant.

5.4 Passing vectors to functions as arguments

If a whole vector is to be passed to a function as an argument, the name of the vector (excluding the [] brackets) is used. In the function itself, a vector with empty [] brackets is defined for it as a parameter:

```
# include <stdio.h>
void set (int vec[], int n)
{
    int i;
    for (i = 0 ; i < n ; ++i)
```

```
         vec[i] = i + 1;
}
int main (void)
{
    int i;
    int numbers[5];
    set (numbers, 5);
    for (i = 0 ; i < 5 ; ++i)
        printf ("%d ", numbers[i]);
    putchar ('\n');
    return 0;
}
```

The output when the program runs is 1 2 3 4 5. The vector numbers is passed to vec as an argument when the function set() is called, where vec is defined as a vector without declaring the number of elements. The number of elements is also passed from numbers to n as the second argument, virtually as information on how big the transferred vector is.

In the function set(), one of the numbers 1, 2, 3, etc... is assigned to each element.

The elements of the vector are output in the main() function after return from the function set().

It would be meaningless to write:

```
void set (int vec[5], int n)
```

although the compiler would permit it. But it would ignore the information: 5!

In the list of the formal parameters of a function, a vector should only appear with empty [] brackets. There is a practical reason for that: you may wish to call the function set() with a vector with 12 or 25 elements.

It is therefore usually necessary to transfer the number of elements as the second argument.

The reader may have noticed at this point that the author cheated slightly.

We know from Chapter 1 that when an argument is passed to a function, a copy is created (call by value). The vector vec must therefore be a complete copy of the vector numbers. If I then assign values to the elements of vec, this should not assign any values to the elements of numbers.

But that is the way it is. When vectors are transferred, different techniques of argument transfer pertain than in the case of simple variables.

This mystery will be unraveled when we discuss pointers (Chapter 6). Then all these remaining questions will be answered.

Now let us deal with some useful functions as applications of vectors. Our initial problem included the sub-problem of reading a string into a `char` vector. We solved it by a characterwise input loop. When you consider how often a string has to be read in a program, it would be tedious to have to program a loop for it every time. The easiest way would be to write a function for it once, which can then be called.

There are some ready-made standard functions for this purpose, such as `gets()` and `fgets()`, as well as `scanf()`. We will look at the different effect of these functions, and come to the conclusion that it is better to write your own function for reading in a string.

Consider this example of reading in a string using `gets()` or `fgets()`:

```
char line[80 + 1];
gets (line);
...
fgets (line, 81, stdin);
```

The function `gets()` receives the vector `line` as an argument, and reads an input string into it. A newline is not saved, but replaced by a `'\0'`. So the string is properly terminated.

The function `fgets()` operates in a similar manner. But it expects three arguments. The first argument is the vector to be read to, and the second one is the information as to how big the vector is.

The third, `stdin`, stands for standard input; this relates to the fact that `fgets()` can also read lines from files (see Chapter 14). The symbol `stdin` is defined in the header file `stdio.h`, which therefore has to be included. In contrast to `gets()`, `fgets()` stores new-line characters in the vector and adds a `'\0'` at the end.

The advantages and disadvantages of both functions are evident: `gets()` is very simple to call. It is usually quite convenient that it does not save the new-line character, since only the string itself is actually of interest.

The big disadvantage is that it cannot know the size of vectors it receives. A user does not have to know how big the vector is, and if too many characters are inputted, the string is relentlessly stored beyond the end of the vector. So you would only use `gets()` if you were sure that the vector received is big enough for all likely user inputs. (hope for the best!).

`fgets()` rectifies this defect, and therefore seems ideal. But in most cases it is inconvenient that the new-line is stored in the vector. For example, if you read in several individual strings with several `fgets()` calls, and they are then to be output in one line, this creates problems that it takes some effort to solve.

It is therefore advisable (and for a C programmer it is a quite reasonable solution) to write your own function. Slightly adapting a suggestion of Kernighan & Ritchie [2], let us call this function `getline()`. Here it is:

```
/*------------------- getline.c -----------------*/
# include <stdio.h>
int getline (char s[], int lim)
{
    int i,
        c;
/* character-wise reading. Terminate when
   limit of char vector exceeded, on input of
   <Ctrl>Z or <Return>                    */
    for (i = 0 ; i < lim - 1 && (c = getchar())!= EOF
         && c!= '\n' ; ++i)
      s[i] = c;
    s[i] = '\0'; /* terminate string with
                    ASCII ZERO    */
    fflush (stdin); /* clear the keyboard buffer */
    if (i==0 && c==EOF) /* if EOF 1st character
                          entered ....... */
      i = EOF;            /* Return value: EOF */
    return i; /* otherwise return value: number of
                characters read  */
}
/*--------------------------------------------------*/
```

This function receives the vector and its size as an argument.

We have already used the for loop that reads characterwise into the vector elements. We have just added the EOF query. An input line can thus be terminated either with Ctrl z (MS/DOS) or Ctrl d (UNIX). But input is also terminated when the end of the vector is reached, which is the shortcoming of the gets() function.

But the new-line character is not stored in the vector either, avoiding the shortcoming of the fgets() function.

The string is also cleanly terminated with '\0'. The function call fflush (stdin); clears the keyboard buffer. So if a user enters more characters than fit into the vector, the superfluous characters are rejected.

In other words, if you omitted the instruction fflush (stdin);, the superfluous characters would remain in the keyboard buffer and be read by the next getline() call. You can choose what you want. Our solution is likely to be more suitable for most string input problems.

The last remark relates to the return value. A `getline()` call returns the number of characters entered as the return value. It is always a number greater than or equal to 0. It is == 0, if the user only enters newline. If the input consists only of Ctrl z (MS/DOS) or Ctrl d (UNIX), then the return value is `EOF` (== -1), a value less than 0.

It is important to again note at this point that the `getline()` function has two effects:

1 It stores an incoming string in the vector passed as a parameter.
2 It returns the information: how many characters were entered. The function accordingly has the data type int.

The return value of the `getline()` function can be used to control loops. A `main()` function can accordingly contain:

```
char line[80 + 1];
while (getline (line, 81) >= 0)
    . . . .
```

The loop only terminates when the user enters Ctrl z or Ctrl d. Empty lines (just newline) do not terminate the loop.

The following example is different:

```
char line[80 + 1];
while (getline (line, 81) > 0)
    . . . .
```

The loop is terminated the first time a blank line is entered.

The return value from `getline()` can also be used for a test loop:

```
char name[20];
int n;
...
printf ("Name: ");
while ((n = getline (name, 20)) <= 0)
{
    switch (n)
    {
        case 0:
            fprintf (stderr,
                    "A name must be entered!\n");
            fprintf (stderr,
                    "Repeat the input!\n");
            break;
        default:
            fprintf (stderr, "program termination!\n");
```

```
        exit (1);
    }
    printf ("Name: ");
}
....
```

The case clause 0 deals with the case that only newline is entered; then only the value −1 is left for the default clause, i.e. entering Ctrl z or Ctrl d., or EOF.

The error messages are output not with `printf()`, but with `fprintf(stderr, ...)`. The standard function `fprintf()` is more general than `printf()`; it can implement formatted outputs to any files. `stderr` is defined again in `stdio.h`, as the "file": standard error output. If a program is started whilst redirecting the standard output to a file, the standard error output is still linked to the screen. The error messages output with `fprintf(stderr, ...)` can therefore be seen on the screen, and attract the attention of the user, even if all "normal" outputs should disappear to the standard output in a file. (In UNIX you can also redirect the standard error output to a file, apart from the standard output.)

You should get into the habit of always sending error messages to `stderr`.

The system call: `exit()` terminates a program (in UNIX: terminates a process).

So the above test loop is only terminated when the user takes the trouble to enter a name, or has entered an EOF to indicate that he or she does not want to use the program any more.

As we have seen, the function `getline()` is quite serviceable for the day-to-day work of a C programmer, just like `printf()` and other standard functions. But in contrast to the standard functions, the program code of `getline()` must be linked to every program that calls `getline()`. If you do not want to do that every time, you have to do two things:

1   The translated object code of `getline()` has to be transferred to a private function library.

2   The C compiler (more precisely the linkage editor) must be trained to look in this private library for unresolved references, and not just in the standard library. Chapter 8 looks at how this is done.

To illustrate another application for (char) vectors, let us write a function for converting strings of digits into the `int` numbers that the strings of digits represent. If the problem is not evident, consider that:

```
printf ("%d\n", 13);
```

converts and outputs the internal representation of the `int` number 13 into a string of digits.

Whereas the int constant is represented in memory by 00 0D, the memory map of the string of digits is : 31 33 (ASCII code). Conversely, in the case of:

```
int n;
scanf ("%d", &n);
```

the user enters an integer in the form of individual digits that are converted by scanf() into an int number, and must be stored in n as such.

It is precisely this last operation that is to be achieved by a function, as the following example shows:

```
char s[] = "-27";
int n;
n = asctoint (s);
++n;
printf ("%s\n", n);       Output: -26
```

(In this case the string of digits is terminated by a '\0', which we wish to assume for this task.)

The function asctoint() could be written as follows:

```
int asctoint (char s[])
{
    inz z = 0,    /* sum field for the
                     int number to be returned */
        f = 1,    /* Factor for a sign */
        i;        /* counter */
    /* loop for skipping leading
       "whitespace characters"  */
    for (i = 0 ; s[i] == ' ' || s[i] == '\t' ; ++i)
        ;
    /* if sign minus .... */
    if (s[i] == '-')
    {
        f = -1;   /* correct factor */
        i++;      /* skip sign */
    }
    /* as long as digits occur ....  */
    for ( ; s[i] >= '0' && s[i] <= '9' ; ++i)
        z = 10 * z + (s[i] - '0');
    return f * z; /* return int number */
}
```

The function asctoint() should still work when the string of digits starts with leading blanks or tab characters. There can be a minus sign, which is then held as the factor –1; otherwise `f = 1` as per initialization. The conditions of the digit loop assumes that the numeric characters from '0' to '9' for a coherent area in the computer's internal code table, which is the case with ASCII and EBCDIC code.

The loop body requires explanation. The expression `s[i] - '0'` represents the numerical value of the digit stored in `s[i]`. Consider for example the digit '4' to illustrate this (see Figure 5.10).

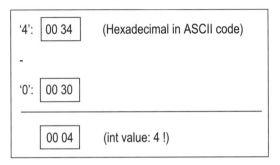

Figure 5.10 *Converting a digit into its value*

The expression `z = 10 * z + (s[i] - '0');` adds this value to ten times what was previously stored in `z`. Do not forget the numerical significance of the individual digits.

It is best to carry out a hand run, e.g. for the following call: `asctoint ("-2149")`.

f	i	s[i]	s[i] – '0'	z
1				0
-1	0	'0'		0
	1	'2'	2	2
	2	'1'	1	21
	3	'4'	4	214
	4	'9'	9	2149
	5	'\0'		

Table 5.1 *Dry run for asctoint("-2149");*

The return value is: (-1) * 2149 = –2149

The loop terminates when it encounters '\0', because it is not a digit.

The loop terminates whenever it encounters any character in a string that is not a digit. This means that no blanks are permitted between the digits, since this would abort the conversion.

So the following result will come as no surprise:

```
printf ("%d\n", asctoint ("12 34"));      Output: 12
printf ("%d\n", asctoint ("1 000"));      Output: 1
printf ("%d\n", asctoint ("-14E37"));     Output: -14
```

In contrast to the function `getline()`, you do not need to create `asctoint()` and add it to your private library. It already exists as a standard function, and as such has the name `atoi()`. Its prototype is to be found in the header file `std-lib.h`, which should therefore be incorporated.

A similar standard function, namely `atof()`, converts sequences of digits into `double` numbers, for example

```
# include <stdio.h>
# include <stdlib.h>

....
char ds[] = "-3.5";
printf ("%lf\n", atof (ds) + 1.0);      Output: -2.500000
```

Since this function has the data type `double`, it is essential to incorporate `std-lib.h`, since the compiler will otherwise assume it is an `int` function when the function is called. It will then only provide an `int` memory location for the return value, returning a false result for `atof()`. This also causes programmers to spend hours looking for a logical error in their program causing incorrect number outputs, until they notice that `# include <stdlib.h>` has been omitted.

The program code of the function `atof()` is described in Kernighan & Ritchie [2].

With the two standard functions `atoi()` and `atof()`, we are in a position to write two further useful functions to read in an integer or a decimal number from the standard input.

```
# include <stdlib.h>
int get_int (void) /* read in an integer */
{
   char s[20];
   getline (s, 20);
   return atoi (s);
}
```

```
# include <stdlib.h>
double get_double (void) /* read in a decimal number */
{
    char s[50];
    getline (s, 50);
    return atof (s);
}
```

Of course you can also use scanf() for this (see Chapter 2 on typical scanf problems.)

The functions get_int() and get_double() are two further candidates for a private function library.

And now another application for char vectors that is also available in similar form as a standard function:

```
void strcpy (char s[], char t[])
{
    int i;
    for (i = 0 ; (s[i] = t[i]) != '\0' ; ++i)
    ;
}
```

Short as this function is, it carries out a frequently used string operation. It copies its second argument (the char vector t) into the first argument (the char vector s). It does this characterwise, by assignment. It is important to recognize that the '\0' terminating t is also copied to s, and the loop is only then terminated.

The function has the data type void, because it returns no return value. (This distinguishes it from the standard function of the same name).

5.5 Multidimensional arrays

A multidimensional array is a data aggregate consisting of associated elements of the same data type that can be accessed using 2, 3, 4, ... indices.

The vectors considered above thus represent a special case of arrays, namely one-dimensional arrays.

Two-dimensional arrays are now considered as an example, known by their mathematical name of matrices. (This leads on logically to the processing of higher dimensional arrays.)

The following instruction defines a matrix with 2 x 3 = 6 int elements:

```
int matrix[2][3];
```

The compiler finds the `[]` operator twice in this instruction. This operator is level 1, and is grouped from the left if it occurs more than once.

The compiler therefore first reads: `matrix[2]`, and observes that: `matrix` is first a vector with 2 elements. Then it reads the brackets `[3]` and interprets as follows: Each of the two elements of the vector `matrix` is in turn a vector of 3 `int` elements. (The keyword `int` is read first, but determines the data type of each individual element when the expression as a whole is evaluated.)

The internal memory map of this matrix could therefore be drawn as in Figure 5.11,

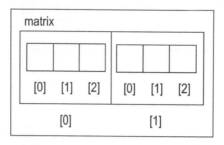

Figure 5.11 *Memory map of matrix*

or as in Figure 5.12.

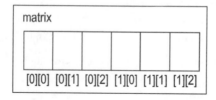

Figure 5.12 *Linear memory map of matrix*

(For the sake of simplicity, the individual bytes of an `int` element have been omitted here.)

When you define a matrix, another representation often suggests itself, a two-dimensional representation. Nobody can prevent you depicting the above matrix accordingly (see Figure 5.13).

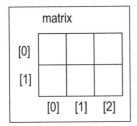

Figure 5.13 *Two-dimensional map of matrix*

The only important thing is:

1 The natural sequence of the elements is as in the first map.

2 Each element of the matrix must be addressed indicating 2 indices.

Such a matrix could be mapped with `int` values by the following program extract:

```
int matrix[2][3];
int i,
    k,
    z = 0;
for (i = 0 ; i < 2 ; ++i)
   for (k = 0 ; k < 3 ; ++k)
      matrix[i][k] = ++z;
```

Satisfy yourself that the contents of the matrix are as shown in Figure 5.14,

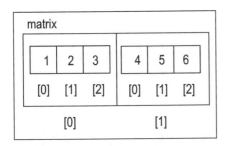

Figure 5.14 *Map of the elements of matrix*

or the contents of Figure 5.15...

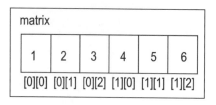

Figure 5.15 *Linear map*

or Figure 5.16

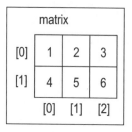

Figure 5.16 *Two-dimensional map*

and that the following program extract:

```
for (k = 0 ; k < 3 ; ++k)
   for (i = 0 ; i < 2 ; ++i)
      printf ("%d:", matrix[i][k]);
```

generates the following output:

```
1:4:2:5:3:6:
```

The traveling salesman is commonly used to illustrate the use of matrices. To store the monthly sales of the 17 salesmen of a company over a year, you would define:

```
float sales[17][12];
```

Where the first index represents one salesman, and the second a month of the year.

But employers of salesmen are not the only people with an interest in multidimensional arrays. They are of much greater interest in the field of mathematics and physics. If a mathematician wishes to convert a matrix into an inverse, transposed, adjunct or some other form, he requires suitable subroutines (or "C functions"). And function libraries of this type are in fact available.

But we do not want to stray into the realms of higher mathematics; we just need to know how a matrix is passed to a function, the question we considered with vectors.

Simple. As with vectors, by indicating the simple name of the matrix. But here too, additional information must be provided on the size of the matrix.

Let us write our function set() again, but this time for matrices; then the following call be located in a main() function:

```
int matrix[2][3];
set (matrix, 2);
```

The function itself could be defined thus:

```
void set (int m[][3], int n)
{
    int i,
        k,
        z = 0;
    for (i = 0 ; i < n ; ++i)
        for (k = 0 ; k < 3 ; ++k)
            m[i][k] = ++z;
}
```

This definition header is somewhat unexpected. You might have expected a function header like:

```
void set (int m[][], int n, int m)  /* invalid! */
```

But that sort of thing is not permitted in C. This is basically because a matrix is a vector of vectors, and the function has to know what sort of a vector or what size of vectors it is dealing with. We will return to this when we have become familiar with pointers.

The following rule should be noted:

→ If a matrix is passed to a function, then the first [] bracket must stay empty when the matrix concerned is defined in the function header; the second matrix should have the same number as the transferred one. The dimensioning of the first [] bracket must be passed to the function as an additional argument.

The general rule for an n-dimensional array is:

→ If an array is passed to a function, then the first [] bracket must remain empty when the corresponding array is defined in the function header; thereafter they should have the same number as the transferred array. The dimensioning of the first [] bracket must be passed to the function as an additional argument.

We still have to discuss initializing a matrix. For example:

```
int matrix[2][3] = { { 13, -4, 195 }, { 25, 37, 2 } };
```

In other words, the initialization list of a matrix consists of an enumeration in { } of initialization lists for the individual vectors making up the matrix.

The initialization list of a 3-dimensional, 4-dimensional, etc arrays would appear progressively nested in this way.

In the case of a matrix of data type `char`, the alternative string notation would look like this:

```
char menu[][20] =
    {
        "Input",
        "Output",
        "End of program"
    };
```

Be aware that if the matrix is initialized immediately, the first [] bracket can remain empty at definition too, as in the case of vectors. The compiler deduces from the number of initialization strings that the following matrix is to be defined:

```
char menu[3][20];
```

This example is very popular in dialog programs where a menu of program services is to be displayed. Its only disadvantage is that it can take up a lot of memory if the menu item strings are of different length.

In the next chapter we will see how you can solve the same problem more economically and more elegantly.

5.6 Exercises

I   Given the following program:

```
# include <stdio.h>
int main (void)
{
    int vec[] = { 98, 13, 24, -20, 18 };
    int tab[5];
    int i;
    tab[0] = 3;
    tab[1] = 1;
```

```
    tab[2] = 4;
    tab[3] = 2;
    tab[4] = 0;
    for (i = 0 ; i < 5 ; ++i)
        printf ("%d\n", vec[tab[i]]);
    return 0;
}
```

What is the output?

2   Can the standard function `strcpy()` that copies the content of a char
    vector to another one, be transferred to copying a double vector to
    another one just by changing the data type char to double?
    If so, write the function (name: `doubcpy()`) and test it by appropriate
    calls from a `main()` function.
    If not, why not? What changes need to be made?

3   Write the C function `stringlen()` to which a char vector is passed,
    and which returns the length of the string stored in the vector as return
    value. This length is defined as the number of characters before the
    `'\0'`.

Tip This function also exists as a standard function called `strlen()`, prototype in the header
file `string.h`.

---

4   Jon Bentley [7], in his very clever book *Programming Pearls*, describes
    how a programmer asked him for help in sorting a maximum of 27000
    positive integers in main memory as quickly as possible. The largest of
    the numbers was just 27000. None of the numbers could occur more
    than once. The main problem was that the memory available was not suf-
    ficient to accommodate a vector of 27000 unsigned int elements, but
    could accommodate a vector with 27000 / 8 = 3375 elements.

    Bentley suggested the following solution: Define a vector of 3375
    unsigned-char elements.

    Read in all the numbers, and store each one using the following
    procedure: The 3375 unsigned-char elements consist of 3375 * 8
    = 27000 bits. All these bits should initially be set to 0. If the num-
    ber to be stored is now, for example, 1034, then the 1034th bit is
    set to 1, etc. When all the numbers have been stored in this way,
    there is in each vector a bit pattern in which the bit position of
    every bit set to 1 represents a number. Now all you need to do is

access all the bit positions, see whether the corresponding bit is set to 1, and if so output the bit position as a number.

This must be the fastest sorting algorithm of all time.

Hint: Define an unsigned char vector with 3375 elements, globally. The definition instruction of the vector is outside each function, preferably at the beginning of the program file.

This has two advantages:

1   All the functions of the program file can access this vector without it having to be defined inside the functions, or having to be passed to the function as an argument.

2   Global data are automatically initialized with 0, i.e. all the bits of the vector are also initially set to 0. (There is further information on global variables in Chapter 7).

Write a function set() to which the number to be stored is passed. In the function, ensure that the bit corresponding to the number is set to 1 (with bit operators, see Chapter 3).

Write a function out() that passes an index to the vector that checks for all the 8 bits of this vector element whether it is set, and outputs the bit position as a number if it is.

Write a main() function that reads in a positive integer as often as required (with scanf() or get_int ()), and stores each individual number with set().

Then use a counting loop to pass all 3375 indices of the vector to the function out().

Pointers

6.1 Simple pointers

Now let us address the question alluded to several times in the last chapter. What are pointers? The answer is basically quite simple:

Pointers are variables in which the memory addresses of other variables can be stored.

Let us explore the question by first examining the memory addresses of variables and other Lvalues. The basic fact to bear in mind is that each program has to be loaded into the computer's main memory to be executed.

The main memory can be conceived as a long strip of memory locations (bytes in the case of byte computers), sequentially numbered from 0 through to the end, like house numbers in a street.

(This ignores the peculiarities of the MS/DOS operating system that operates segmented addressing internally to take account of the architecture of the INTEL processor. For present purposes, we are assuming linear addressing.)

C has the unary operator & (level 2) that determines the starting address of an Lvalue in the memory. We have already met this operator in Chapter 2 with the standard function `scanf()`.

Here is a small demonstration of how to display the contents and addresses of some variables on the screen:

```
int x = 13;
double z = 3.5;
char s[] = "Text";
printf ("Address and contents of x: %p: %d\n", &x, x);
printf ("Address and contents of z: %p: %lf\n", &z, z);
printf ("Address and contents of s: %p: %s\n", &s[0], s);
```

The program run (in MS/DOS) produces:

```
Address and contents of x: FFF4: 13
Address and contents of z: FFEC: 3.500000
Address and contents of s: FFE6: Text
```

(If the %p format descriptor of the printf() function used here to output addresses is not known to your C compiler, you can use %X instead.)

The expression &x is evaluated with the starting address of the variable x. Since int variables are 2 bytes long in MS/DOS, the variable x therefore uses the two bytes with the addresses FFF4 and FFF5.

The variable z likewise uses the 8 bytes of FFEC through FFF3 inclusive, and the vector s uses the 5 (!) bytes from FFE6 through FFEA inclusive.

The address operator & thus initially tells us what we need to know, by telling us the whereabouts in the memory of the variables we have defined.

But the program run reveals two things:

If you compare the starting addresses of the variables with the sequence in which the variables were defined, you see that the variables are evidently allocated memory addresses ranging from higher to lower. This technique is used in many C compilers and operating systems, but not necessarily in all.

Between the memory occupied by the vector s and the variable z there is (at the address FFEB) a "slack byte" that cannot be used by a variable. It results from the compiler placing every variable at the start of a machine word (in MS/DOS = 16 bits = 2 bytes). This word alignment facilitates processor access to the main memory areas. But you do not need to know these internal addressing rules to use addresses and pointers in C.

Now let us meet our first pointer variable:

```
int z = 13;
int .* ip;
ip = &z;
```

Whereas z is a normal int variable containing 13, ip is a pointer variable. ip is set to have the data type int * (in words, "pointer to int").

Since pointer variables are there to store addresses, ip = &z; assigns the starting address of the variable z to the pointer ip. The memory map in Figure 6.1 illustrates the relationship.

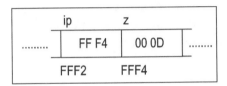

Figure 6.1   *Memory map of ip and z*

The variable z begins at the starting address FFF4 in the main memory, and contains the numerical value D (decimal: 13) in hexadecimal notation.

The pointer variable ip happens to start here at the address FFF2, and contains FFF4, the starting address of z. You can also say: "ip "points to z". (Hence the name pointer.) This relationship can be illustrated as in Figure 6.2.

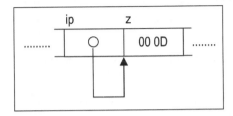

Figure 6.2   *Typical pointer representation*

The advantage of this is that you do not have to keep working out specific memory addresses.

But remember that the pointer ip and the variable z to which ip points do not necessarily have to be together in the memory, as this representation might suggest. Figure 6.3 represents the situation more accurately.

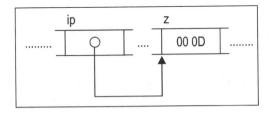

Figure 6.3   *ip points to z*

The only important thing is that ip contains the starting address of z, regardless of where the variable z is stored relative to ip.

The immediate question then is the use of pointers. We will not get a completely satisfactory answer to this question until the end of this chapter. But we can now see how the pointer `ip` can be used to access the contents of the variable z:

```
int z = 13;
int * ip;
ip = &z;
printf ("Address of z: %p\n", &z);      ---> FFF4
printf ("Address of z: %p\n", ip);      ---> FFF4
printf ("Contents of z: %d\n", z);      ---> 13
printf ("Contents of z: %d\n", *ip);    ---> 13
```

The expression `*ip` in the last instruction contains the unary operator `*` (level 2) that arose in the pointer definition (`int * ip;`).

The expression `*ip` in this last instruction is interpreted as follows: In the main memory go to the address contained in `ip`, and evaluate the memory contents from this address onwards as an int value (because `ip` is a pointer to int).

The unary operator `*` is called the reference operator because it refers to the content at an address .

Thus it is clear that the expression `*ip` is assigned the same value as the expression z, because both relate to the contents of the same memory location.

But `ip` first has to be set to the starting address of z. The following example demonstrates that `ip` can point to different int variables in succession:

```
int z = 13,
    y = 24;
int * ip;
ip = &z;
printf ("Contents of z: %d\n", z);      ---> 13
printf ("Contents of z: %d\n", *ip);    ---> 13
ip = &y;
printf ("Contents of y: %d\n", y);      ---> 24
printf ("Contents of y: %d\n", *ip);    ---> 24
```

When `ip` has been set to the starting address of y, `*ip` naturally refers to the content of y.

At this point we need to return to the definition of our pointer `ip`. How is the expression `int * ip;` to be interpreted? `int z;` is straightforward: z is a variable of the data type int. So now we could say that in `int (* ip);` the data type of the variable `ip` is such as its contents (application of the reference operator) returns an int value. This means that: `ip` is a pointer to an int variable. The actual or notional bracket in the expression `int (* ip);` unfortunately does not fully express the evaluation actually carried out by the compiler. More correct would be the grouping `(int *) ip;` and we will meet the expression `(int *)` frequently as a data type pointer to `int`.

This is not just splitting hairs. C beginners typically have great difficulty with two program extracts that have the same effect:

```
int z = 13;
int * ip;
ip = &z;
printf ("%d\n", *ip)
```

and:

```
int z = 13;
int * ip = &z;
printf ("%d\n", *ip)
```

We have met the first extract before; in the second extract, `ip` is defined as a pointer to `int`, and is immediately initialized with the starting address of `z`. But note that `ip` (data type `(int *)`) is initialized with `&z`, not with `* ip`. And that would be wrong, because only the pointer variable itself can be initialized with an address. In other words it has to be either:

```
int * ip = &z; (as in the second program extract)
```

or

```
int * ip;
ip = &z;          (as in the first program extract).
```

Another problem that frequently gives rise to run-time errors with C beginners (and even professionals) is this:

```
int z = 13;
int * ip;
*ip = 24;
```

The further course of the program can bring some surprising results, at least in MS/DOS. A program like this will very probably abort in UNIX, and produce the alarming error message: `Bus error, core dumped`. What has happened?

The instruction `*ip = 24;` has assigned the value 24 to the `int` memory location to which `ip` points. But which `int` memory location does `ip` point to? Although `ip` was defined as a pointer to `int`, nowhere was the starting address of an `int` variable initialized. The pointer variable `ip` contains a random value (perhaps the contents of a variable from an earlier program run.)

The instruction `*ip = 24;` then stores the value 24 in this random address. In UNIX, this address could be outside the address space assigned to the process, which prompts the UNIX kernel to terminate the process. MS/DOS does not offer this security, and you could overwrite an important memory area of the operating system or your own program, which could have disastrous results.

Hence the following important programming rule:

Every pointer must be assigned the starting address of a defined memory location before the reference operator can be applied to this pointer.

So far we have only considered a pointer to int. But in C you can define pointers to all possible data types, including self-defined data types (see Chapter 11). A few examples:

```
short sx = 17;
long lx = 134L;
unsigned char uc = 0x41;
short * sp = &sx;
long * lp = &lx;
unsigned char * ucp = &uc;
printf ("%d\n", * sp);   ---> 17
printf ("%ld\n", * lp);  ---> 134
printf ("%u\n", * ucp);  ---> 65 (decimal form of 0x41)
```

6.2 Pointers and vectors. Pointer arithmetic

You might ask why C does not just have a data type pointer instead of pointers to int, pointers to long, ... etc.? After all, all pointers are the same length, big enough to contain a memory address.

We already have one answer to this question. The expression (*pointer) accesses the contents of the memory location, and we have to define whether the memory location to be accessed is int, long ... etc..

But having different data type pointers also has consequences for another operation, pointer arithmetic. Pointer arithmetic is explored below in connection with vectors, which will solve some puzzles relating to vectors.

Let us take the following example:

```
int tab[5] = { 13, 4, 128, 97, -9 };
int * ip = &tab[0];
```

Here an int vector tab is defined with five elements, all of which have to be initialized immediately. Also an int pointer that is initialized with the starting address of the first vector element of tab.

First of all an abbreviated way of writing the expression; instead of:

```
int * ip = &tab[0];
```

you can write:

```
int * ip = tab;
```

The actual name of a vector (excluding the index operator [ ]) is identical to the starting address of the first element of the vector.

The memory map can be represented as in Figure 6.4.

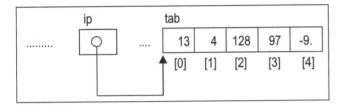

Figure 6.4 *ip points to tab*

(The contents are not shown in hexadecimal, for the sake of simplicity.)

We have generalized by again assuming that `ip` and `tab` do not have to be adjacent in the memory, although they probably are. But it is now essential that all five elements of the vector `tab` are contiguous in the memory. Because that is how a vector is defined – a contiguous memory area of similar elements.

The instruction `printf ("%d\n", *ip);` outputs the number 13, because `ip` points to the starting address of the first element, and `*ip` accesses the contents of the first element.

Calculation operations are now permitted to a limited degree for the pointer variable `ip`, e.g.:

```
++ip;
```

Based on our knowledge of the increment operator, this means that the contents of `ip` are incremented "by 1"; the question is just "by 1 what?". The contents of `ip` is an address, so you might assume that the address is incremented by 1 byte. Unfortunately that is wrong. Here the data type to which the pointer points comes into effect: Since `ip` is a pointer to `int`, `++ip` means that the contents are incremented by the length of an `int` unit. If `ip` was a pointer to double, `++ip` would mean increasing the stored address by the length of a `double` value.

With the initialization given, our operation `++ip;` gives rise to the relationships shown in Figure 6.5.

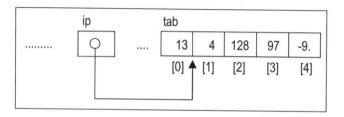

Figure 6.5 *ip after the first incrementation*

ip now points to the second element of the vector tab, and with the instruction printf ("%d\n", *ip); would output the value 4. But if we had instead carried out the operation ip += 3;, the result would be as shown in Figure 6.6.

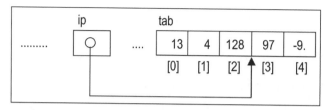

Figure 6.6 *ip after the second change*

One begins to appreciate the important connection between a vector or a particular data type, and a pointer to the same data type. With a pointer you can successively work through all elements of a vector, just by incrementing the contents of the pointer.

But you do not need to increment the pointer permanently; simple, temporary expressions can of course also be formed without changing the pointer variable itself, as in the following example:

```
int tab[5] = { 13, 4, 128, 97, -9 };
int * ip = tab;
printf ("%d\n", tab[1]);        ---> 4
printf ("%d\n", *(ip + 1));     ---> 4
printf ("%d\n", tab[3]);        ---> 97
printf ("%d\n", *(ip + 3));     ---> 97
```

In the second printf() call, (ip + 1) refers to the address of the second element, and the expression *(ip + 1) refers to the contents of this element.

As you can see, and as the program run demonstrates, *(ip + 1) is evaluated with the same memory location as tab[1]. The same applies to the expressions *(ip + 3) and tab[3]. The same number appears in both expressions, and so the same vector element is evaluated.

This analogy between pointer expressions and indexed vector expressions goes much further than one might suppose.

Consider the expression `tab[3]`. The first part of the expression, namely `tab`, represents a short form of the starting address of the vector, as we now know. The question is what is the actual data type of the expression `tab`, or the identical expression `&tab[0]`? Since it represents the starting address of an `int` memory location, it has the same data type as the variable to which it could be assigned, pointer to `int` (`int *`). But if the expression `tab` has the data type (`int *`), then the following expression:

```
tab + 3
```

has to be evaluated with an address 3 `int` units after the starting address of the vector, and

```
*(tab + 3)
```

has to be evaluated with the contents of the memory location.

So we can see that there are good reasons for using the pointer expression `*(tab + 3)` instead of `tab[3]`, although `tab` is not a pointer variable, but a vector name. This clearly shows why the indices for vectors in C start with 0; they are nothing other than the distance from the start of the vector.

The analogy between pointer vector expressions and indexed vector expressions goes further still. `ip[3]` is also a valid equivalent to `*(ip + 3)`, although `ip` is not a vector but a pointer variable.

In other words, under the following conditions:

```
int tab[5] = { 13, 4, 128, 97, -9 };
int * ip = tab;
```

the following four expressions are completely equivalent, and are evaluated with the same memory location:

```
tab[3] <---> *(tab + 3) <---> *(ip + 3) <---> ip[3]
```

This analogy takes effect in the operation of the C compiler as follows: The compiler replaces every indexed vector expression with the corresponding pointer expression. (No surprise for readers familiar with ASSEMBLER.)

But for precisely this reason, the compiler has no problem dealing with the expression `3[tab]`. This is not a printing error; your eyes do not deceive you. The compiler converts:

```
3[tab] ---> *(3 + tab) ---> *(tab + 3),
```

which is the same as `tab[3]`.

(3 + tab is obviously the same as tab + 3. Mathematicians would say the commutative law applies to the addition of a pointer and an integer value.)

The almost perfect analogy between vector expressions and pointer expressions has a limit. In the above example, ip is a pointer variable (emphasizing the word variable), whereas tab represents the constant starting address of the vector, representing a constant, like all expressions formed with the address operator like &tab[3].

The instruction: ++ip; used above cannot be done with tab, i.e. ++tab; is invalid in the above circumstances.

To summarize systematically:

→ The address operator & can only be applied to variables or Lvalues, and itself returns a constant address.

→ The indirection operator * can be applied to any address expressions (data type: pointer to ...), and then refers to an Lvalue.

To demonstrate this last observation:

```
int tab[5] = { 13, 4, 128, 97, -9 };
int * ip = tab;
*(ip + 3) = 105;
printf ("%d\n", tab[3]);          ---> 105
```

The instruction *(ip + 3) = 105; assigns a new value, namely 105, to the fourth element of the vector, overwriting the old value 97. That is possible, because *(ip + 3) refers to an Lvalue, just like the corresponding expression tab[3] or *(tab + 3), whereas (tab + 3) represents a constant address expression.

As regards pointer arithmetic, i.e. the option of calculating with pointers, you can also subtract an int number from a pointer expression, as in the following program extract:

```
int tab[5] = { 13, 4, 128, 97, -9 };
int * ip = tab;
ip += 3;
printf ("%d\n", *ip);     ---> 97
printf ("%d\n", *(ip - 2));     ---> 4
```

The following expressions are generally possible in pointer arithmetic:

→ pointer + iexpr   ---> pointer

→ pointer - iexpr   ---> pointer

→ pointer - pointer ---> ivalue

Where:

`pointer`: means any pointer (address) expression.

`iexpr`: means an integer expression (e.g. `long` is also possible.)

`ivalue`: means an `int` value.

The last of these three formulae requires more detailed explanation:

```
int tab[5] = { 13, 4, 128, 97, -9 };
int * ip = tab;
ip += 3;
printf ("%d\n", ip - tab);          ---> 3
printf ("%d\n", tab[ip - tab]);   ---> 97
```

The expression `ip - tab` returns the difference between `ip` and `tab`, measured not in bytes but in `int` units, i.e: 3. In `tab[ip - tab]` this value 3 is again used as an index for the vector `tab`.

This now explains why negative indices can make perfect sense, as the following example illustrates:

```
int tab[5] = { 13, 4, 128, 97, -9 };
int * ip = tab;
ip += 3;
printf ("%d\n", ip[-1]);          ---> 128
```

The compiler converts the expression `ip[-1]` into `*(ip - 1)`. The memory map is shown in Figure 6.7.

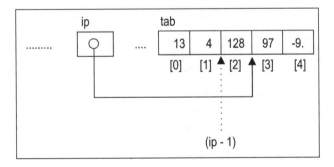

Figure 6.7 *Access using expressions with ip*

But negative indices should logically only be used with pointer variables, and then only on condition that the pointer is not pointing to the start of the vector.

6.3 Pointers to various data types

This section explores the behavior of various pointers that point to memory locations with different data types. In the field of elemental data types, assigning a variable to another one of a different data type is not a problem, as in this example:

```
int x = 15;
double w;
w = x;
```

The assignment w = x; implicitly converts the int content 15 of the variable x into the data type double, i.e. the value 15.0, and then stores it in w.

Where, for example, a pointer to int is assigned to a pointer to an unsigned char, the situation should really be much more straightforward, since a memory address is only transferred to another pointer variable, without converting a value. An address remains an address, you might think.

But the behavior of the C compiler is much more critical in the case of pointer assignments. It always remembers that addresses are only used to access the storage locations of a particular data type. It therefore gives a warning for the following program extract:

```
int z = 25,
    * ip = &z;
unsigned char * ucp;
printf ("%d\n", *ip);        ---> 25
ucp = ip; /* "Warning: Suspicious pointer conversion" */
```

The contents of the int pointer ip, the starting address of z, is assigned to ucp (a pointer to unsigned char), prompting the compiler warning. This warning is really for the programmer's sake, to point out that he or she cannot use the expression *ucp to access the whole int memory location of the variable z.

The programmer may nevertheless deliberately intend to interpret a memory location differently than was intended when it was defined. In order to reassure the C compiler by warning it of this intention, you can use the cast operator (unsigned char *):

```
int z = 25,
    * ip = &z;
unsigned char * ucp;
printf ("%d\n", *ip);        ---> 25
ucp = (unsigned char *)ip; /* No warning! */
printf ("%u\n", *ucp);      ---> 25
ucp++;
printf ("%u\n", *ucp);      ---> 0
```

The compiler now omits the warning.

So a pointer can be assigned to another pointer of a different data type using a cast to point out the change of type.

There are two exceptions to this rule, as explained below.

First consider the effects of this pointer assignment. The expression *ucp is now assigned the value of an unsigned char memory location (just 1 byte). The operation ++ucp; then sets the pointer to the next byte of our int variables z. All the bytes of an extensive area of memory can be individually displayed in this way.

The attentive reader may be surprised at this point that in the above program run the higher-order byte contains the value 25 and the lower-order byte contains the value 0, although you would expect exactly the opposite.

This is because the above program was running on a computer with an INTEL processor (in MS/DOS). It is a peculiarity of the INTEL processor that it stores the bytes of all contiguous memory locations such as int, long, double variables in reverse order. This is connected with the way this processor processes such memory locations.

The contents of an int location 00 19 (hexadecimal value of 25) is stored in an INTEL computer in the form 19 00. Calculations involving the memory location are nevertheless correctly carried out, so a C programmer does not have to be concerned with this INTEL convention. It just has to be taken into account for a small number of hardware-related problems.

Now for the two exceptions for casting with pointer assignments. You do not get a compiler warning in two cases. First, if the assigned address is given in the form of a direct address (e.g. int constants), and, second, if a pointer is assigned to void or if void is assigned to a pointer. The following program extract demonstrates this:

```
int z = 25,
    * ip = &z;
unsigned char * ucp;
void * p;                    /* Pointer to void */
ucp = ip;        /* Warning: Suspicious pointer conversion */
ucp = (unsigned char *)ip; /* No warning! */
ucp = 0x0;                   /* No warning! */
p = ip;                      /* No warning! */
ucp = p;                     /* No warning! */
```

As regards the first case: ucp = 0x0; allocates the memory address 0. In the MS/DOS operating system, you could (if the program compiles with the memory model large) use the expression *ucp to access the first byte of the interrupt vectors. Such an access would not be permitted in UNIX, or only for a privileged process.

Direct addressing of memory locations is really only of importance for hardware-related programming, e.g. if the program is to be written directly to the screen memory for faster screen output on an IBM PC, and a pointer is set to the starting address of the screen memory for this purpose.

Precisely because direct addressing otherwise has no relevance, it is conventional to declare one particular address, namely 0, as the identifier for invalid address, and define the `define` constant NULL in `stdio.h`. So if a pointer variable contains the value NULL, this means that this pointer does not contain a valid address, and the indirection operator should not be used to access the memory contents at this address. (We will be seeing more of this use of NULL.)

As regards the second case: We have so far only encountered the reserved word void in the form of `int main (void)`, where it means that the parameter list of the `main()` function is empty.

But there are more `void` type functions than that, e.g.:

```
void func (int x)

{

    printf ("%d\n", x);

}
```

Here `void` means that the `func()` function has no data type, because it does not return a return value. These `void` functions in C correspond to procedures in PASCAL and subroutines in FORTRAN. They do something, but do not return a function value.

The word `void` thus always seems to mean something like "nothing".

There are no variables in C of the type `void`! (What sort of variables would they be anyway?) But there are certainly pointers to `void`, i.e. variables of the type `void *`. These variables are capable of holding addresses of any storage location. They are known as untyped pointers. Assignments involving pointers to `void`, either left or right of the assignment operator, do not require the use of a cast operator. (see above program example).

But you must not apply the indirection operator * to these pointers.

Pointers to `void` are therefore always used where a memory address is to be stored and we do not (yet) know which object's starting address it represents. (There is an application in Chapter 9 when considering the standard function `qsort()`.)

Let us stop at this point to consolidate the material we have learned about pointers, with a practical exercise. Experience indicates that the material on this subject cannot all be assimilated in one go. Pointers and their use are very much a matter of practice, so we recommend that you work through Exercise 1 before reading on.

6.4 Pointers as function parameters

The problem here will be illustrated by a program that unfortunately does not do what it is supposed to do – a program with a bug:

```c
/* swap.c: "wrong" version */
# include <stdio.h>
void swap (int x, int y)
{
    int h;
    h = x;
    x = y;
    y = h;
}
int main (void)
{
    int a = 27,
        b = 14;
    swap (a, b);
    printf ("%d:%d\n", a, b);
    return 0;
}
```

The void function swap() assigns two integers to the parameters x and y, and exchanges their content using the variable h.

In the main() function, the variables a and b defined and initialized there are passed to the function swap(). After this function call, the contents of a and b are displayed. When the program runs, what appears on the screen is 27:14, and not 14:27 as the programmer intended.

What has happened? The mistake should be explicable in the light of what we have learned about function calls. When the variables a and b are transferred as current arguments when swap() is called, they are passed to the function parameters x and y. x and y thus receive a copy of a and b ("call by value", see Chapter 1). The function swap() then does its job, namely exchanging x and y, and not a and b.

On return from the function swap(), the variables a and b defined in the main() function are completely untouched by the exchange operations, and still contain their original initialization values.

After what we have learned about pointers in this chapter, it may be possible to see how the following program does the job correctly:

```c
/* swap.c: "right" version */
# include <stdio.h>
void swap (int * x, int * y)
{
    int h;
    h = *x;
    *x = *y;
    *y = h;
}
int main (void)
{
    int a = 27,
        b = 14;
    swap (&a, &b);
    printf ("%d:%d\n", a, b);
    return 0;
}
```

The starting addresses a and b are now passed to the pointers x and y when swap() is called. In other words, the pointers x and y point to the variables a and b of the main() function, although the latter are unknown by their name in the function swap(). Swapping *x and *y in swap() in fact swaps the contents of a and b. The programmer is now relieved to see the desired result 14:27.

It is worth briefly considering the function concept in the context of swap().

The purpose of a function subroutine in programming is really to process the data passed to it, and to return just one function value as the result. The whole purpose of a function concentrates on this one function value (for example, in FORTRAN function subroutines it is actually forbidden to change the parameters.). But now swap() is a function that does not even return a value. Yet something is still returned; swap() "leaves behind" two (changed) values.

In this form, as a void function, swap() is actually not a typical function subroutine, but rather what in PASCAL is called a procedure. A procedure does not return a value, but enables several transferred arguments to be changed. The transfer technique involved is not really "call by value", but rather "call by reference", since it is not memory contents that are passed to the parameters of a function, but addresses of memory locations.

One typical procedure can be implemented in C in pure form, as a `void` function. There are of course also mixed forms of function and procedure, the C standard library is full of them; our `getline()` function is basically a procedure, as we will now see.

Let us first consider the following `getline()` call:

```
char line[80];
getline (line, 80);
```

Here we note that the return value of `getline()`, the number of lines entered, is not used at all. And in fact we could also have written `getline()` as a `void` function, because the number of characters entered as a return value is just another waste product. But the main task of this function is to read in a number of characters from the standard input, and to store each character in an element of the vector `line`.

We noted when defining the function that the author had cheated a bit when the argument transfer was declared, namely in the first argument. We are now in a position to clarify this.

The first argument, `line`, represents the starting address of the vector, and the call could have been:

```
getline (&line[0], 80);
```

Knowing what we do about pointers, this argument must be passed to a pointer to char, so we should have formulated the function header of `getline()` thus:

```
int getline (char * s, int lim)
```

instead of:

```
int getline (char s[], int lim).
```

The expression `char s[]` is only an alternative way of writing `char * s`, and the compiler makes this conversion. So it was not right to say "The vector line is transferred", but only its starting address is passed to a pointer.

The whole definition of getline() could accordingly be formulated in pointer form thus:

```
/*--------------- getline.c -----------------------*/
# include <stdio.h>

int getline (char * s, int lim)
{
    int i,
        c;

/* read characterwise. Terminate when limit
   of char vector exceeded, on entry of
   <Ctrl>Z or <return> */

    for (i = 0 ; i < lim - 1 && (c = getchar()) != EOF
        && c != '\n' ; ++i)
        *(s + i) = c;

    *(s + i) = '\0';        /* termination of the string
                               with ASCII NULL    */

    fflush (stdin);         /* Clear keyboard
                               buffer   */

    if (i==0 && c==EOF)     /* If EOF entered as 1st
                               character ....... */
        i = EOF;            /* Return value: EOF     */
    return i;               /* Otherwise return value: number
                               of characters read   */
}
```

We could have used a mixed form, defining the formal parameter s as a pointer, and still have been able to use the indexed vector notation s[i] in the function, which is indeed a very common practice.

The important thing is that when getline() is called, a starting address is passed to a pointer, whether or not the definition of the first parameter is char s[] or char * s. And that also explains why the getline() call can result in so many elements of line being changed, although as a function it can only return a single value.

You might wonder why the notation char s[] was ever introduced in C, since it is really superfluous because of the pointer concept. Perhaps as an aid for C beginners who have not yet learned to use pointers? It is more likely that the intention was to create a means of passing vectors that is compatible with other programming languages (e.g. FORTRAN).

Other functions such as asctoint() (from Chapter 5) could be reformulated to pointer notation in this way.

The standard function strcpy() that we encountered in Chapter 5, can now be redefined in two ways in a new guise:

```
char * strcpy (char * s, char * t)
{
   int i;
   for (i = 0 ; (*(s + i) = *(t + i)) != '\0' ; ++i)
      ;
   return s;
}
```

1   Pointers to char have now been defined as formal parameters, and pointer expressions are used to access the individual elements of the two vectors transferred.

2   The function now no longer has the data type void, but pointer to char (char *). The first argument is accordingly returned as a return value (data type: char *), the starting address of the first transferred vector, again as an additional by-product. The purpose of this is that previously (as a void function) it had to be formulated roughly as follows:

```
strcpy (line, string);
printf ("%s\n", line);
```

Whereas now it can be made into an instruction:

```
printf ("%s\n", strcpy (line, string));
```

The nested function call means that first strcpy() is called, which copies string to line. The return value of strcpy(), namely line, is passed straight to printf() after copying, and the copied string is displayed.

Many standard functions work this way, especially in the field of string processing (see Chapter 12).

6.5 Vectors of pointers

Just as it is possible to define `double`, `int`, or `char` vectors, it should be possible to define vectors of pointers. Let us take the following example:

```
long lvec[5] = { 13L, -5L, 24L, 198L, 17L };
long * lvp[5]; /* Vector of 5 long pointers */
lvp[0] = &lvec[1];
lvp[1] = &lvec[0];
lvp[2] = &lvec[4];
lvp[3] = &lvec[2];
lvp[4] = &lvec[3];
```

At this point we should clarify how the pure definition instruction `long lvec[5];` is evaluated by the compiler:

1   `lvec` is a vector with five elements.

2   Each of these five elements has the data type `long`.

The second definition is to be interpreted accordingly, but taking account of the precedence of the `[]` brackets (level 1) over the `*` operator (level 2):

1   `lvp` is a vector with five elements.

2   Each of these five elements has the data type `long *`, i.e. pointer to `long`.

The following assignments give each element of the pointer vector the starting address of one elements of the `long` vector. This results in the memory map shown in Figure 6.8.

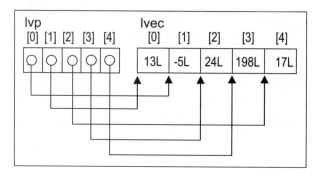

Figure 6.8 *Memory map of lvp and lvec*

Each element of `lvp` represents a `long` pointer variable, and is initialized with the starting address of a `long` variable, namely of an element of the `long` vector `lvec`. The individual elements of `lvp` could also be initialized with the starting addresses of individual `long` variables; it does not have to have a `long` vector. It should also be clear that not every element of `lvp` has to point to the corresponding element of `lvec`, and this is not the case in our example.

You may have now seen the purpose of the remarkable "pointering" of the vector `lvec`, which is illustrated in the output of the following extended program extract:

```
long lvec[5] = { 13L, -5L, 24L, 198L, 17L };
long * lvp[5]; /* Vector of 5 long pointers */
int i;

lvp[0] = &lvec[1];
lvp[1] = &lvec[0];
lvp[2] = &lvec[4];
lvp[3] = &lvec[2];
lvp[4] = &lvec[3];

for (i = 0 ; i < 5 ; ++i)
    printf ("%ld:", lvec[i]); ---> 13:-5:24:198:17:
putchar ('\n');

for (i = 0 ; i < 5 ; ++i)
    printf ("%ld:", *lvp[i]); ---> -5:13:17:24:198:
putchar ('\n');
```

Whereas the first loop in which `lvec[i]` is used displays the stored numbers in their natural memory sequence, the second loop using `*lvp[i]` outputs the numbers in sorted sequence. This is naturally because the elements of `lvp` are initialized with the elements of `lvec` precisely so as to provide sorted access to `lvec`. (See Exercise 1 in Chapter 5.)

Accordingly you can also define a second vector of `long` pointers that is initialized by the elements of `lvec` in such a way that you have access to `lvec` sorted in descending order.

This aspect constitutes an important application of pointer vectors: You define a vector of a particular data type that is to be initialized by the data to be processed. For each desired sorting criterion, you then define a vector of pointers to this data type, which is initialized with the elements of the base vector according to the sorting criterion. Depending in the sorting sequence desired, you then use one pointer vector or another to access the data. This application becomes even more interesting when we come to structures (Chapter 11).

A second application of pointer vectors is frequently used with strings (and can only be used there). Let us revisit the following example from the previous chapter:

```
char menu[][20] =
        {
            "Input",
            "Output",
            "Program end"
        };
```

The corresponding memory map is shown in Figure 6.9.

```
menu
[0]  I  n  p  u  t  \0 \0 \0 \0 \0 \0 \0 \0 \0 \0 \0 \0 \0 \0 \0
[1]  O  u  t  p  u  t  \0 \0 \0 \0 \0 \0 \0 \0 \0 \0 \0 \0 \0 \0
[2]  P  r  o  g  r  a  m     e  n  d  \0 \0 \0 \0 \0 \0 \0 \0 \0
    [0] [1] [2] [3] [4] [5] [6] [7] [8] [9]........              [19]
```

Figure 6.9 *Menu as two-dimensional array*

Here a two-dimensional `char` array `menu` has been used to store three strings. The length of one line has been defined as 20 characters, because the programmer did not want to count the longest of the strings character by character (12 would have been enough!). But even with minimal dimensioning of the array, memory space would have been wasted with the first two lines. Here the pointer vectors help:

```
char * menu[] =
        {
            "Input",
            "Output",
            "Program end"
        };
```

This defines a vector of three `char` pointers that uses only 3 * the length of a pointer in the memory. Each element of `menu` is initialized with the starting address of one string constant at a time. The string constants are also placed by the compiler in a special area of the memory, the data segment, leaving no empty gaps. This results in the memory map shown in Figure 6.10.

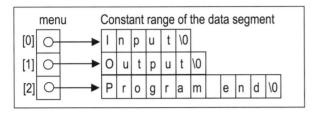

Figure 6.10 *Menu as pointer vector*

(The individual memory locations are not shown as a linear sequence for technical printing reasons.)

The important thing is that the string constants also occupy their place in the data segment in the first array version. But whereas the array for menu requires 3 * 20 = 60 bytes, the pointer vector needs only 3 * 2 = 6 or 3 * 4 = 12 bytes, assuming a pointer length of 2 or 4 bytes.

But the pointer vector variant has the one disadvantage that you have to take care not to overwrite the strings to which the elements of menu point. You would then change constants, which could have disastrous consequences.

The following program has broken this rule, with strange results:

```
# include <stdio.h>
# include <string.h>

int main (void)
{

    char * menu[] =
        {
            "Input",
            "Output",
            "Program end"
        };
    strcpy (menu[0], "Input of values");
    printf ("%s\n", menu[1]);       ---> of values
    printf ("%s\n", menu[2]);       ---> it
    printf ("%s\n", menu[2] + 3); ---> gram end
    return 0;

}
```

The result is not surprising if you consider the changes that strcpy () makes to the memory map (Figure 6.11):

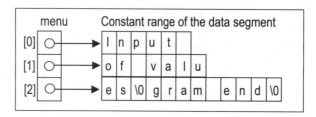

Figure 6.11 *Impermissible overwriting of string constants*

Hence the programming rule:

If the vectors of char pointers are initialized directly with the starting addresses of string constants, the program must never write to the strings. If the problem requires write access, the char array variant must be used.

Despite this restriction, char pointer vectors are widely used, when the strings they manage are only to be displayed (read-only access).

6.6 Pointers to pointers

When we looked at pointers and vectors, we saw that a vector can also be processed with the aid of a pointer. An int vector needs an int pointer, a long vector needs a long pointer, etc. As a general rule, you can use a pointer of data type (type *) to process a vector with elements of data type type.

If we transfer this abstract mechanism to pointer vectors, then we first have to note that type is now (int *), (long *) etc. If I define a pointer to process a corresponding vector, it must be of the data type pointer to (int *), pointer to (long *), etc, or in words, pointer to pointer to int, pointer to pointer to long, etc.

Let us revisit our long program as an example:

```
long lvec[5] = { 13L, -5L, 24L, 198L, 17L };
long * lvp[5]; /* Vector of 5 long pointers */
long ** lvpp = lvp; /* Pointer to pointer to long */
int i;

lvp[0] = &lvec[1];
lvp[1] = &lvec[0];
lvp[2] = &lvec[4];
lvp[3] = &lvec[2];
lvp[4] = &lvec[3];
```

```
for (i = 0 ; i < 5 ; ++i)
    printf ("%ld:", **(lvpp + i)); ---> -5:13:17:24:198:
putchar ('\n');
```

`lvpp` is a pointer to pointer to `long`, which is immediately initialized with the starting address of the vector `lvp`.

Consider the alternative formulation

```
long ** lvpp = &lvp[0];
```

To appreciate what `lvpp` is initialized with, the starting address of the first element of `lvp`, which in turn is a pointer to `long`. The starting address of this element is then of the data type pointer to pointer to `long`, which is why you can also assign it to `lvpp`.

The memory map is shown in Figure 6.12.

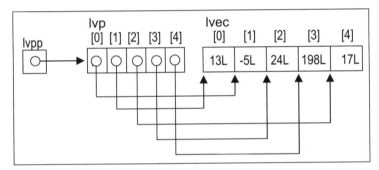

Figure 6.12 *lvpp points to the pointer vector lvp*

Now you can use `lvpp` to process both the vector `lvp` and also the vector `lvec`. First consider that the expression `*lvpp` is identical to `lvp[0]`, just as `lvpp` is identical to `&lvp[0]`, or equally to `lvp + 0`.

`*(lvpp + 1)` is likewise evaluated with the same content as `lvp[1]`. Of course you can also represent it as: `lvpp[1]`, although `lvpp` is not a vector, but a simple pointer variable (remember the analogy of pointer vector expressions and indexed vector expressions). But the content assigned to `*(lvpp + 1)` (and also `lvp[1]`) is an address. In this case `&lvec[0]`. To output the content of `lvec[0]`, you need double indirection:

```
printf ("%ld\n", **(lvpp + 1)); ---> 13
```

Let us construct the evaluation of the expression `**(lvpp + 1)` step by step:

→ `lvpp` is assigned the value `&lvp[0]`, data type: `long **`
→ `lvpp + 1` is assigned the value `&lvp[1]`, data type: `long **`
→ `*(lvpp + 1)` is assigned the value `lvp[1]` = `&lvec[0]`, data type: `long *`
→ `**(lvpp + 1)` is assigned the value `lvec[0]`, data type: `long`, value: 13

This illustrates the output of the `for` loop of the program extract. The following three instructions make a good exercise:

```
printf ("%ld\n", *(*(lvpp + 1) + 2)); ---> 24
```
→ `lvpp` is assigned the value `&lvp[0]`, data type: `long **`
→ `lvpp + 1` is assigned the value `&lvp[1]`, data type: `long **`
→ `*(lvpp + 1)` is assigned the value `lvp[1]` = `&lvec[0]`, data type: `long *`
→ `*(lvpp + 1) + 2` is assigned the value `&lvec[2]`, data type: `long *` (But only because `lvec` is a vector. If the elements of `lvp` pointed to the starting addresses of individual `long` variables that were not contiguous in the memory, this expression would be assigned the value of the starting address of an undefined area of memory.)
→ `*(*(lvpp + 1) + 2)` is assigned the value `lvec[2]`, data type: `long`, value: 24

```
printf ("%ld\n", *(*(lvpp + 3) + 1)); ---> 198
```

→ `lvpp` is assigned the value `&lvp[0]`, data type: `long **`
→ `lvpp + 3` is assigned the value `&lvp[3]`, data type: `long **`
→ `*(lvpp + 3)` is assigned the value `lvp[3]` = `&lvec[2]`, data type: `long *`
→ `*(lvpp + 3) + 1` is assigned the value `&lvec[3]`, data type: `long *`
→ `*(*(lvpp + 3) + 1)` is assigned the value `lvec[3]`, data type: `long`, value: 198

```
printf ("%ld\n", **(lvpp + 3) + 1); ---> 25
```

→ `lvpp` is assigned the value `&lvp[0]`, data type: `long **`
→ `lvpp + 3` is assigned the value `&lvp[3]`, data type: `long **`
→ `*(lvpp + 3)` is assigned the value `lvp[3]` = `&lvec[2]`, data type: `long *`
→ `**(lvpp + 3)` is assigned the value `lvec[2]`, data type: `long`, value: 24
→ `**(lvpp + 3) + 1` is assigned the value `lvec[2]` + 1, data type: `long`, value: 25

6.7 Pointers to pointers as function parameters

The next problem is how to pass an array of pointers to a function. A program that passes our `long` pointer vector to a function `set()` could be formulated like this:

```
void set (long * p[], int n)      /* Definition of set () */
{
   int i;
   for (i = 0 ; i < n ; ++i)
      * p[i] = i + 1;
}
int main (void)
{
   long lvec[5] = { 13L, -5L, 24L, 198L, 17L };
   long * lvp[5]; /* vector of 5 long pointers */
   int i;
   lvp[0] = &lvec[1];
   lvp[1] = &lvec[0];
   lvp[2] = &lvec[4];
   lvp[3] = &lvec[2];
   lvp[4] = &lvec[3];
   set (lvp, 5);             /* call set () */
   for (i = 0 ; i < 5 ; ++i)
      printf ("%ld:", *lvp[i]); ---> 1:2:3:4:5:
   putchar ('\n');
   return 0;
}
```

When `set()` is called, the starting address of the pointer vector is transferred to the formal parameter of the function `set()` defined by `long * p[]`, by means of `lvp`. So `p` is a vector of long pointers whose number of elements has been omitted, or so it seems. This form of definition of the formal parameter is reminiscent of our first version of the function `getline()`, where the first parameter had the form `char s[]`.

But we know from our discussion of `getline()` that in reality a pointer is being defined, not a vector. Applied to our `long` pointer vector, this means that when the compiler reads the expression `long * p[]` in the header of the function `set()`, then it really turns it into a pointer variable. It should be clear from the preceding section what sort of pointer that is. The following version of `set()` uses a pure pointer notation:

```
void set (long ** p, int n)        /* definition of set () */
{
    int i;
    for (i = 0 ; i < n ; ++i)
        ** (p + i) = i + 1;
}
```

When the function set () is called, you get the memory map shown in Figure 6.13.

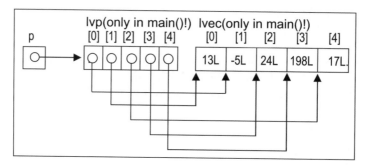

Figure 6.13   *Assignment of lvp to p*

Although the variable names lvp and lvec only occur in the main() function, since the starting address was transferred from lvp to p, it is possible to access the content of the lvec elements with the above pointer expressions ** (p + i).

At the end of the function set (), the numbers stored in lvec have changed (see Figure 6.14).

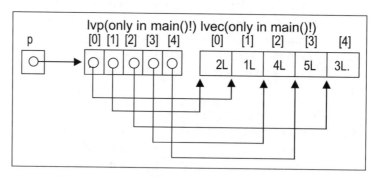

Figure 6.14   *Effect of set() on lvec*

Although the pure pointer expressions used in the second version of set () more accurately express what has really happened, the first version of set () is nevertheless easier to read and to program. When passing pointer vectors to functions, the beginner need have no inhibitions about preferring the first indexed version. Many professionals do the same thing.

> **Warning** We will round off this topic by introducing another common programming error. Consider first the following program:

```
# include <stdio.h>
int z = 13;      /* global variable! All functions
                    may access z   */
void set (int * ip)
{
   ip = &z;
   *ip = 24;
}
int main (void)
{
   int * ip;
   set (ip);
   printf ("%d\n", z);    ---> 24
   printf ("%d\n", *ip); ---> 8447 /* (random!) */
   return 0;
}
```

That is now the second sample program with a global variable. Remember you can access a global variable (defined outside each function) from all functions (at least from the same program file).

The programmer had used the function set() so elegantly to achieve two effects:

1 A transferred int pointer was to be initialized with the starting address of the global variable z.

2 The new value 24 was then to be assigned to the global variable z.

First set() is called in the main() function with an int pointer. The first printf() call, which actually outputs 24 as the new contents of z, shows that set() has at least carried out the second part of its task.

But when *ip is output, it is not the content of z that is output as expected, but some random number.

What has happened?

The pointer variable `ip` was defined in the `main()` function, but not initialized there, so it therefore contains a random number as the stored address.

This random address is passed to the formal parameter `ip` of the function `set()`. The formal parameter of the same name thus contains a copy of the pointer variable `ip` from `main()`.

The starting address of `z` is then assigned to the formal parameter `ip` in `set()`, but not to the `ip` from `main()`. Whereas `*ip = 24;` in the function `set()` really assigns the new value to the variable `z`, `ip` from `main()` still contains the original random address. After returning from `set()`, the `int` numerical value is output at this random address with `*ip`, again not a predictable number.

The correct solution looks like this:

```
# include <stdio.h>
int z = 13;
void set (int ** ipp)
{
    *ipp = &z;
    **ipp = 24;
}
int main (void)
{
    int * ip;
    set (&ip);
    printf ("%d\n", z);    ---> 24
    printf ("%d\n", *ip); ---> 24
    return 0;
}
```

The key difference is that in `main()` the starting address of `ip` is passed to the function `set()` and not the content, and logically to a pointer to pointer to `int`. The `ipp` from `set()` now points to the pointer variable `ip` from `main()`, and the starting address of `z` is assigned to the pointer variable `ip` from `main()` with `*ipp = &z;`, exactly as if `main()` had contained the expression : `ip = &z;`.

Logically, the double indirection (`**ipp`) also has to be used with `ipp` to assign the value 24 to `z`.

Hence the following programming rule:

If the address of a variable of data type `type` is to be assigned to a pointer variable of data type `type *`, and if this process is to occur in a function written specially for that purpose, then the starting address of the pointer variable must be passed to the function, and in the function header the formal parameter must contain the data type `type **`.

It is admittedly somewhat contrived that the programming error described here is demonstrated on the basis of a global variable. In practice the error frequently occurs when a function is required to allocate dynamic memory space, and the starting address of this memory is to be stored in a pointer variable outside the function. We will return to this problem in Chapter 13.

6.8 Pointers to vectors

As well as vectors of pointers, pointers to vectors play a certain minor role. As the name implies, such a pointer points to a whole vector. That means that if this pointer is incremented by 1, the address stored in it is incremented by a whole vector. That requires this pointer to have been initialized with the starting address of a two-dimensional array, if it is to be sensibly used. You can process a two-dimensional array line by line by successively incrementing the pointer.

Let us first deal with the syntax of such a pointer definition. Let us consider the two following definition instructions:

```
int * vp[10];          (1)
```

and

```
int (* pv)[10];        (2)
```

The sequence in which the operators are evaluated plays an important role in distinguishing the two forms. We have already met instruction (1): vp is a vector of ten elements. Each element has the data type int *. So this defines a vector of 10 int pointers.

In instruction (2), the bracketing forces the compiler to interpret it differently:

1   (* pv) means pv is a pointer!

2   (* pv)[10]: pv is a pointer to a vector of 10 elements!

3   int (* pv)[10]: pv is a pointer to a vector of 10 int elements.

Everything there is to be said about this new type of pointer will be illustrated using the following program:

```c
# include <stdio.h>
void init (int (* pv)[4], int n)
{
    int i,
        k;
    for (i = 0 ; i < n ; ++i)
        for (k = 0 ; k < 4 ; ++k)
            (*(pv + i))[k] = i + k;
            /* or:  pv[i][k] = i + k; */
}
void initline (int * ip, int n)
{
    int i;
    for (i = 0 ; i < n ; ++i)
        *(ip + i) = 99;
}
void display (int (* pv)[4], int n)
{
    int i,
        k;
    for (i = 0 ; i < n ; ++i)
    {
        for (k = 0 ; k < 4 ; ++k)
            printf ("%2d ", arr[i][k]);
        putchar ('\n');
    }
    putchar ('\n');
}
int main (void)
{
    int arr[3][4];
    init (arr, 3);
    display (arr, 3);
    initline (arr[2], 4);
    display (arr, 3);
    initline (arr[0], 3);
    display (arr, 3);
    return 0;
}
```

Let us start in the `main()` function. There a two-dimensional array `arr` is defined. In the following call, the expression `arr` is passed to the function `init()` as the first argument. What is the data type of this expression, or what does it represent? Remember that `int arr[3][4]` can be understood as `arr` representing a one-dimensional vector of three one-dimensional vectors of four `int` values. The expression `arr` or `&arr[0]` refers to the starting address of the one-dimensional vector whose three elements contain a one-dimensional vector with four `int` elements. The expression `arr` or `&arr[0]` thus has the data type pointer to a vector of four `int` elements. So it can only be assigned to such a pointer. And in the function `init()`, the first formal parameter is in fact accordingly defined: `int (* pv)[4]`.

In the context of such a definition, it is important that the `[]` brackets must now not be empty, and a definition such as `int (* pv)[]` is invalid. It must be defined how many elements the vector has to which `pv` is to point. How should the compiler otherwise e.g. be able to assign a value to the address expression `pv + 1`?

The function `init()` serves to initialize all the `int` elements of a two-dimensional array comprising any number of vectors of four elements. The number of vectors must therefore be passed to `init()` as the second argument. An element is initialized in the instruction:

```
(*(pv + i))[k] = i + k;
```

Since the program is only intended to illustrate the basic use of pointers to vectors, the expression `i + k` is arbitrarily defined as the initialization value, and is of no further interest.

We need to clarify the expression for the Lvalue to which this initialization value is assigned. For example, if we assume `i` is 1 and `k` is 2, then a value has to be assigned to the following expression:

```
(*(pv + 1))[2] = i + k;
```

1 `pv` is assigned the value `arr`, data type: `int (*)[4]`

2 `pv + 1` is assigned the value of an address that exceeds `pv` by the length of an `int` vector of 4 elements, data type: `int (*)[4]`. So this is the starting address of the second of the vectors constituting the array.

3 `*(pv + 1)` is assigned the value of the second vector of the arrays, data type: `int [4]`, or `int *`, which is the same thing.

4 `(*(pv + 1))[2]` is assigned the value of the third element of the second vector of `arr`, data type: `int`

Note that since indexed vector expressions and pointer expressions are equivalent, the following two notations would also be possible:

```
*(*(pv + 1) + 2)          /* pure pointer expression */
pv[1][2]                  /* pure index expression */
```

The second form treats pv as a two-dimensional array, quite rightly, because you can use pv just as well as arr to process the whole array.

The function display() works with the same expressions as init(); in this case all the elements of the array are output to the standard output using the pointer.

For the sake of completeness we have included the call of a function init-line(). The first argument passed to this function is the expression arr[2]. You can easily establish the data type of this expression by converting it to pointer form: *(arr + 2). Since arr, the starting address of the array, is of data type int (*)[4] , arr + 2 designates the starting address of the third vector of the array. *(arr + 2) then designates the third vector, which has the data type int [4] or int *. The first formal parameter of initline() is then logically a normal int pointer.

The function initline() permits the elements of an int vector to be initialized, in this case with 99. The number of elements must naturally be passed as the second argument.

To summarize: If a matrix with 3 × 4 int elements is defined by int arr[3][4]; , then the expression arr[2] represents the starting address of the third vector constituting the array.

The second initline() call demonstrates that you do not have to have all the elements of the vectors processed.

The overall result of the program run is :

```
 0   1   2   3
 1   2   3   4
 2   3   4   5

 0   1   2   3
 1   2   3   4
99  99  99  99

99  99  99   3
 1   2   3   4
99  99  99  99
```

Finally a word on the remarkable data type expressions used when explaining evaluation, e.g. `int (*) [4]` as data type pointer to an `int` vector with four elements. It is certainly strange that no variable name appears. But this is not some imaginary symbolism invoked by the author for heuristic reasons; an expression like this represents a real, valid syntax form for the data type, used mainly in the cast operator. The following example shows how a `long` matrix can be interpreted as an `unsigned char matrix` using an appropriate pointer:

```
long arr[3][4];
unsigned char (* ucp)[4 * sizeof(long)];
ucp = (unsigned char (*)[4 * sizeof(long)])arr;
.....
```

`arr` is assigned to the pointer `ucp` using the corresponding cast operator.

The remaining topic of pointers to functions will be considered in Chapter 9, and Chapter 11 deals with pointers in connection with structures.

6.9 Some consolation

If you have labored through this chapter thus far with some success, you can now relax, and begin to think of yourself as a proper C programmer, because mastering pointers is probably the most difficult but also a crucially important component of C.

But if you have found this chapter a struggle and sometimes felt the urge to scream and jump out of the window, or if your mental contortions seem like convoluted pointers, then you may console yourself with the following considerations:

1   Generations of C programmers have trodden this path before you.

2   Pointers are very much a matter of practice. Revisiting this chapter, and using pointers in practical programs will heal some wounds.

3   Not all types of pointer expressions occur in day-to-day C programming, for example pointers to vectors, discussed last.

4   You may also console yourself that it could be worse, e.g. "pointers to pointers to ..." or "pointers to pointers to pointers to pointers to ....". But who could do things like that? Unless you are working as a mathematical researcher with an astrophysics professor seeking to simulate cosmological world models in 10-dimensional space.

For those who do not read these lines because they have already thrown this book away, and with it the whole idea of C, it lies beyond the author's power to exercise any influence on this fateful existential decision.

6.10 Exercises

1 Try to trace the documented program run of the following program. Note down the memory locations.

```c
# include <stdio.h>
int main (void)
{
    double dvec[] = { 17.9, -34.07, 100.5, 8.125 };
    char line[] = "hieroglyphics";
    long lvec[5];
    int i;

    double * dp = dvec;
    char * cp = line;
    long * lp = lvec + 4;

    printf ("%lf\n", *(dp + 2));      ---> 100.500000
    printf ("%lf\n", dp[1]);          ---> -34.070000
    printf ("%lf\n", *(dvec + 3));    ---> 8.125000
    *dp = 24.4;
    printf ("%lf\n", dvec[0]);        ---> 24.400000

    putchar (*(cp + 7));                  ---> y
    putchar ('\n');
    printf ("%c\n", *(cp + 7));           ---> y
    printf ("%s\n", line + 7);        ---> yphics

    for (i = 0 ; i < 5 ; ++i)
        lvec[i] = 1L + i * 2L;
    for (--i ; i >= 0 ; --i)
    {
        printf ("%ld:", *lp);             ---> 9:7:5:3:1:
        lp--;
    }
    putchar ('\n');
    lp += 4;
    printf ("%ld\n", lvec[lp - lvec + 1]);  ---> 9

    putchar (*(cp + 6));                  ---> 1
    putchar ('\n');
    putchar (*cp - 6);                ---> b
```

```
   putchar ('\n');
   putchar (*(cp + 7) + 1);              ---> z
   putchar ('\n');

   for (dp = dvec + 3 ; dp >= dvec ; dp--)
      printf ("%.3lf:", *dp); ---> 8.125:100.500:-
      34.070:24.400:
   putchar ('\n');
   return 0;
}
```

Tip Observe the evaluation sequence of the operators concerned in the expressions *(cp + 6) and *cp - 6, and be aware that they mean something completely different. Likewise with the expression: *(cp + 7) + 1.

START UP!

2 Test the following program:

```
/* size.c */
# include <stdio.h>
void size (char s[])
{
   printf ("%u\n", sizeof(s));
}
int main (void)
{
   char s[100];
   printf ("%u\n", sizeof(s));
   size (s);
   return 0;
}
```

Look at the screen outputs when the program runs, and note that the compiler actually replaces char s[] with char * s. size() should output 2 or 4 for the length of a pointer (depending on the operating system of the memory model).

3 Rewrite the function asctoint() so that it only contains pure pointer expressions.

4 Write a function palindrome() in the program file palindro.c, to which a single argument is passed in the form of a string, which exam-

ines the string to see whether the it is a palindrome. If it is, return the value 1 as return value, otherwise 0.

A palindrome is a text that reads equally well back to front. For example: MADAM, DEIFIED.

Write a `main()` function for this that reads in any number of strings (using `getline()`), until `<Ctrl>z` or `<Ctrl>d`) is entered, and outputs after each line of text "Palindrome!" or "Not a palindrome!". Use pointer expressions as far as possible.

5 In the program file `found.c` write the function `found()` that searches in a string transferred as the first argument for the occurrence of a search string transferred as the second argument. When the search string has been found, return the starting address of its location as the return value, otherwise NULL. (What data type does the function have to have?)

This involves writing a `main()` function that first reads a search string into a `char` vector using `getline()`, and then reads any number of lines of text into another `char` vector. Each of these text lines must be examined using `found()` to determine whether it contains the search string. If it does, the whole line of text is displayed, otherwise not.

(The attentive reader may have noticed that this task contains the germ of a useful tool, which exists in UNIX as the command `grep`. To create a program resembling `grep` you need to separate the input of the search string from the input of the text lines. The `grep` command solves this problem by requesting entry of the search string as the first command-line argument when the command is called, then the text lines are read from the standard input or from files. But this goes beyond the programming techniques we have covered. After working through Chapter 14 we will be able to write a better `found` command more closely representing the `grep` command.)

6 If the reader's enthusiasm for the lottery has not been dampened by the results of Exercise 7 in Chapter 2, the following daunting task may be of interest, which can be solved using vectors of pointers.

In the program file `lotto.c`, write a `main()` function to simulate the lottery draw. The program run might look like this:

```
Lottery draw:

Number 1:   3
Number 2:  13
Number 3:  30
Number 4:  39
```

```
Number 5:   7
Number 6: 47
Bonus number: 10

Result of the draw:
 3, 7, 13, 30, 39, 47
Bonus number: 10
```

Note that lottery numbers naturally have to be generated by a random number generator. The C standard library provides the standard function rand() for this purpose. Every time rand() is called, it returns a random number derived from a pseudo-random-number algorithm.

But if you call this lottery program with its seven rand() calls several times, you will get the same sequence of seven random numbers every time. You can avoid this by using the standard function srand() to initialize the random number generator with a different seed every time. The prototype of both functions:

```
# include <stdlib.h>
int rand (void);
void srand (unsigned seed);
```

rand() returns the random value. srand() has to be initialized with a random value. The best thing is to use the current time provided by the standard function time():

```
# include <time.h>
time_t time (time_t * timer);
```

The derived data type (see Chapter 11) time_t comprises the data type long in most compilers. So you have to define a variable of type time_t, and pass its starting address to time(). time() then files the number of seconds since 1.1.1970, 0:00:00 (Greenwich Mean Time) (the moment of the birth of UNIX) in the time_t variable. This number is the return value.

Method:

1 Initialize the generator with srand() with the return value of time() as argument;

2 Create one or more random numbers with rand().

The function rand() returns a random number in the range 0 to RAND_MAX to a define constant, that is defined in stdlib.h. This number must of course be normalized to the valid lottery number range. Since the smallest random number is 0 and not 1, it is advisable to make the number range 0 to 48, and to use each number in this range as an index in a suitably dimensioned int vector for the numbers 1 to 49.

Now comes the main programming problem. You cannot just generate a random number in the range 1 to 49 seven times in a row, because the same number may be "drawn" more than once.

A solution of this problem could be as shown in Figure 6.15.

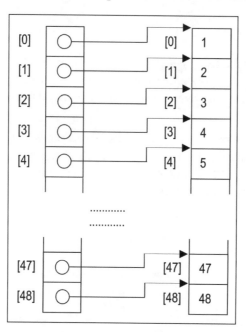

Figure 6.15   *The situation before the first draw*

Each of the elements of a pointer vector `ip` points to each element of the vector `number` containing the numbers to be drawn. Let us assume that the first number drawn is the number 4 (index: 3). Apart from the fact that this number has to be stored in a special vector as the first element, it must not be available when the next lottery number is determined. The best thing is to move it to the end of the list (see Figure 6.16).

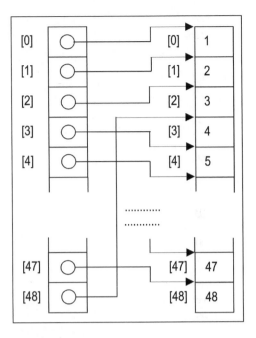

Figure 6.16 *The situation after the first draw*

When the next number is drawn, you can only take a random number in the range 0 to 47 (!) etc. The upper limit of the random number is this decremented by 1 for each draw.

Also consider that at the end of the draw, all six numbers are to be sorted again and displayed.

To make the draw more exciting, you can call sleep (3); after each number is drawn, to pause the program for 3 seconds. (Prototype in dos.h in MS/DOS C compilers; in UNIX, sleep() is a system call).

Memory classes

Memory classes play an important role in defining variables in C, and also play a minor role in functions. They affect:

→ the scope (of functions too);
→ the lifetime;
→ the memory location;
→ whether variables can be automatically initialized.

You can influence the type of memory class in two ways:

1 by where the variables are defined within a program;
2 by special additional keywords.

As regards (1):

A variable defined inside a function is called a local variable. A variable defined outside all functions is called a global variable.

The different characteristics of local and global variables are described below.

As regards (2):

The variable definitions we have encountered so far have been in the form:

```
datatype variable;
```

But a definition instruction like this can be extended by adding a keyword:

```
[memory class] datatype variable;
```

The [] brackets mean that it is not essential to specify a memory class; a default memory class is assumed if no keyword is given.

Keywords that affect the memory class are:

→ auto: local (stack) variables (default memory class);
→ register: request to the compiler to use the processor's internal registers;
→ static: static variables, both local and global;
→ extern: external declaration of global variables;

The instruction sequence:

```
int main (void)
{
    auto int x;
    ...
}
```

is identical to:

```
int main (void)
{
    int x;
    ...
}
```

Automatic variables, i.e. variables of the memory class `auto`, exist only as local variables. Specifying the keyword `auto` is optional, and is therefore almost always omitted. In other words, all local variables are `auto` where no memory class keyword is stipulated. This also applies to the definition of formal parameters of functions (one exception, see below).

So what exactly is an auto memory class?

The memory location of automatic variables is a special area of memory called a stack. You have to know that each program loaded into main memory occupies three different areas of memory there:

1 Text segment: containing the program code, the machine instructions constituting the program.

2 Data segment: containing certain non-automatic variables and constants of a program.

3 Stack: containing all the automatic variables, possibly including temporary memory areas for function return values.

The stack is managed according to a particular procedure called LIFO ("last in, first out"). That means that when a second variable is installed in the stack, it occupies the memory location after the first. If these variables are then deleted, the first location to be cleared is that of the second variable, the one entered last. Any area of memory operating on this principle, whereby whatever was pushed onto the stack last is the first to be taken off, is called a stack.

The operating system also establishes a stack for every program to be executed (in UNIX: for every process). But you can also set up a private stack for your own purposes, which we will do in Chapter 8.

Most operating systems start filling their stack from the top at high memory locations, then work downwards to low memory locations.

The following program extract then creates the memory map shown in Figure 7.1:

```c
int main (void)
{
   short x;
   long w;
   ...
}
```

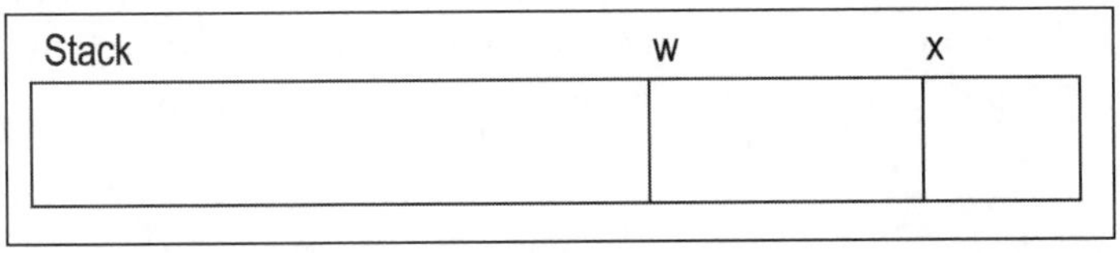

Figure 7.1   *The LIFO method of occupying the stack*

Scope: Automatic variables can be accessed by name only within the function or within the block they are defined in.

The following program demonstrates this:

```c
void func (void)
{
   int s = 0;                    /* within function */
   {
      int i;                     /* within block    */
      while (s < 1000)
      {
         s += i;
         printf ("%d\n", s);    /* valid!          */
      }
      printf ("%d\n", i);       /* valid!          */
   }
   printf ("%d\n", i);          /* invalid!        */
   printf ("%d\n", s);          /* valid!          */
}
int main (void)
{
   func ();
   printf ("%d\n", s);          /* invalid!        */
   return 0;
}
```

The penultimate `printf()` call in `func()` is invalid because the variable i is addressed outside the block in which it is defined.

The `printf()` call in the `main()` function is likewise invalid since it uses the variable s whose scope only extends to the function block of `func()`.

But note that the variable s is valid within the nested block, being defined within `func()` but outside the block nested in `func()`. However many blocks are nested together, variables defined anywhere are valid in all the inner blocks.

Lifetime: Automatic variables are only created at run time, when their definition instructions are carried out. They expire on termination of the function or block in which they were defined. The local definition instructions used above:

```
short x;
long w;
```

are for this purpose executable instructions that the compiler translates into program code, and reserves storage space for in the stack at run time.

Corresponding machine instructions release the reserved stack storage space at the end of the function, to make it available for other variables.

This limited lifetime of `auto` variables has important consequences. For example, if the above function `func()` is called twice in succession, we cannot assume that the variables s and i will still contain the same values the second time they are called.

Automatic initialization: All auto variables are not automatically initialized. After an instruction like `int i;` has been executed, the variable i thus created contains a random value – whatever a previously called function or perhaps a previous program left in this memory location.

So if automatic variables are to contain a defined value the first time they are used, they must be specifically initialized at the time of definition.

Variables of the memory class register differ hardly at all from automatic variables, except that the storage location can differ. The instruction

```
register int i;
```

represents a polite request to the compiler to use a processor register to set up the `int` variable i. Unfortunately the compiler does not always comply with such polite requests. If the remaining program code means it cannot spare any of its few registers, it rejects the request, and establishes the variable as an automatic variable on the stack. So a programmer can only request a register; he or she cannot be certain that the compiler will comply.

The practical purpose of register variables arises from the rapid access to registers in contrast to main memory locations. Integer variables are frequently found in heavily used loops, and speed up a program significantly as register variables, provided the compiler obliges.

Everything we have said about `auto` variables as regards scope, lifetime, and automatic initialization also applies to register variables.

> **Tip** Formal function parameters may have the memory class register (the exception referred to above for `auto`).

The next thing is to discuss global variables that are characterized not by a memory class keyword, but just by being defined outside each function.

In the following program

```
int z = 100;            /* Global variable          */

int main (void)
{
   int x = 13;           /* local, automatic variable */
   ...
}
```

z is a global variable, whereas the variable x is local. They both differ externally only in having a different variable name. The decisive difference is the position where they are defined: the variable z outside `main()`, and the variable x inside it.

Global variables are distinguished by the following characteristics:

→ Memory location: the data segment of the program code.
→ Scope: in all functions of the same module (i.e. the same program file) in which the global variable is defined. They are then called module global.

A global variable can also be used by functions of another module provided it is declared with an external declaration.

If a global variable is valid in all modules of a program, it is called program global. A program global variable `number` is defined in the following program example:

```
/* Module: prog1.c */
# include <stdio.h>
void incr (void);
void decr (void);
int number = 99;
int main (void)
```

```
{
    printf ("%d\n", number);  ---> 99
    incr ();
    printf ("%d\n", number);  ---> 100
    decr ();
    printf ("%d\n", number);  ---> 99
    return 0;
}
/* Module: prog2.c */
external int number;
void incr (void)
{
    number++;
}
void decr (void)
{
    number--;
}
```

The whole program consists of the functions main(), incr() and decr(), distributed over two modules prog1.c and prog2.c. In prog1.c, the global int variable number is defined. The instruction: external int number; declares number in prog2.c as well – it is "externally declared". Since there are no other modules for this program, this makes number program global. All three functions access this same variable number.

The external instruction is only a declaration of a variable defined elsewhere.

If the C compiler is to make an executable program out of the two source program files, then it first compiles both files individually and separately into object files.

When prog1.c is compiled, it reserves the variable number in the data area. When prog2.c is compiled, it replaces the access to number by a place holder or unresolved reference, because of the external declaration. It is then the business of the linkage editor to resolve this unresolved reference, so that incr() and decr() access number from prog1.o(bj).

Lifetime: All the time the program runs. This characteristic clearly arises from what has already been said on the subject of memory location and scope. Since the compiler reserves the storage space for number in the object code data area when prog1.c is compiled, the variable exists as soon as the program to be executed is loaded into memory. Since the distribution of variables in the data segment does not change, unlike the stack, the variable number stays there until the end of the program run.

Automatic initialization: All global variables are automatically initialized with 0 (by the compiler) unless they are explicitly initialized in some other way. That means an uninitialized global int variable contains the value 0, an uninitialized double variable contains the value 0.0, a char variable the value '\0', a pointer the value NULL, etc.

The above sample program demonstrates what global variables can be used for. Whenever data from several functions is to be available, either for reading or writing access, it can be stored in global variables. To dispense with global variables in the above program, the interfaces of the functions would have to be changed, for example, as follows:

```
/* Module: prog1.c */
# include <stdio.h>
void incr (int * p);
void decr (int * p);
int main (void)
{
    int number = 99;
    printf ("%d\n", number); ---> 99
    incr (&number);
    printf ("%d\n", number); ---> 100
    decr (&number);
    printf ("%d\n", number); ---> 99
    return 0;
}
/* Module:prog2.c */
void incr (int * p)
{
    (*p)++;
}
void decr (int * p)
{
    (*p)--;
}
```

If functions are to have read/write access to variables defined elsewhere, then either the starting addresses of these variables must be passed to corresponding function pointers, or the variables must allow the functions access through a global definition.

Variables of the memory class static behave like global variables:

→ Storage location: in the data segment of the program code.

➜ Scope: the decisive factor here is whether the static variables are defined locally or globally. As local variables, they are valid only in the function or the block in which they are defined. As global variables, they are always module global. Global static variables cannot be declared externally.

This is an important difference from "normal" global variables. Global static variables are in practice used whenever only functions of the same module are supposed to have access to this variable, but not functions of other modules. This blocking of access from other modules is an important programming aid in C to achieve data encapsulation, which is of great significance to modular programming.

Data encapsulation is demonstrated in the following sample program of a "sorted stack" (see Chapter 8).

Lifetime: The entire program run time. This again is derived from the data segment memory location. But the fact that the scope for local static variables is restricted, has the following interesting consequence: the second time a function is called or a block is run for the second time, a related local static variable still contains the same values it was given the first time. The simplest application of this fact is demonstrated by the following sample program that uses a local static variable as a function "call counter":

```
# include <stdio.h>
void func (void)
{
    static int count = 0;
    printf ("%d. call!\n", ++count);
    . . .
}
int main (void)
{
    func ();        ---> 1st call!
    . . .
    func ();        ---> 2nd call!
    . . .
    func ();        ---> 3rd call!
    . . .
    return 0;
}
```

Automatic initialization: All static variables are automatically initialized with 0 (by the compiler) unless they are explicitly otherwise initialized. The explicit initialization of count with 0 is therefore really superfluous in the above example.

We did it for documentary reasons, to remind ourselves of the value this counter is starting from.

To conclude, this account of memory classes, a "reverse" overview of the key points is given below, with an additional commentary on explicit initialization:

Scope:
1. **local** variables:
   → within the function (block) they are defined in.
2. **global** variables:
   → within the module (program file) they are defined in (module global);
   → also within every other module if they are declared with external (program global if they are declared in all modules of a program);
   → global `static` variables cannot be declared external.

Lifetime:
1. **auto:** only as long as the function or block in which it is defined is carried out;
2. **register:** only as long as the function or block in which it is defined is carried out;
3. **static:** throughout the entire run time;
4. **global:** throughout the entire run time.

Memory location:
1. **auto:** stack;
2. **register:** register (if possible, otherwise stack);
3. **static:** data area for the program code;
4. **global:** data area for the program code.

Explicit initialization:

All variables can be initialized with values at the time of definition.

<u>Exception</u>:

In the K&R standard vectors (tables) and structures can only be initialized at the time of definition if they are global or of the memory class `static`. (But this restriction no longer applies for the ANSI standard.)

Automatic initialization:
1. global: variables are automatically initialized with 0;
2. static: variables are automatically initialized with 0;
3. all others are not.

The following supplement concerns the problem of variables with the same names:

```
# include <stdio.h>

int z = 13;
void func (void)
{
    printf ("%d\n", z);
}
int main (void)
{
    int z = 98;
    func ();                    ---> 13
    printf ("%d\n", z);   ---> 98
    return 0;
}
```

A variable with the name z is defined twice in this program, once as a global variable, and then as a local variable in main().

In main(), z addresses the local variable, i.e. a local variable conceals a global variable of the same name. There is no local variable z defined in the function func(), so the global variable is therefore addressed as z. There is no facility in C for addressing the global variable z within this main() function (unlike in C++).

If global variables with the same name are defined in several modules, the linkage editor gives an error message. Rightly, because if there were any contradictory external declarations, it would not be clear which of the variables was being referred to.

The following case is permitted. Only one of the global variables with the same name is a "normal" global variable. All the others are global static variables. Here the static variable concerned conceals the access to the "normal" global variable for all functions of the module concerned.

A further supplement is required to the external declaration of functions. This is covered in Chapter 9.

I   What is the output from the following program?

```
/* Module: prog1.c */
# include <stdio.h>
int k = 0, m = 1, n = 2;
int main (void)
{
    void fun1 (void);
    int fun2 (void);
    int fun3 (int x, int y, int z);
    k++;
    m += k;
    printf ("%d %d %d\n", k, m, n);
    fun1();
    printf ("%d %d %d\n", k, m, n);
    printf ("%d\n", fun2());
    printf ("%d\n", (k = fun3(k, m, n)));
    printf ("%d %d %d\n", k, m, n);
    return 0;
}
void fun1 (void)
{
    int k = n;
    m += k;
    n = m - ++k;
}


/* Module: prog2.c */
extern int k, m, n;
int fun2 (void)
{
    int p = 2;
    k -= p;
    m = (k!= p);
    n += m++;
    return n;
}
```

```
/* Module: prog3.c */
static int k = 1, m = 2, n = 3;
int fun3 (int x, int y, int z)
{
    k += x++;
    return k + y - z + ++n;
}
```

Hint: write down all the variables, and note down every changed value to keep track. The program is only for training purposes.

2   What is the output from the following program?

```
# include <stdio.h>
void func (void)
{
    static int z = 0;
    printf ("%d. call this function!\n", ++z);
}
int main (void)
{
    int i;
    for (i = 0 ; i < 7 ; ++i)
        func ();
    return 0;
}
```

3   Look at the following program:

```
# include <stdio.h>        /* next.c */
char * next (char * sp);   /* Prototype */
char s1[] = "This is a sentence",  /* global */
     s2[] = "   with many words   ";
int main (void)
{
    char * strp;
    printf ("here comes s1:\n");
    strp = next (s1);
    while (strp!= NULL)
    {
        printf ("%s\n", strp);
        strp = next (NULL);
    }
    printf ("here comes s2:\n");
```

```
    strp = next (s2);
    while (strp!= NULL)
    {
        printf ("%s\n", strp);
        strp = next (NULL);
    }
    return 0;
}
```

And the program run:

```
here comes s1:
This is a sentence
is a sentence
a sentence
sentence
here comes s2:
with many words
many words
words
```

Unfortunately, the function next (), declared above has no definition. Your task is to write this definition so that the program
produces the output shown above.

The function derives the starting address of the next "word" from
a string, as shown above. Words are defined as being separated by
a sequence of blanks or tab characters.

Please note that the first call of next () receives the starting
address of the string to be investigated, whilst every call after that
(in a loop) supplies the address value NULL for the same string. So
if next () receives NULL as an argument, it knows that it should
continue its word search where it left off from the previous call.
How can next () know that?

By a char pointer of course, defined as a local static variable,
and keeping its stored address until the next function call.

Note also the run condition of the loop; next () returns NULL, if
it does not find another word.

Tip (Some standard functions, e.g. strtok ()) use this method of local static variables.

Modular programming libraries

8.1 What is modular programming?

Modular programming is a paradigm of C programming without which any description of C would be incomplete. That is why there is a whole chapter devoted to it.

The issue here is not the language structure of C, but the "philosophy" of programming with C.

The language resources required for this subject (global variables, global `static` variables, etc.) were dealt with in the last chapter, so this is really about applying what you learnt there.

Let's first consider the concept **module**. A module is a self-contained component which can be communicated with via defined interfaces, but of which the internal workings are concealed from the environment. People also talk about "public" interfaces and "private" internal workings. By carefully assembling different modules, a functioning whole can be created which fulfils a specific purpose.

Working in reverse, if you start with a specific purpose, the solution required to achieve that purpose can be divided into various modules, with each module fulfilling part of the function.

When these two procedures are applied to program development, they are known as **bottom-up** and **top-down processes**.

If the attentive reader now thinks that the term module equals function in C, then that is only correct in that the procedural subdivision of a program into various functions is of course in a sense modular.

In C, however, a module consists of a program file which contains some data (mostly global variables) and a series of functions to manipulate that data.

The data and functions of a program should be divided into different modules according to the following criteria:

| Each module should deal with a particular aspect of the problem;

2 The details of the implementation should be hidden from other modules ("data encapsulation", "information hiding").

A largish program should therefore consist of several program files (modules). For example, one of the modules deals with all the file accesses, another handles screen output, a third controls access to dynamic main memory areas, etc. The functions could also be divided up in other ways.

To demonstrate a modular program in practice, you should really apply it to quite a large-scale problem. It is only because of lack of space and to provide an overview that modularity will be demonstrated here applied to a small, concise program.

8.2 A "sorted stack"

This program is designed to store a series of decimal numbers occurring in any sequence and to make the stored numbers available at any time. However, the numbers should not be retrieved in the sequence in which they were stored (as in a QUEUE), nor in reverse order (as in a STACK), but it must always be the smallest of the remaining stored numbers which is retrieved.

The data structure used here could best be described as a "sorted stack".

The program consists of two modules, with one containing the data and functions for the storage of the numbers as described above and the other an application program which uses the first module – in this case a `main()` function to test our number management. We therefore have the following files:

```
  /* srmem.h */
 void clear (void);
 double put (double f);
 double fetch (void);


/* Module: srmem.c */
# include <stdio.h>
# define MAXMEM 200            /* max. memory length */
static double mem[MAXMEM];     /* memory */
static double * mp = mem;      /* memory pointer */
static double * hp;            /* auxiliary pointer */
void clear (void)             /* initialize memory*/
{
   mp = mem;
}
double put (double f)         /* put f in the memory */
{
   if (mp >= mem + MAXMEM)
```

```
   {
       fprintf (stderr, "\007Error: memory is full!\n");
       return 0.0;
   }
   for (hp = mp - 1 ; hp >= mem ; --hp)
       if (f > *hp)
           *(hp + 1) = *hp;
       else
       {
           *(hp + 1) = f;
           mp++;
           return f;
       }
   *(hp + 1) = f;
   mp++;
   return f;
}
double fetch (void) /* fetch value from memory */
{
   if (mp > mem)
       return *--mp;
   else
   {
       fprintf (stderr, "\007Error: memory is empty!\n");
       return 0.0;
   }
}
/* Module: memsort.c */
# include <stdio.h>
# include "srmem.h"
int main (void)
{
   double x;
   if (put (23.4) == 0.0)
       return 1;
   if (put (248.7) == 0.0)
       return 1;
   if (put (-3.6) == 0.0)
       return 1;
   if (put (44.4) == 0.0)
       return 1;
   if (put (17.5) == 0.0)
```

```
            return 1;
    if (put (-39.2) == 0.0)
            return 1;
    if (put (15.2) == 0.0)
            return 1;
    while ((x = fetch ())!= 0.0)
            printf ("%lf\n", x);
    return 0;
}
```

Regarding the header file srmem.h, all we will say for now is that it contains functions prototypes. We will consider later how it fits into modular programming.

The module srmem.c contains all our material for sorted stack management. The global static vector mem is our sorted stack. This is the area of the memory where all the values "thrown" on to the stack are stored. Its size can easily be adjusted to suit the required amount of data by redefining the constant MAXMEM.

The second global static variable mp is a double pointer, with the following practical purpose: it always indicates the next free, i.e. unoccupied element of the vector mem. At the start mp indicates the start of the vector, that is to say the first element. The first value thrown on the stack would be stored there and mp would then have to be directed to the address of the next element. mp is therefore our "sorted stack pointer".

It is certainly not essential for the third stack variable, the auxiliary pointer hp to be also defined globally. It could equally well have been defined as a local variable in the function put (), because it is only there that it is used.

Let's first consider the first of the three functions of this module, namely clear (): this initializes the stack, by directing the stack pointer mp to the start of the vector mem.

However, as mp was already initialized in this way when it was defined, it should be clear that the purpose of clear () is to initialize the stack again at any point while the program is running, i.e. to discard all previously stored values.

That once again sheds light on the significance of the pointer mp: it is not the content of the vector mem which indicates which double values are currently stored on the sorted stack, but the position of the pointer mp. Everything coming before the address stored in mp counts as being "stored on the sorted stack", while everything after the address stored in mp counts as not yet occupied memory space. So when a program has thrown about 24 double values on the stack with put () and then invokes clear (), all these 24 double values count as being "deleted from the stack" (although they do still temporarily exist in the relevant elements of mem).

The put() function carries out the actual job of sorting and storing a double value on the sorted stack. When the double value which has been passed to the parameter f is to be stored on the sorted stack, a check must first be made that there is still free space in the mem vector. That is the case if mp indicates an amount of storage space which is less than mem + MAXMEM – the upper limit. Otherwise an error message is generated and the function is exited with 0.0.

If there is sufficient memory space, the value passed to f must be stored in an element of the mem vector in such a way that it is only followed by smaller values. The sorted stack should therefore insert each value thrown on to the stack in such a way among the values already stored that, from the start of the mem vector, all stored values are stored sorted in descending order.

The for loop therefore begins in the last (and smallest) element with hp = mp - 1; and then works its way "forwards". Each element is thereby copied one element further "backwards", freeing up the element itself. However, should the value passed to f now be smaller than that element, then f is stored in the last freed element and the function is quitted.

To illustrate this algorithm, the last put() call of the main() function is shown as it is stored (see Figure 8.1).

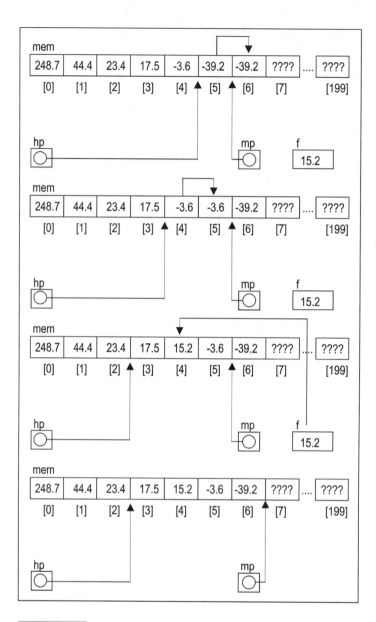

Figure 8.1 *put(): Sorted insertion of a new element*

Finally, mp is always updated, by being increased by one element and the newly stored value is returned as the return value.

It should be clear that the put () function also fulfils its task correctly in the following three limiting cases:

1 The value which has been passed is the first, i.e. the stack is previously still empty.

2 The value which has been passed is smaller than all previously stored values, so it must be stored after the last element.

3 The value which has been passed is larger than all previously stored values, so it must be stored at the start of the mem vector.

The return value is always the value which has been successfully thrown on the stack, or 0.0, if the stack was already full. That causes a problem: what happens if the stack is not full, but the value 0.0 is thrown on the stack?

You can't tell from the return value of the put() function whether a value of 0.0 which was passed has been successfully stored on the stack or whether the stack was full, even though the user only sees an error message in the latter case.

A loop with put() calls would have no unambiguous criterion for canceling the function in the case of a full stack.

We will tackle this problem later; for now we must just tell the user of our sorted stack function not to store the value 0.0.

The third function, fetch(), moves the sorted stack pointer mp back by one element and returns the value which it finds there as the return value. Because of the logic of the way our sorted stack is built up using put(), that is always the smallest of all the stored values.

Of course, that can only happen if mp > mem, i.e. the sorted stack is not empty. If it is empty, the user receives a message and the return value of 0.0 is sent.

If the above instruction not to throw the value 0.0 on the stack has been observed, then the return value 0.0 following a fetch() call must always mean that the stack is empty. This feature is used in the main() function of memsort.c to retrieve and display all stored values from the stack.

The program run then generates the following screen output:

```
-39.2
-3.6
15.2
17.5
23.4
44.4
248.7
Error: memory is empty!
```

The last line of output may be irritating for the user of our sorted stack. The intention was to empty the stack using fetch(), so an error message is not expected. However, the error message was built in by the programmer to distinguish an empty stack from the situation where a stored value of 0.0 has been removed from the stack.

This is another indication that there is room for improvement in our program (see below).

8.3 Project management

So much for the logic behind the individual functions of our "sorted stack". Now we come to the real nitty-gritty, where we establish that the above program consists of two modules: `srmem.c` and `memsort.c`. There is also the header file `srmem.h`, but that is not counted as a module of the program. Both modules must be specified when invoking the compiler.

In UNIX:

```
cc memsort.c srmem.c -omemsort
```

In MS/DOS (e.g. BORLAND-C):

```
bcc memsort.c srmem.c
```

These commands have the effect of making the compiler translate each individual module, separately from the others, and file it in the relevant object file. It then invokes the linkage editor, which links all the object files (by linking other object functions from the standard library) to a executable program `memsort` (with UNIX) or `memsort.exe` (with MS/DOS). This fact opens up two new problem areas which should be discussed here:

1 Efficient maintenance of a program (project files);
2 Provision of individual modules in the form of object libraries.

Efficient maintenance of a program

Imagine that our program consisted of not two but twenty modules. After a successful test run, it later emerges that the program would be slightly improved if there were a little tweaking of the seventeenth module. After this slight modification to the seventeenth module, a new executable program would have to be created.

The easiest thing to do would be for the programmer to have all twenty modules retranslated and bound by the linkage editor.

If these little modifications crop up quite frequently, it may occur to the programmer how much time it is taking to translate all twenty modules – despite the high speeds of modern C compilers and computers.

The programmer hits on the ruse of just retranslating the seventeenth module, which brings about a useful reduction in the translation time, although the linkage editor still has to link all twenty modules again.

Let us assume that our program consisted of the modules: mod1.c, mod2.c, ..., mod20.c, then in UNIX for example the following command calls would be needed:

```
$ cc -c mod17.c
$ cc mod1.o mod2.o ... mod20.o -oprog
```

The first call instructs the compiler cc, through the option -c ("compile only") only to translate mod17.c and save it in the file mod17.o without then invoking the linkage editor. With the second call, cc recognizes from the filename messages .o that it is only being sent object files. As no single file has been specified which ends with .c in its name, the actual C compiler is not invoked, but instead the linkage editor straightaway, which links all the object modules to an executable program prog.

If the programmer has made small changes in modules mod4.c, mod11.c and mod18.c at the same time, it could be that by the time of the last change he or she has forgotten which modules have been changed and which are now to be retranslated. He or she could make good use of the command ls -ltr (in UNIX) or DIR /OD (in MS/DOS), to obtain a file list sorted in ascending order by the time stamp of the last change. From that it is possible to see which .c files have been changed since the creation of the relevant .o(bj) files. All in all, this is a very long-winded procedure.

A utility program is needed to relieve the programmer of this work. In UNIX a tool like this is known by the name make, and some C compilers in MS/DOS also have make among the accessories. This command uses a dependency description file – known for short as a make file to check which source code modules must be retranslated because they have a more recent time stamp than the relevant object modules and also whether the linkage editor should be invoked, because perhaps only one object module has a later timestamp than the destination – the executable program file.

In other words: make means that only the most essential operations to make the executable program file up-to-date are carried out. As an example of how make can be applied, let us look here – in a simplified form – at the make file memsort.m for our sorted stack program:

```
# memsort.m
#
memsort:        memsort.o srmem.o
        cc memsort.o srmem.o -omemsort
memsort.o:      memsort.c srmem.h
```

```
        cc -c memsort.c
srmem.o:      srmem.c
        cc -c srmem.c
```

Apart from the comment lines, which must always start with #, this make file consists of three groups of two lines each. The structure is the same for all three groups: the first line describes for a specific file the other files on which it depends. Thus, memsort depends on the two object files memsort.o and srmem.o. That means that it is checked whether only one of the two files memsort.o and srmem.o has a later time stamp than the file memsort. If that is the case, then the line below will invoke cc memsort.o srmem.o -omemsort as a command. Otherwise this command is not called.

The first line of the second group states that the object module memsort.o is dependent on the files memsort.c and srmem.h (in the sense described above). If so, then again the relevant second line cc -c memsort.c is carried out, but otherwise not. This guarantees that the object module memsort.o is kept up-to-date. It should be understood why in this case there is a dependency on srmem.h. Because this header file is included in memsort.c, with # include "srmem.h", even if there is a change only to srmem.h, the file memsort.c should be retranslated.

The third group of pairs of lines is structured in exactly the same way and ensures that srmem.o is up to date.

Regarding syntax, it is important to know that each second line (the action line then) must begin with one or more tab characters. No leading blanks allowed here.

Let us now assume that the program memsort is up-to-date and has already been invoked for use several times. Now the programmer makes a change to srmem.c, by for example setting the constant MAXMEM to 300 instead of 200 as previously.

Then make is invoked, to update the program, and the following happens on the screen:

```
$ make -fmemsort.m
cc -c srmem.c
cc memsort.o srmem.o -omemsort
$
```

make, having been provided with the name of the make file after the option -f (for "file"), indicates all the actions which have actually been carried out.

As was to be expected, out of the source code modules only srmem.c was retranslated, and with the last action the linkage editor is invoked to generate the executable program. It is worth noticing the sequence of the actions which have been carried out, which makes sense logically, but appears to contradict the content of the make file. There, invoking the linkage editor was a component of the first group. make processes the specified description file "recursively", which is why the groups have to be structured in this way.

make can also do a lot more than we have shown here. It can cope with the most complex of projects, where not only the C compiler is invoked but all manner of commands may be used. It understands a powerful macro language which can be used drastically to reduce huge make files, but it would be beyond the scope of this book to go into that. The reader who is interested in make should refer to a somewhat more detailed introduction in Bach et al. (1987) [8] where there are also other references to the literature.

Modern C compilers also have – as well as make – a project management system incorporated in a mainly graphics "integrated development environment", which has the same functionality as make. There it is generally only the modules which are involved in a project which have to be included in a Project (BOR-LAND) or Workspace (MICROSOFT). When the compiler is activated, only the really necessary operations are then automatically carried out. The dependency of the user-defined header files is also automatically recognized from the #include instructions and no longer needs to be specified separately.

Provision of individual modules in the form of object libraries

Let's imagine that the "inventor" of our "sorted stack" would like to make his product available to other programmers. All he has to do is pass on the two files srmem.h and srmem.c. Anyone acquiring this software product then has to insert the module srmem.c in his project if the "sorted stack" is to be used there.

However, the acquirer can also change the functions of the "sorted stack" or improve the whole way it works and market it as his own product.

Perhaps the original inventor of the product would have something against that. In that case he does not give away the source code, but only the files srmem.o (or srmem.obj), i.e. the object code and the header file srmem.h.

The new user can now incorporate the object file in his project without being able to change the functions in the source code. The only thing he or she has access to in the source code is now the header file srmem.h with the prototypes of the three functions.

It is now necessary to provide a description for the user-programmer of how the three functions of the "sorted stack" work, and the provider could make this available in a readme.doc file. Its contents could read as follows:

readme.doc

"Sorted stack"

For storing a maximum of 200 double figures. The double figures can be stored in any order on the "sorted stack", but they are always retrieved from the "sorted stack" in ascending order.

Public interfaces:

```
# include "srmem.h"
```

void clear (void);

Initializes the stack, i.e. discards (deletes) all previously stored figures and makes the complete memory space of 200 storage slots available again.

```
# include "srmem.h"
```

double put (double f);

Stores the parameter f on the "sorted stack".

Return value: value f if it has been successfully stored on the stack, otherwise, if the stack is full, 0.0. (In this case an error message indicates that the stack is full.)

```
# include "srmem.h"
```

double fetch (void);

Retrieves the smallest of all values stored on the "sorted stack". This value is then removed from the stack. When the stack is empty fetch() returns the value: 0.0 and indicates with an error message that the stack is empty.

That is all a programmer needs to know to use the functions of the "sorted stack". Note: no explanation is given about the actual implementation. Whether the stored figures are stored in a vector (as in our case), a concatenated list, or a binary tree, and what the access algorithms are remains hidden.

That is the most important feature of modular programming: a module is a "black box" which you cannot see into, and can only communicate with via "public interfaces ", ensuring a well-defined functionality.

Here we should explain the importance referred to above of the header file srmem.h: it represents the official interfaces of the sorted stack in the form of prototypes.

8.4 Libraries

Now we come to the real subject of this section: libraries.

Let's imagine that a module contained not three functions but three hundred. A user of this module, however, may only invoke twenty-eight of these three hundred functions in his user program. Is it then necessary to link the whole object module to the program?

It is not only since C that compilers (or more precisely linkage editors) have had the ability to find missing functions from object libraries, extract them and link them to the rest of the program. In the example given above, the linkage editor would copy the object code of the twenty-eight functions – but only these – from a suitable library, if all three hundred functions were stored not in an object file but in an object library.

These libraries have to be constructed in a specific format, to allow for individual functions to be extracted. Each C compiler therefore generally also has a Library Manager, which allows it to insert object modules in libraries, replace old versions with new ones, extract copies of individual object modules from a library or delete them there.

To return to our example of the sorted stack, it would require the following steps to make a library:

In UNIX:

```
cc -c srmem.c
ar r $HOME/lib/libsrmem.a srmem.o
```

In MS/DOS (using the example of BORLAND-C):

```
bcc -c srmem.c
tlib \lib\srmem.lib +srmem.obj
```

First, an object file must be created (`srmem.o` in UNIX, `srmem.obj` in MS/DOS), using the option `-c`.

The Library Manager in UNIX is called `ar` (for archiver). Its other arguments are:

➔ `r`: replace a previous module version by the new one which has been specified. If there is no old version, the new one is added;
➔ `libsrmem.a`: name of the library in which the module should be replaced;
➔ `srmem.o`: name of the new object module.

If the library which is specified does not exist, it will be created. In principle the library can have any filename you like. However, to keep to the conventions of the UNIX C compiler, the name should always begin with `lib` and end with `.a`. Then the compiler for our `memsort` program could be invoked like this:

```
cc memsort.c -L$HOME/lib -lsrmem -omemsort
```

In this call, when `srmem` is specified after `-l` (for libraries), `cc` forms the complete library name `libsrmem.a`.

The option `-L` means that directories can be specified where `cc` should look for libraries specified by `-l`.

It should be understood that the last compiler call does something different from the following one:

```
cc memsort.c srmem.o -omemsort
```

Here it is always the entire (!) object file `srmem.o` which is bound, while the call with `-lsrmem` only extracts from the library and links those functions which are really invoked in `memsort`.

In the Library Manager `tlib` from BORLAND, the new module is added to the library `srmem.lib` using `+srmem.obj`. If you wanted to replace an old version by a new one here, you would specify:

```
+-srmem.obj
```

The names convention for libraries for the C compiler in MS/DOS only expects that the names will end with `.lib`.

A call for our `memsort` project would look like this (for the BORLAND C compiler):

```
bcc -L\lib memsort.c srmem.lib
```

Two important tips about C libraries in MS/DOS:

1. With MS/DOS C compilers there are generally not one but several libraries with the same content for the different memory models of executable programs. This problem of memory models is a reflection of the special way MS/DOS deals with INTEL processors. All we shall say here is that with the above `tlib` call, a library for the standard memory model Small would be generated.

2. The "integrated development environments" of modern C compilers in MS/DOS and WINDOWS generally make it much easier both to specify the libraries which should be searched and also to specify the directories which should be searched for libraries. Entry fields on a menu system then replace command line options. (Further information can be found in the relevant compiler manuals.)

Tip A collection of functions in a closed problem cycle can be packaged in the form of one or more object files in a library. This then allows application programmers who only want to invoke certain ones of these functions to include just those functions in their programs.

In fact we have been using this option from the start - since "Hello, world!" -, because even using `printf()` causes the linkage editor to fetch the program code for this function from a library: the standard library. With the UNIX C compiler the standard library is called `libc.a`. With MS/DOS (e.g. BORLAND) there is a different version for each memory model: `CS.LIB`, `CM.LIB`, ... or in WIN-DOWS: `CWS.LIB`, `CWM.LIB` ....

So long as the linkage editor continues to find unresolved references, it continues to search in the standard library for the program code for the relevant functions. That applies to all standard functions which we have used so far, regardless of whether their prototypes are located in `stdio.h`, in `string.h` or in any other header file. It is important to make this clear, because there is a widespread misconception that the `stdio.h` file is the standard library. No, `stdio.h` is only a header file, which only contains the prototypes of just a small number of the standard functions.

The standard library is always searched by the linkage editor. However, when you invoke the compiler you can also specify other additional libraries which should be searched for functions. That may be libraries which – like the standard library – are supplied by the compiler manufacturer or other software manufacturers, or libraries you have created yourself, which we have just learnt about.

As an example of the former type, let us take the famous Curses library in UNIX, which contains a multitude of functions for terminal control. It would have to be specified separately each time the compiler is invoked:

```
cc ...... -lcurses ....
```

We should now consider the question: as a programmer, when do you set up a library for a set of functions? There are two criteria for this:

1 Depending on the situation, it is likely that an application program could only invoke some of the functions contained in the set. To put it another way: if you can foresee that when you invoke one of the functions (nearly) all the others will be invoked too, you would be better creating an object file instead of a library.

2 The functions of the set deal with a generally applicable problem cycle, of interest to all kinds of application programs. If a package of functions has only been designed for one special application, and it cannot be envisaged that it could ever be of interest to any other application, you would not create a library. However, in that case the first criterion would probably also not be met.

A good example which is suitable for a library because it is generally applicable would be a functions package for date management. It could contain functions which:

1   check if a date is plausible;

2   identify if a date is in a leap year;

3   calculate from one date the date of the next day or of a given day (30 days later);

4   calculate the difference between two dates.

8.5 An improved "sorted stack"

At the end of this chapter we want to try to improve our sorted stack library. Let us consider again which defects could be subject to improvement.

During the above main() function, the user sees at the end of the program: `Error: memory is empty!` on the screen. The main problem lies in the fact that this is more of an error message for the application programmer rather than for the user.

Now the application programmer is not really to blame for this situation, because the error message is generated by `fetch()`, which is part of the library, and for which he does not have access to the source code. It is actually up to the application programmer to decide whether to tell users at the end: "That was all the stored numbers!" or whether there is no such message at all. Unfortunately, the author of the sorted stack library does not leave the programmer this freedom.

A second deficiency is that under no circumstances should one throw the value 0.0 on the stack. The application programmer did adhere to that in the above `main()` function. However, if he or she had at any point also inserted the call:

```
if (put (0.0) == 0.0)
    return 1;
```

the program would have stopped at once.

But if the programmer was not defining the numbers personally, but had left it to the user to enter the figures to be stored on the "sorted stack", he or she could never have been certain the users would not do what they had been forbidden to do and enter the figure 0.0. It could even be essential to the job to store the value 0.0.

So the main problem is that both functions, `put()` and `fetch()`, produce as the return value the value which has been stored or removed from the stack. However, as the return value is also to be used to control the relevant loop – so long as the stack is not yet full nor yet empty – it is necessary to make one of the double figure values the identifying character for just these special cases. But that would mean that this value (0.0) would no longer be a figure which could be stored. An unacceptable limitation. It should be understood that the inventors of the getchar() macro were also dealing with this problem. This macro gives the character which has been read as the return value. At the same time however you need to be able to tell from the return value if the user no longer wanted to enter any characters, using the end of input key combination.

We know how the programmers of getchar() solved this problem: instead of returning the character which was read as a char value, they returned it as an int value. They then had the option of indicating the end of input character by returning the int value -1 (EOF), which could never be the code for a valid character, i.e. is different from all the characters in the code table.

Unfortunately, we cannot follow this route. Which even bigger value than any double value could we return, to indicate a full or empty stack?

We use a different technique to solve our problem. Here is the improved "sorted stack":

```
/* srmem.h */
# define SRSTACK_OK 0
# define SRSTACK_FULL 1
# define SRSTACK_EMPTY 2
extern int srstack_error;
void clear(void);
double push (double f);
double pop (void);
/*-------------------------------------------------*/
/* Module: srmem.c */
# include <stdio.h>
# include "srmem.h"
# define MAXVAL 200                /* Max. stack length */
static double val[MAXVAL];         /* Stack */
static double * vp = val;          /* Stack pointer */
static double * hp;                /* Auxiliary pointer */
int srstack_error = SRSTACK_EMPTY; /* Error variable */
void clear (void) /* Initialize stack*/
{
    vp = val;
    srstack_error = SRSTACK_EMPTY;
}
double put (double f) /* Add f to the stack */
{
```

```
        if (vp >= val + MAXVAL)
        {
            srstack_error = SRSTACK_FULL;
            return 0.0;
        }
        if (srstack_error == SRSTACK_EMPTY)
            srstack_error = SRSTACK_OK;
        for (hp = vp - 1 ; hp >= val ; --hp)
            if (f > *hp)
                *(hp + 1) = *hp;
            else
            {
                *(hp + 1) = f;
                vp++;
                return f;
            }
        *(hp + 1) = f;
        vp++;
        return f;
    }
double fetch (void) /* Retrieve value from stack*/
{
    if (vp > val)
    {
        if (srstack_error == SRSTACK_FULL)
            srstack_error = SRSTACK_OK;
        return *--vp;
    }
    else
    {
        srstack_error = SRSTACK_EMPTY;
        return 0.0;
    }
}
/*-------------------------------------------------*/
/* Module: memsort.c */
# include <stdio.h>
# include "srmem.h"
int main (void)
{
    double x;
    if (put (23.4) == 0.0 && srstack_error == SRSTACK_FULL)
```

```
        return 1;
    if (put (248.7) == 0.0 && srstack_error == SRSTACK_FULL)
        return 1;
    if (put (-3.6) == 0.0 && srstack_error == SRSTACK_FULL)
        return 1;
    if (put (0.0) == 0.0 && srstack_error == SRSTACK_FULL)
        return 1;
    if (put (17.5) == 0.0 && srstack_error == SRSTACK_FULL)
        return 1;
    if (put (-39.2) == 0.0 && srstack_error == SRSTACK_FULL)
        return 1;
    if (put (15.2) == 0.0 && srstack_error == SRSTACK_FULL)
        return 1;
    while (x = fetch (), srstack_error != SRSTACK_EMPTY)
        printf ("%lf\n", x);
    return 0;
}
```

With three `define` constants in `srmem.h`, three different states are defined for the stack: Everything OK, stack is full and stack is empty. At the same time an `int` variable `srstack_error` is declared externally.

This variable is defined globally in `srmem.c`, but deliberately not as a `static` variable. Access to it should be possible to it from all functions in which `sr-mem.h` is bound. It is initialized with the initial status of the stack, namely: "stack is empty".

By communicating with this variable we will be able to find out the status of the sorted stack at any time. It is important that all stack operations ensure that this variable is up-to-date. That is why all three functions set `srstack_error` to one of the three values, depending on the situation. In particular:

`clear()` must of course set `srstack_error` to the value `SRSTACK_EMPTY`.

The `put()` function sets `srstack_error` to the value `SRSTACK_FULL`, if the stack is full. However, that also means that the value passed to the parameter f could not be stored. Otherwise it must always be checked whether the stack is empty. Then the value f is stored as the first value and the status of the stack must be changed to `SRSTACK_OK`.

On the other hand, the `fetch()` function must set `srstack_error` to `SRSTACK_ OK` if the stack was full, but it no longer is full if `fetch()` has been invoked. Equally, `SRSTACK_EMPTY` must be set if `fetch()` is invoked for an empty stack.

Note that neither put(), nor fetch() now produce an error message. The question of whether a message should be sent about a full or empty stack is now left entirely to the application programmer, who can obtain information about these limiting cases after each put() or fetch() command by evaluating the srstack_error variable.

Let us now consider how the application programmer should evaluate the result of a put() or of a fetch() call. The changed main() function contains instructions such as these for put() calls:

```
if (put (23.4) == 0.0 && srstack_error == SRSTACK_FULL)
    return 1;
```

The program stops if put() comes back with the return value 0.0 and srstack_error indicates a full stack. Note that put() still returns the value 0.0 if the stack is full. The absence of a corresponding return instruction would lead to a compiler error for syntax reasons. However, the following program lines would also fulfill the purpose of making sure the return value from put() is not evaluated at all:

```
put (23.4);
if (srstack_error == SRSTACK_FULL)
    return 1;
```

In this application we can see that put() could equally well have been defined as a void function: we no longer need the return value.

The case is a little different with the fetch() call. Here the return value must be retrieved, for without it you would not need to invoke fetch() at all. However, it is no longer used to find out if the stack is empty. Accordingly, the fetch() call is also no longer used to evaluate the loop conditions.

Note that in

```
while (x = fetch (), srstack_error!= SRSTACK_EMPTY)
    printf ("%lf\n", x);
```

the expression x = fetch () is evaluated, but – because of the sequence operator ",", the whole loop condition is only created by the evaluation value of srstack_error!= SRSTACK_EMPTY (see "Sequence operator" on p. 60).

It is of course assumed in all this that the header file srmem.h is bound using external declaration of srstack_error, otherwise it would not be possible to access this variable. It should be clear that information about this externally declared variable must also have its place in a README.DOC file. It is part of the library's public interface.

This technique of dealing with error statuses or exceptions by globally defined and externally declared variables is also used for example in system programming with system calls. These are C functions which directly invoke certain subroutines of the operating system. In the event of an error, a code for the type of error is filed in a predefined global variable, giving access even to the original error messages of the operating system.

However, it should not be denied that "lugging around a global variable" could possibly be seen as rather cumbersome. That is why another solution should be suggested for our original problem. For example, what about the int functions put() and fetch(), which always give either SRSTACK_OK, SRSTACK_FULL or SRSTACK_EMPTY as a return value?

The only problem then would be fetch(), which cannot give the double value which it has retrieved from the sorted stack as the return value. But this problem can be easily solved by the following prototypes:

```
int fetch (double * dp);
```

and the following usage:

```
.....
double x;
.....
while (fetch (&x) != SRSTACK_EMPTY)
    ....
```

Here, fetch() puts the value it has retrieved from the stack in a variable to which it has access via the pointer dp. Only the status of the sorted stack is now given as the return value.

This technique is also used by standard functions such as scanf(). (Further information can be found from the online help for the C compiler on the return value of scanf().)

8.6 Exercises

The following exercises relate to the second, improved version of our sorted stack. You are strongly recommended to work through all the exercises in order without going straight to sneak a look at the specimen answers!

I   Create the necessary files for our sorted stack. Change the main() function, so that the figures thrown on the stack by the user are read in using get_double(). The inputting process should be stopped if the user enters 0.0 or if the stack turns out to be full when a user figure is stored. (Here we again have the unfortunate situation that the user cannot store the figure 0.0. But now it is not the fault of our sorted stack, but of `get_double()`. This problem too can be solved (see Exercises 6 and 7).

Create a header file `my.h` containing the prototypes of the three previously developed functions `getline()`, `get_int()` and `get_double()`.

Don't forget to link the header file `my.h` to `memsort.c`.

To make the program run now either:

I a project (in an "integrated development environment") or

2 a make file (if `make` is available)

must be set up.

Remember that now `getdbl.c` and `getline.c` are also part of the project.

Update the project by selecting the menu item `Build` (or similar) (in an integrated development environment) or invoking `make`.

Test the program!

2 Set up a library for the sorted stack called `srmem.lib` (in MS/DOS) or `libsrmem.a` (in UNIX). Note: it is still essential to have a project file or `make` file. But their content must be adapted to the new situation.

Delete the object and executable files and have the project updated again. Test the program!

3 Incorporate three new functions `total()`, `avail()` and `status()` in our sorted stack.

The `total()` function should give the total size of the sorted stack as a return value (i.e. the value of MAXMEM).

The `avail()` function gives the number of `double` elements which are not currently occupied, i.e. are available, as the return value.

The `status()` function gives the content of the global variable `srstack_error`. Make this variable into a static-global variable and remove the corresponding external declaration from `srmem.h`. (Why is that now possible?)

Replace the old version by the new one in the library. Change the previous `main()` function, avoiding all access to `srstack_error` (that is now forbidden) and work only by invoking `status()`.

In the `main()` function, when user input is finished, say how many of the figures have been stored on the `sorted stack`. Test the program!

4 Based on the example in this chapter, create a `readme.doc` file with a description of the "sorted stack" in the version in Exercise 3!

5 Assuming you didn't miss out on creating the lottery program in Exercise 6 of Chapter 6, change this program so that the first 6 numbers drawn are thrown on the sorted stack using `put()`, from where they can be retrieved again to display the results of the draw using `fetch()`. (Some slight evidence that our sorted stack could actually serve some useful purpose!)

Create a corresponding project or `make` file. Test the program!

6 Exercise 1 threw up a problem for us: if the user enters the value 0.0 when he invokes `get_double()` (or only Return), the loop will be ended, although he perhaps wanted to throw 0.0 on the stack and then add other numbers. We can see that `get_double()` suffers from the same limitations as our first `fetch()` version.

Change the `get_double()` function so that you define a global variable there too, `doub_error`, which can be occupied by the `define` constants `DOUB_OK` (value: 0), `DOUB_NOTHING` (value: 1) and `DOUB_EOF` (value: 2). Then: `doub_error` contains

1 the value: `DOUB_OK` when a number is entered

2 the value: `DOUB_NOTHING` when only Return is entered

3 the value: `DOUB_EOF` when Ctrl z or Crtl d is entered.

Remember that `get_double()` itself invokes `getline()`. A distinction is made between the three above cases depending on the `getline()` call.

The three `define` constants and an external declaration of `doub_error` are to be defined in the header file `my.h`.

Change the read loop in `memsort.c` accordingly. From now on the user should be able to throw the value 0.0 on the stack. The read loop should only be broken for `DOUB_NOTHING` or `DOUB_EOF`.

7 For reasons of completeness, the same change should be made to the `get_int()` function. Here the global variable should be called `int_error` and the corresponding `define` constants `INT_OK`, `INT_NOTHING` and `INT_EOF`.

8 Create a new library my.lib (in MS/DOS) or libmy.a (in UNIX), into which you put the object modules from getline.c, getint.c and getdbl.c.

How should the project or make file now be changed for the memsort project?

Update the project again, after you have deleted the relevant object and executable files, and test the memsort program again!

Functions

9.1 Definition, declaration, calling

Let's summarize once again what we know about functions.

Definition of a function:

```
[static] type fname (plist)
{
    ...
    ... /* Instructions from the functions structure */
    ...
}
```

Meanings are as follows:

1   type:
→   void, if the function does not give a return value or
→   the data type of the return value.

2   fname: the name of the function, which must be made up according to the same rules as variable names.

3   plist:
→   void or no data (i.e. empty brackets), if the function has no parameters or
→   a list of parameter definitions of the form: [register] type variable, separated by the list operator ",". (Parameters may be of the register memory class.)

In principle all function definitions are global, i.e. they can be declared externally in any number of modules and then also called there unless they are defined as static functions. A static function is automatically module-global, i.e. it can only be called from functions which belong to the same module as the static function.

Declaration of a function (prototype):

```
[external | static] type fname (plist);
```

A prototype for a `static` function must be identified with the keyword `static`. Otherwise, the keyword external can be specified, but does not have to be.

(However, a `static` declaration can of course only be specified in the same module as where the `static` function is also defined.)

The prototype:

```
external int getline (char * s, int lim);
```

is also the same as:

```
int getline (char * s, int lim);
```

Generally external is always omitted from function declarations.

The parameter list either looks exactly the same as it did in the definition, or it consists of a list of data types without variable names. The following declarations are therefore identical:

```
int getline (char * s, int lim);
```

and:

```
int getline (char *, int);
```

The final semicolon is important!

Calling a function:

```
fname (arglist)
```

I   Here `arglist` refers to a list, separated by commas, of the actual arguments which, when they are called, are passed to the formal parameters as defined in the function definition, and which must correspond to these in number and data type.

2   The call itself is an expression which is evaluated with the return value of the function. However, if it is a `void` function which is being called, which does not give a return value, the call expression can also not be evaluated.

With regard to (1): The compiler does not take too seriously the requirement for the arguments passed to the function to be of the same data type as the corresponding parameters. However, the data types of the arguments must be convertible into the data types of the formal parameters, according to the type conversion rules which are implicitly built into the compiler.

However, before any conversion of differing data types, the following must apply:

All arguments of the type char, unsigned char, short and unsigned short are always converted to the data type int, and all float arguments are always converted to the data type double and added to the stack. The relevant parameters then occupy the lowest value section of these int or double arguments. (In MS/DOS the conversion from short to int is not necessary, because both data types have the same memory length in any case).

The following program shows examples of function calls which the compiler accepts without any problem, those which it marks with a warning and those which are strictly forbidden:

```c
# include <stdio.h>
void func1 (double z)
{
   printf ("%lf\n", z);
}
void func2 (char * p)
{
   printf ("%c\n", *p);
}
int main (void)
{
   long z = 0x41424344L;

   func1 (3.5);
   func1 (3.5f);
   func1 (12);
   func1 (-18L);
   func1 ((short)7);
   func1 ('A');
/* func1 ("A");    Error!
                char pointer: no conversion into double! */
   func2 ("ABC");
/* func2 (1);      Error!
   int: no conversion into char *! */
   func2 (&z);     /* Warning: "Suspicious pointer conver-
sion"! */
   return 0;
}
/* ---- Program run: ---------- *
3.500000
```

```
3.500000
12.000000
-18.000000
7.000000
65.000000
A
D
 *  ----------------------------  */
```

As can be seen from the program run, simple numerical data types are straightaway converted into other numerical data types implicitly. It is more problematic with pointers: the last call `func2 (&z);` passes a pointer to `long` to a pointer to `char`. We know that the same operation would not be permitted as an assignment (at least not without using a cast operator). When it is passed as an argument, however, there is just a warning to the programmer about the discrepancy. The compiler carries out the conversion which is obviously intended, as if the programmer had written:

```
func2 ((char *)&z);
```

(Incidentally, in C++ the compiler is much more particular. Because the C++ rules for checking the consistency of prototypes are much stricter, it would have reacted in this situation with a proper error message ("Error").)

What even the C compiler rejects as an error is the attempt to convert a pointer to `char` into the data type `double`.

With regard to (2): Let us assume for example the following function:

```
int incr (int x)
{
    return ++x;
}
```

Then the expression `incr (3)` is evaluated with 4!

We have seen before that functions can also be called in nests. For example, take the following function:

```
int quad (int z)
{
    return z * z;
}
```

Then the expression `quad (incr (3))` is evaluated with 16. Here it is important to understand that `incr()` is called before `quad()`. Because `quad()` receives as the actual argument the return value from calling `incr()`. This situation is clearly demonstrated if we add a screen output to both functions, thus:

```
int incr (int x)
{
   printf ("Function: incr()\n");
   return ++x;
}
int quad (int z)
{
   printf ("Function: quad()\n");
   return z * z;
}
```

The call quad (incr (3)) then provides the following output:

```
Function: incr()
Function: quad()
```

Incidentally, the implicit conversion rules which we have already described for passing arguments to the parameters of a function also apply to the return value of a function. That is demonstrated in the following programming example:

```
# include <stdio.h>
double func1 (void) /* Note: Double function! */
{
   return 1;       /* Note: Conversion of 1 (int) into dou-
ble! */
}
unsigned char * func2 (void)
{
   static long z = 0x4041L;
   return &z;      /* Warning: "Suspicious pointer conver-
sion"! */
}
int main (void)
{
   unsigned char * p;
   printf ("%lf\n", func1 ());
   p = func2 ();
   printf ("%c\n", * p);
   return 0;
}
```

```
/* ---- Program run: ------------------- *
1.000000
A
 * ------------------------------------- */
```

So, even when the `int` constant 1 is returned with `return`, a conversion into the `double` value 1.0 still takes place on the return, because – and only because – the function `func1()` is of the `double` type.

In `func2()` the return value `&z` has the data type pointer to `long`, but this is implicitly converted into the data type of the function, namely pointer to `unsigned char`, which incidentally is not translated without a warning from the C compiler.

9.2 Processes on the stack

Now that we have discussed passing arguments and return values from the point of view of their effect, we must now consider internal aspects. What happens to arguments or parameters and the return value in the main memory when a function is called and processed?

We have already learnt in Chapter 7 that the formal parameters of a function – just like normal, automatic variables – are placed on the stack. That is true, at least, so long as the parameters are not of the memory class `register`, i.e. are possibly stored in a register.

In one way, however, function parameters are different from normal, automatic variables, and that is in the sequence in which they are added to the stack. Let us take the following program as an example:

```
void printsum (int x, int y)
{
    printf ("Sum: %d\n", x + y);
}
int main (void)
{
    int a = 3,
        b = 5;
    printsum (a, b);
    return 0;
}
```

When `printsum()` is called, the core image of the stack looks as in Figure 9.1.

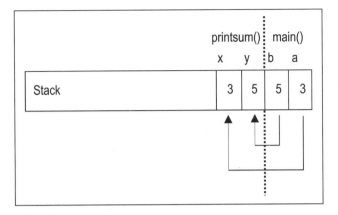

Figure 9.1 *Stack allocation when printsum() is called*

(The dotted line indicates what comes from variables from `main()` and what comes from `printsum()`.)

So, whereas the variables a and b are added to the stack in the order in which they were defined (going of course from the upper limit of the stack to the lower addresses), with the function parameters x and y, it is exactly the other way round.

So, first the content of the variable b is copied into the newly-created variable y, and after that the content of a is copied into the variable x, which is also newly-created.

The fact that function parameters are created in reverse order, i.e. "back-to-front" in the parameter list, is an important feature of C language, which does have its practical significance. This makes it easy, for example, to write functions which can be called with any number of arguments, such as `printf()`. But there will be more on this later (see Chapter 19).

The fact that this sequence applies not only to the formal parameters, but that the actual arguments are evaluated in the same sequence is remarkable, because it contradicts everything we have learnt about the sequence operator. Consider the following program and its outcome:

```
# include <stdio.h>
void printargs (int x, int y, int z)
{
    printf ("%d:%d:%d\n", x, y, z);
}
```

```
int main (void)
{
    int a = 0;
    printargs (++a, ++a, ++a);
    printf ("But: %d\n", (++a, ++a, ++a));
    return 0;
}
/* ---- Program run: ----------- *
3:2:1
But: 6
 * ------------------------------ */
```

The task carried out by `printargs()` demonstrates the above statement about the evaluation sequence for the argument list ++a, ++a, ++a. It is quite different in the `printf()` call, where, through the brackets around the same list, we can see the usual, normal effect of the sequence operator. This peculiarity of argument lists should always be borne in mind.

We had already referred to the fact that function parameters occur as completely new variables, which receive as their content a copy of the arguments which are passed, as **Call by Value** (see Chapter 1). In particular, it follows from this that a function cannot use its parameters to change the original data which is passed as arguments to the parameters.

If you really want to do so, you have to define pointers as formal parameters, as we saw in Chapter 6, to which the starting addresses of the variables must be passed as actual arguments. This means that in C you can perform something like **Call by Reference** (see function: `swap()` on p. 123).

Let's now turn our attention again to the return value of a function. An unnamed, temporary storage area is assigned for generating a return value. Temporary because the return value only has to be stored somewhere for a short time before it is immediately allocated to a variable, issued or used in some other way. It may be that the C compiler – depending on the situation or data type – uses a register or a memory slot on the stack for it. As these internal workings of the C compiler are not supposed to be of concern to us here, let us assume for all that follows that, when a function is called, the compiler first generates a storage area for the return value on the stack. In order to be able to set up this storage area with the correct data type, it must know the data type of the function. (Hence the need for function declarations.)

We will use the program above with one small change to show the processes involving the memory in connection with the return value:

```
int sum (int x, int y)
{
    return x + y;
}
int main (void)
{
    int a = 3,
        b = 5,
        c;
    c = sum (a, b);
    return 0;
}
```

Here `printsum()` has been replaced by the `sum()` function, which produces nothing, but gives the sum of the two parameters as the return value.

Figure 9.2 shows what is happening on the stack.

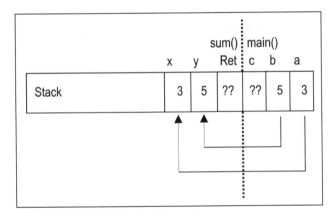

Figure 9.2 *Stack assignment when sum() is called*

In this diagram `Ret` indicates the temporary storage place for the return value. This storage place is assigned the calculated value 8 by the return instruction (Figure 9.3), to which an assignment is made after the return to the `main()` function of the variable c (Figure 9.4).

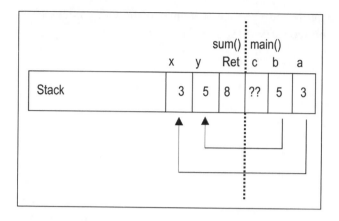

Figure 9.3 *sum(): effect of the return instruction*

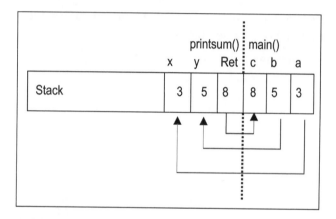

Figure 9.4 *sum(): return to the main() function*

Only then is all the memory on the stack which was occupied by calling the function sum() freed again (Figure 9.5).

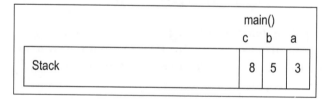

Figure 9.5 *Freeing of the stack by main()*

So in C it is always the calling function (i.e. here `main()`), which cleans up the stack again after the called function has been called.

An understanding of these processes on the stack is essential for the next subject.

9.3 Recursive functions

The fact that from a `functionA()`, a `functionB()` can be called, and from that in turn a `functionC()` etc. is not new to us. However, C also supports recursive function calls, i.e: `functionA()` calls in turn `functionA()`, i.e. itself.

A new, namely recursive, function `sum()` will now be used to explain the processes on the stack, in order then to clarify some logical aspects of recursive functions.

```c
# include <stdio.h>
int sum (int n)
{
   if (n > 0)
      return n + sum (n - 1); /* recursive call! */
   return n;
}
int main (void)
{
   int x;
   x = sum (3); /* non-recursive call! */
   printf ("sum from 1 to 3: %d\n", x);
   x = sum (5); /* non-recursive call! */
   printf ("sum from 1 to 5: %d\n", x);
   return 0;
}
```

The function `sum()` defined in this program is a recursive function because with the expression `sum (n - 1)` it calls itself! The two calls of `sum()` in the `main()` function are non-recursive calls, because they do not result from `sum()` but from `main()`.

In order to understand the special features of recursive calls, let us now work gradually through the `main()` function until the first `printf()` call:

I Before `x = sum (3);` is called (Figure 9.6).

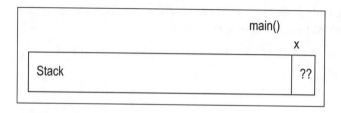

Figure 9.6 *Before sum() is called*

2 First call of sum (3) (Figure 9.7).

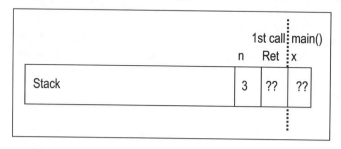

Figure 9.7 *First call of sum()*

3 Because n is >0, the second call of sum (2) occurs (Figure 9.8).

	2nd call		1st call		main()
	n	Ret	n	Ret	x
Stack	2	??	3	??	??

Figure 9.8 *Second call of sum()*

4 Because n is >0 is, the third call of sum (1) takes place (Figure 9.9).

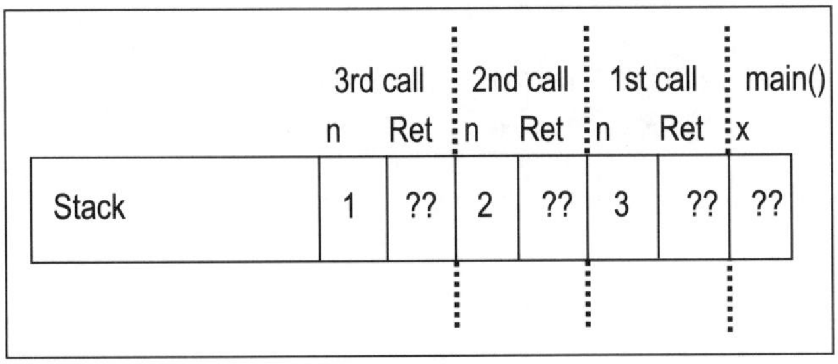

Stack	3rd call n	3rd call Ret	2nd call n	2nd call Ret	1st call n	1st call Ret	main() x
	1	??	2	??	3	??	??

Figure 9.9 *Third call of sum()*

5 Because n is >0, the fourth call of sum (0) takes place (Figure 9.10).

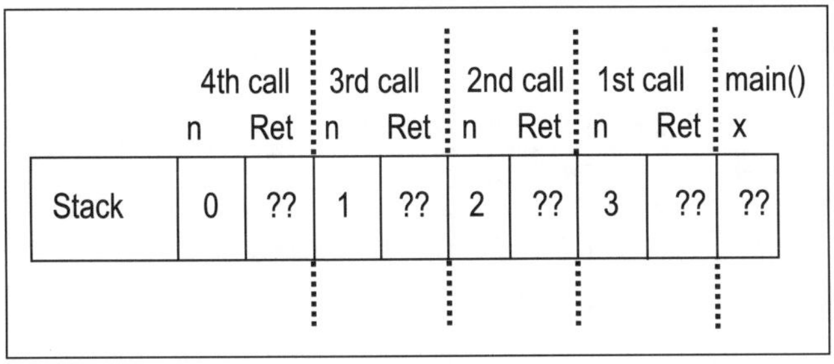

Stack	4th call n	4th call Ret	3rd call n	3rd call Ret	2nd call n	2nd call Ret	1st call n	1st call Ret	main() x
	0	??	1	??	2	??	3	??	??

Figure 9.10 *Fourth call of sum()*

6 Because n==0, this function call is quitted with n (i.e. 0) (Figure 9.11).

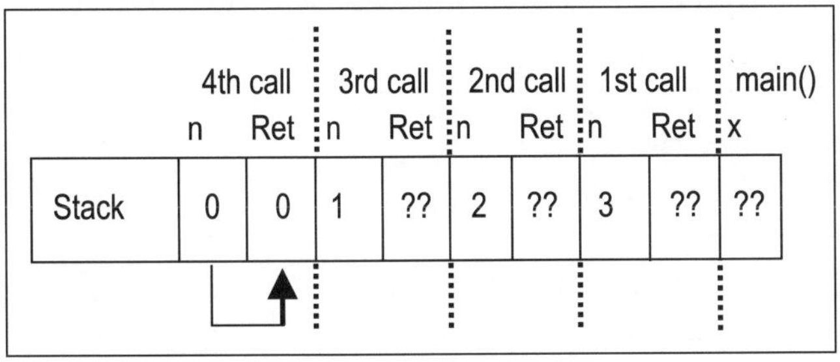

Stack	4th call n	4th call Ret	3rd call n	3rd call Ret	2nd call n	2nd call Ret	1st call n	1st call Ret	main() x
	0	0	1	??	2	??	3	??	??

Figure 9.11 *Quitting the fourth sum() call*

7 In the third function call, n (i.e. 1) + the last return value (i.e. 0) = 1 is returned (Figure 9.12).

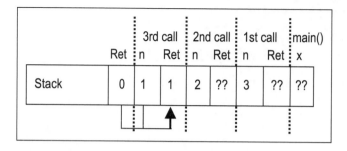

Figure 9.12 *Quitting the third sum() call*

8 In the second function call n (i.e. 2) + the last return value (i.e. 1) = 3 is returned (Figure 9.13).

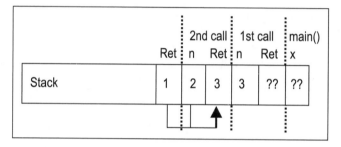

Figure 9.13 *Quitting the second sum() call*

9 In the first function call n (i.e. 3) + the last return value (i.e. 3) = 6 is returned (Figure 9.14).

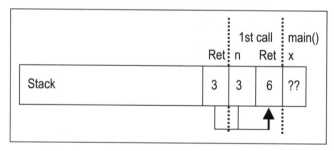

Figure 9.14 *Quitting the first sum() call*

10 In the main() function, this return value (i.e. 6) is assigned to x (Figure 9.15).

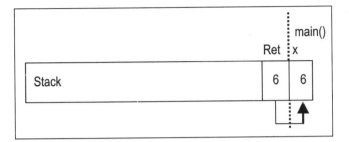

Figure 9.15 *Assigning the return value to x from main()*

The reader can check that the whole program sequence produces the following result:

```
sum of 1 to 3: 6
sum of 1 to 5: 15
```

by also working out all the individual stages on the stack for the second call x = sum (5).

What is important in all this is:

> **Tip** Each repeated recursive call puts all local variables including the parameters and a memory space for the return value back on the stack again.
>
> After returning from a recursive call, you arrive back at the point where the call started. And for all recursive calls that is a point within the same function.

It is this second point which causes the greatest difficulties for "recursion programming beginners" and you can only get used to it through repeated practice.

Having now considered the technical side of the matter, let's have an explanation of recursive program logic.

The reader is bound to have noticed what our recursive function sum() is actually doing: it calculates the sum of the numbers from 1 up to a number passed to the first, non-recursive function call.

We have already solved this problem once, in Chapter 1, in that case with an iterative solution, i.e. with a loop. It is very interesting to compare the iterative and the recursive solutions because recursion also solves the problem by repeated totaling of the numbers. And yet it achieves it without a loop. The repetition here occurs directly because of the recursive call.

In the iterative solution the repeating of the summation process was limited by the conditions of the loop, while in the recursive solution it is by the conditions of a branch. You could summarize it thus: what in an iterative solution is the loop, in a recursive solution is the branch.

What would actually happen if a recursive function had no branch? Take the following example:

```c
# include <stdio.h>
void print (char * s)
{
    printf ("%s\n", s);
    print (s);     /* recursive call */
}
int main (void)
{
    print ("zero");
    return 0;
}
```

Here there is no condition under which the recursive calls would ever come to an end. Just like in an endless loop you will see a great many zeros. So from the logic point of view, a recursive function without condition equates to an endless loop. And yet it is possible for a program like this to come to an end. Unlike in the iterative endless loop, for each recursive call a new parameter s is added to the stack, just like `printf()` adds new arguments to the stack each time, and it can be foreseen that sometime the whole stack will be full. What happens then is called **stack overflow**. Whether the program then stops or carries on after the overflow of the stack addresses – with disastrous results - can generally be regulated by the relevant compiler option when translating the program.

And that shows us the limitations of the otherwise so useful recursive programming: it significantly loads up the stack and where there is a large number of recursive calls it can lead to the dreaded stack overflow. In other words: a recursive solution should only be chosen for problems like this if the number of recursive function calls remains manageable.

One of the handiest applications of recursive program logic is to output the directory structure in operating systems with directory hierarchies (such as UNIX and MS/DOS. See for example the command TREE in MS/DOS.).

Also for processing all data in a tree-type structure and can actually only be processed with recursive logic (see also binary trees in Chapter 13.)

In Chapter 6 we learnt that pointers can be defined to point to anything you like, so why not to functions too. We will consider the idea using a formal comparison between vectors and functions :

1 The expression `char str[80];` represents the definition of a vector. By analogy to that, let's consider the expression `int getline (char * s, int n)` as the head of the definition of a function. What the two expressions have in common is that they are structured in the pattern data type name brackets. The differences are in the type of brackets and in the content of the brackets. In what follows we intend to disregard these differences and build the analogy between them on what they have in common.

2 The expression `str[5]` describes a concrete vector element , and the expression `getline (s, 80)` a concrete call to the function.

3 The expression `str` is evaluated with the starting address of the vector. By analogy, the expression `getline` describes the "starting address of the function", whatever that may be!

4 With `char * sp;` a pointer is defined which can point to a `char` vector. Similarly, with `int (*f)()` a pointer is defined which can point to an `int` function. What is important here is the additional pair of brackets. The compiler interprets this expression step by step according to the precedence of the operators:

1 `(*f)` f is a pointer

2 `(*f)()` f is a pointer to a function

3 `int (*f)()` f is a pointer to a function of type: `int`

Without the first pair of brackets, namely int *f(), we would have something quite different, namely `f` as a function of type pointer to `int`.

5 The expression `sp = str;` assigns to the pointer `sp` the starting address of the vector `str`. In exactly the same way the expression `f = getline;` assigns to the function pointer the starting address of the int function `getline()`.

6 With `*(sp + 5)` a concrete vector element is interpreted with the help of the pointer `sp`. Similarly to this, `(*f)(s, 80)` describes the concrete call to the function getline with the help of the function pointer `f`. The following analogy is also possible: instead of `*(sp + 5)` you can also write: `sp[5]`. Correspondingly you should also be able to say: `f(s, 80)`. And indeed the expressions `(*f)(s, 80)` and `f(s, 80)` are iden-

tical in their effect. Both, assuming the initialization of 5., lead to the call: getline(s, 80).

Let's summarize everything again in a little programming example:

```
int getline (char *, int); /* Prototype */
int get_int (void);        /* Prototype */
char s[80];                /* Vector definition */
int x;                     /* Variable definition */
int (*f) () = getline; /* Definition of the function pointer
f,
 which is initialized with the starting address of get-
line()*/
(*f) (s, 80); /* Call for getline() */
f = get_int; /* Assignment of the starting address of
get_int() */
x = f (); /* Call for get_int() */
```

For the two function calls with the function pointer f, different types of call were selected (see 6.). We could equally well have chosen the other way round:

```
f (s, 80);
```

and:

```
x = (*f) ();
```

Before we go on to demonstrate the practical use of function pointers in a first application example, we should note another, very important differentiation in the definition:

Warning

```
int (*f)();
```

This pointer f can point to the address of any int function, regardless of the number and data type of the arguments of that function. However, they must be taken into account when calling the function.

So:

```
f = getline;
(*f)(s, 80);     /* or: getline (s, 80); */
```

```
f = get_int;
x = (*f)();        /* or: x = get_int ();  */
```

Warning but:

```
int (*f)(char *, int);
```

This pointer can only point to an `int` function in which two parameters are defined, the first as pointer to `char`, the second as `int`.

So:

```
f = getline;
(*f)(s, 80);     /* or: getline (s, 80); */
```

What is now forbidden is: `f = get_int;`!

Now for the first application example:

```
int sum (int x, int y)
{
   return x + y;
}
int dif (int x, int y)
{
   return x - y;
}
int mul (int x, int y)
{
   return x * y;
}
int div (int x, int y)
{
   if (y)
      return x / y;
   return 0;
}
int square (int x, int y, int (*ff)(int, int))
{
   int z;
   z = (*ff) (x, y);
   return z * z;
```

```c
}
void menu (void)
{
    printf ("Square calculations:\n\n");
    printf ("< a >   Addition\n");
    printf ("< s >   Subtraction\n");
    printf ("< m >   Multiplication\n");
    printf ("< d >   Division\n");
    printf ("<Return>   Program end\n\n");
    printf ("Required operation: ");
}
int main (void)
{
    char input [2];
    int a,
        b;
    int (*f) (int, int);
    menu ();
    while (getline (input, 2) > 0)
    {
        switch (input[0])
        {
            case 'a':
                f = sum;
                break;
            case 's':
                f = dif;
                break;
            case 'm':
                f = mul;
                break;
            case 'd':
                f = div;
                break;
            default:
                fprintf (stderr, "Incorrect input! Termina-
tion!\n");
                return 1;
        }
        printf ("Integer 1: ");
        a = get_int ();
        printf ("Integer 2: ");
```

```
        b = get_int ();
        printf ("\nResult: %d\n\n", square (a, b, f));
        menu ();
    }
    return 0;
}
```

Apart from defining the four functions for the basic arithmetical operations, the `square()` function should also attract our interest. As well as the two parameters x and y for two integers, a third parameter `ff` is defined as a pointer to an `int` function with two `int` parameters. It should be noted that this pointer is specifically designed so that it can point at any one of our four basic arithmetical functions.

However, let's first consider the `main()` function. There the user is allowed to select one of the four basic arithmetic types. According to this selection, a function pointer f which is defined there is pointed at the starting address of one of these four functions. When the user has entered two `int` digits, the function `square()` is then called by passing the two integers which were entered to x and y and the function pointer to `ff`.

The `square()` function calls this function to which the `ff` is pointing, by passing the two integers, calculates the sum, the difference, the product or the quotient of the two numbers and sends the square of this calculated value back as the return value.

In other words: the `square()` function only needs to be defined once, and the square of which basic arithmetical operation it calculates is determined by the caller by its third argument.

Of course, the same problem could have been solved more easily, without the function pointer. With the following function:

```
double square (double w)
{
    return w * w;
}
```

the square of a sum could also be calculated by a nested function call:

```
printf ("\nresult: %d\n\n", square (sum (a, b)));
```

9.5 An application: sorting with qsort()

However, the standard function `qsort()` shows that pointers to functions can be essential. This function sorts everything which is a vector, using the quick-sort algorithm, one of the fastest sorting algorithms (References: [2], [3]).

We do not need to concern ourselves here with this algorithm, `qsort()` does that for us. But what `qsort()` needs to know is: what is the sort criterion by which the user would like to have his vector sorted? For this purpose this function has a function parameter defined as a parameter to which the user of `qsort()` must pass the starting address of a self-defined comparison function. The programmer who is using `qsort()` uses his comparison function to define the criterion by which the sorting should take place.

Let us first consider the prototypes:

```
# include <stdlib.h>
void qsort (void * base, size_t elem, size_t size,
            int (*vf)(const void *, const void *));
```

These mean:

→ **base:** starting address of the vector which is to be sorted;
→ **elem:** number of elements in this vector;
→ **size:** size of an element in bytes;
→ **vf:** pointer to an `int` function which compares two elements. This function expects the starting addresses of two elements which are to be compared.

`vf` must be defined by the user of the `qsort()` function with a return value:

→ >0, when the first element is > than the second element
→ =0, when the first element = the second element
→ <0, when the first element is < than the second element.

Two further explanations are required in order to understand the prototypes:

1. The data type `size_t` is not an elementary data type but a derived data type. We will learn in Chapter 11 how derived data types are defined. Here all we need to know is that in most C compilers `size_t` is defined as an `unsigned int`. Under these circumstances it therefore does not matter whether you say for example `size_t elem` or `unsigned int elem`.

2. The key word `const` is described in Appendix 16.3. A pointer to `const void` means that the memory content at the address to which such a pointer is pointing should be considered as a "constant", i.e. this memory content must not be overwritten! People also refer to "read only" access.

The attentive reader may be surprised by this restriction, because we know from Chapter 6 that with pointers to `void` you can't access the material anyway, never mind "read only". However, we will see later that these pointers at const void must be converted to other pointers in our comparison function, and we want to retain the restriction of read-only access in the process.

It can be said in conclusion that if the prototype of a function contains pointers to const data types, that is a guarantee that in this function there will be no write access to the memory content to which the pointers point.

Before we come to our first application example, we must once again be clear about the job of qsort(). It is to sort a vector. To that end it receives as information: the starting address of the vector, the number of elements, the length of an element and the starting address of a comparison function. The first three items of information uniquely identify the position in the memory and the features of the vector which is to be sorted.

(One might be tempted to pass the data type of the elements to qsort() as the third argument. But what data type would the third parameter then have to have? In C there is no data type for data types!)

However the quick-sort algorithm may work, qsort() will also, like the bubble-sort in Chapter 5, keep on comparing two elements with one another, to decide whether these elements should be exchanged. For this comparison, qsort() calls the comparison function (fourth parameter) and passes it the starting addresses of the two elements to be checked. It concludes from the return value whether or not they should be exchanged. To be precise, if the return value is > 0, they are exchanged, otherwise not.

The programmer of the comparison function must take account of this, by working on the basis that the two parameters of his function point to two elements of his vector. Only the programmer knows what kind of elements they are, what data type they are, how they are to be handled, and, because of the sort criterion s, whether the two elements have to be exchanged and can send the relevant return value.

In the following qsort() application example, let's first consider the main() function:

```
# include <stdio.h>
# include <stdlib.h>
# include "my.h"
# define DBANZ 100
int dbcomp (const void * p1, const void * p2)
{
    const double * dp1 = (const double *)p1,
                 * dp2 = (const double *)p2;
    if (* dp1 > * dp2)
        return 1;
```

```
        if (* dp1 < * dp2)
            return -1;
        return 0;
}
int main (void)
{
    static double dbvec[DBANZ];
    int i;
    int n;
    for (i = 0 ; i < DBANZ && (dbvec[i] = get_double ())
!= 0.; ++i)
        ;
    n = i;
for (i = 0 ; i < n ; ++i)
        printf ("%lf\n", dbvec[i]);
    qsort ((void *)dbvec, n, sizeof(double), dbcomp);
    for (i = 0 ; i < n ; ++i)
        printf ("%lf\n", dbvec[i]);
    return 0;
}
```

In a vector with 100 double elements, a number n of decimal numbers is read in. This then occupies the first n elements of the vector.

The qsort() call receives: the starting address of the vector dbvec, the number of elements to be sorted n, the length of an element sizeof(double) and the starting address of the comparison function dbcomp().

After the qsort() call, the numbers which have been entered are shown again, but in the sorted order.

But how have the numbers been sorted? That is determined solely by the comparison function dbcomp(). That has – because qsort() demands it – two parameters of the pointer to const void type. These are each sent the starting addresses of two elements of our vector by qsort(). Because we know that these are double elements, in dbcomp() we assign these pointers immediately to two locally defined pointer to const double.

We examine the two double contents to which the pointers point, and return 1 if the first element is larger than the second. This return value would cause qsort() to exchange the two elements. The other possible return values 0 and -1 have the effect that qsort() leaves the two elements unchanged. This logic of the comparison function therefore has the effect that the vector is sorted in ascending order by qsort().

However, if the programmer had written the comparison function like this:

```
if (* dp1 < * dp2)
    return 1;
if (* dp1 > * dp2)
    return -1;
return 0;
```

then `qsort()` would have sorted the vector in descending order.

We can see from this that, with his comparison function, the user of `qsort()` is in control of the sort criterion, while `qsort()` is only the servant, carrying out its work strictly according to the instructions from the comparison function.

We will see later that `qsort()` only reveals its full power when the sort criterion is outside the data which is to be sorted. You just have to imagine that a vector of pointers is to be sorted, but the sort criterion is to be found not in the addresses stored in the pointers but in the data to which the pointers point.

This interesting situation will be demonstrated once we have discussed structures and pointers to structures (see Chapter 11).

9.6 Search with bsearch()

Another explanation is required. Why are three different return values given in the comparison function, although `qsort()` itself is only interested in two different values, namely > 0 or <= 0?

The answer is simply that the comparison function written for `qsort()` can also be used for another interesting standard function which depends on differentiating between three different return values, namely `bsearch()`. This function makes it possible to search in vector sorted by `qsort()` or in any other way for a vector element with a specific value. Here first is its prototype:

```
# include <stdlib.h>
void *bsearch (const void *key, const void *base, size_t
nelem, size_t width, int (*fcmp)(const void*, const void*));
```

In this function we find again all the parameters of `qsort()`. In addition, however, as the first argument the starting address of a memory area must be passed to `key`, which contains the value to be searched for.

The function then returns as the return value either the address of the vector element containing the value to be searched for or NULL, if there is no such vector element.

It is worth noting that `bsearch()`, works with the same comparison function with which `qsort()` previously sorted the vector.

In its application to bsearch(), however, it is only the return value 0 which is of interest in this comparison function, because it is identity between the value being searched for and a vector element which is required. So we can see: because the comparison function is to be used for both standard functions, qsort() and bsearch(), it must provide three different return values.

As an application for bsearch() we now want to consider whether in our sorted vector dbvec the double value 3.5 is stored and if so in which. Our main() function would have to be supplemented by the following lines:

```
double search = 3.5;
double * searchp;
. . . .
. . . .
searchp = bsearch ((const void *)&search, (void *)dbvec, n,
                  sizeof(double), dbcomp);
if (searchp == NULL)
    fprintf (stderr, "%lf: Not found!\n", search);
else
    printf ("%lf: Found in %d. Element\n", search,
            (searchp - dbvec) + 1);
```

Just as we did earlier for qsort(), we will now shed a little light on the internal workings of bsearch(). The name of the function stands for "binary search". This search process works as follows: first the whole vector is halved. If the middle element created by this halving is the same as the one searched for, the function can be exited with the starting address of this element as the return value.

If the middle element is larger than the value being searched for, then the function for the lower half of the vector is called, recursively, and otherwise the function for the upper half of the vector. By continuous halving of the vector intervals, you reach the element being searched for very quickly, or, if the vector interval only has one element left, which does not contain the searched for value, you arrive at a negative search result with the return value NULL.

It should be clear that this process of binary search which has been described only works with sorted vectors. With an unsorted vector, calling bsearch() leads to meaningless results.

It may be that your C compiler has, in addition to the ANSI standard, functions such as lsearch() or lfind(), which carry out the same search in a linear, that is to say sequential way. With these functions you can search unsorted vectors as well, but of course this can take much longer than the binary search in a sorted vector.

We should also mention a problem in the use of `bsearch()`: if the sorted vector contains the value being searched for more than once, then, because of the binary search process, there is no guarantee that you will receive the starting address of the first of these identical elements.

9.7 Exercises

I Create in `factor.c` the recursive function `factor()`, which calculates the factorial of a `long` number which has been passed. (See also Exercise 3 in Chapter 1).

The only parameter: a `long` variable for the number of which the factorial is to be calculated.

Return value: the calculated factorial as a `long` number!

When it is called with a non-positive value, the function should come back immediately with the return value 0L.

Tip: use in your recursive program logic the fact that the following applies:

```
n! = n * (n - 1)!
```

Also define a `main()` function which calculates and displays all the factorials of the numbers from 1 to a integer specified by the user.

Test the program, by having all the factorials from 1 to 12 displayed!

2 With reference to our `square()` function, write a new `square()` function which works with a `double` value and a `double` function.

In the `main()` function, the user should have the option of selecting one of the functions `sin()`, `cos()`, `exp()` or `log()` and, for a `double` argument entered by him, calculating and displaying the square of the relevant function.

The above mathematical functions exist as standard functions and require the linking of the header file `math.h`. (Warning! In UNIX the mathematical functions are often not found in the standard library but in a special mathematical library `libm.a`! In this case when the compiler is called the option `-lm` must also be specified!)

3 Use the following definitions in a `main()` function:

```
# define DBANZ 100
....
double dbvec[DBANZ];
double * dbvp[DBANZ];
int i;
int n;
....
for (i = 0 ; i < DBANZ ; ++i)        /* Assigning
pointers */
    dbvp[i] = &dbvec[i];
```

Read in any number of decimal numbers (but max. 100) into the vector `dbvec`.

Sort with a `qsort()` call the vector of pointers `dbvp`, so that through it you have access to the numbers stored in `dbvec` sorted in ascending order.

In the `main()` function first display all the decimal numbers you have entered, sorted in ascending order, and then in the original input order.

Of course you have to define a new comparison function for the `qsort()` call, which should now be given the name `upwards()`.

Test the program!

Now extend the `main()` function with a second pointer vector called `dbvp2`, which also gets its pointers as elements from `dbvec`.

Sort `dbvp2` as well. Write a comparison function `downwards()`, which gives access to the elements of `dbvec` sorted in descending order.

Allow users to choose in which order they want to see the numbers previously entered.

Tip In this exercise we have the situation already referred to in this chapter where a pointer vector is to be sorted using `qsort()`, but the sort criterion is somewhere else, namely in the vector `dbvec`.

Having a good crack at solving this exercise should be good practice for further applications of qsort() in Chapter 13.

4 Write the function bdoubsearch(), which works exactly like the standard function bsearch(), with the one simplifying difference that bdoubsearch() should only ever search for a double value in a double vector. The function head should therefore have the same parameters as bsearch() except for the fourth, which you just omit. The length of a vector element therefore does not need to be specified, because we know that we are always dealing with the data type double.

Read again the description of how bsearch() works (see above) and then define bdoubsearch() as a definitely recursive function.

Use the dbcomp() function which was used in this chapter, both to sort a double vector with qsort() and also to search subsequently for a number with bdoubsearch ().

5 At the start of Chapter 5, the following exercise was used to show the importance of vectors: a line of text is to be read in and displayed again backwards. It was pointed out there that this exercise could actually also be solved without vectors, i.e. only with one variable, in fact as a recursive function. The end criterion of the recursion is when newline or EOF in entered.

Write this recursive function and call it getrline(). You should have the data type void and no parameters.

Write a main() function for it, which calls getrline() once and then sends a new-line.

6 The function getrline() could still be improved. If you want to be able to call this function in the main() function as often as you like, e.g. until the user only puts new-line or EOF when he enters a line, then it must become an int function, which gives the number of characters entered (exclusively new-line or EOF) as the return value to the main() function.

Change the function in this way and build a loop into the main() function accordingly.

Tip: in Chapter 7 we learnt how to define a function call counter. However, this tip alone is not enough. This exercise is a real challenge to the recursive programmer!

The C pre-processor

We established back in Chapter 1 that the C pre-processor is a macro processor which does not use C as a language, but the effect of which can, in some ways, be compared with that of a word processing program. It has its own instructions (directives), which can be recognized by their leading character #.

The pre-processor is automatically called by the C compiler, to pre-process the program text to be translated.

It can also usually be called as a separate program and is then usually called cpp (C pre-processor). A call such as:

```
cpp prog1.c prog2.c etc.
```

then produces the files prog1.i and prog2.i etc., which contain the source text of the program converted by the pre-processor, which any C compiler can translate. Instructions beginning with # will no longer occur in these files.

Below, we consider the different pre-processor directives.

10.1 # include

The directive # include <file> has the effect that it is replaced by the content of file. In other words, the content of file is copied into the source text in the place where the include directive was. This copying process can occur recursively, i.e. there can be # include directives within file.

In principle, any file can be copied into the source text by #include. However, an initial selection criterion demands that the content of files bound in this way must be able to be understood by the C compiler or in turn by the pre-processor.

A second, more refined selection criterion relates to program organization. It is a terribly bad habit of some C programmers these days, and not at all the real purpose of the # include directive, to bind other source code files (.c files). Just think about a largish program, consisting for example of twenty modules prog01.c, prog02.c, ..., prog20.c. Here the other nineteen could be bound in the first module by #include. Then all the programmer would have to do to translate would be call:

```
cc prog01.c
```

The simplicity of this compiler call is among the stupidest excuses of that sort of programmer. Just think what would happen if a small change was made in prog17.c; the results of Chapter 8 will show you that it is better instead to set up a project file for this program.

The conclusion of these thoughts can be summed up in the following programming rule.

Only header files (usually .h files) should be bound by #include, containing exclusively the following content:

```
# include ... other header files
  . . . .
# define ... of constants and macros (see below)
  . . . .
type definitions: (see Chapter 11)
  struct ...
  union  ...
  enum   ...
  typedef...
  . . . .
external declarations of global variables
  . . . .
prototypes of functions
  . . . .
```

The sequence of the instructions given here is also significant and should be taken as a recommendation for self-defined header files.

The #include directive has two different syntax forms:

1 # include <fileA>;

2 # include "fileB".

Here the pre-processor looks for fileA in one or more directories known to it as special include directories.

The compiler option -Idirectory enables you to define these include directories.

In contrast to this, fileB is searched for first in the current directory, and only if it is not found there is the search continued as in (1).

An instruction such as:

```
# include "stdio.h"
```

would therefore allow a self-defined file such as `stdio.h` to be bound. However, if there is no such self-defined file in the current directory, again the standard `stdio.h` supplied with the compiler would be bound.

This account requires one small modification if you are working not with a "command line compiler" but with an "integrated development environment". There you have the option of entering not only include directories but also "source code directories" (usually under the menu item "Source") , which are intended for the actual `.c` files. In the above description, "current directory" then has to be replaced by "source code directory", and `fileB` would then be looked for first in these source code directories and only then in the include directories if necessary.

10.2 # define

We already know about the easiest application of this directive: to define pre-processor constants. Let's consider the following simple program:

```
# include <stdio.h>
# define A "Otto"
# define B Anna
int main (void)
{
    printf (A "\n");
    printf ("B\n");
    return 0;
}
```

The first `define` instruction defines the constant A as "Otto". From this line on, the pre-processor replaces each A which occurs in the source code with "Otto". It makes a find in the first `printf()` call and turns it into: `printf ("Otto" "\n");`.

The C compiler then turns this expression into: `printf ("Otto\n");` (see note on string constants on p. 25). The whole program produces the following screen output:

```
Otto
B
```

That demonstrates that the `define` constant B, which was defined as "Anna", was not replaced in the second `printf()` call. However ruthless the pre-processor is in replacing constants, the content of string constants is protected against it.

By convention, `define` constants are written with capital letters. Also, unlike in our rather poor example, longer, more meaningful names should be used. Otherwise the following could happen:

```
# define A Otto
....
void printA ( ... );
....
int main (void)
{
    ....
    printA ( .... );
    ....
}
```

The pre-processor produces: `printOtto ()`, and the linkage editor searches in vain for this function, which doesn't exist at all.

10.3 Macros

A second use of `#define` is in defining pre-processor macros. A macro is a parametrized format for text substitution which appears outwardly like a C function call. A macro is defined using the following syntax:

```
# define name([paramlist]) expression
```

This means:

- → `name`: name of the macro (if possible also with capital letters);
- → `paramlist`: list of parameters, separated by commas, or left blank;
- → `expression`: the expression for substitution.

As regards the syntax, it is important that there is no space between `name` and `(`, at least not in the definition of a macro. Otherwise the pair of brackets would be counted with the parameter list for `expression`, and all you would have done would be define a `define` constant `name`.

Let's take an example:

```
# define QUAD(x) ((x) * (x))
```

The macro `QUAD` has only one parameter, namely x. Unlike the parameters in a C function, a macro parameter has no data type. It just represents a textual wildcard . This macro is used in the following instructions:

```
int i = 10;
double z = 1.3;
printf ("%d\n", QUAD (i));
printf ("%lf\n", QUAD (z));
```

```
printf ("%d\n", QUAD (i + 1));
```

Whatever expression is specified for the QUAD expression as the "argument", it replaces the wildcard x. The pre-processor converts the printf() calls into:

```
printf ("%d\n", ((i) * (i)));          ---> 100
printf ("%lf\n", ((z) * (z)));         ---> 1.690000
printf ("%d\n", ((i + 1) * (i + 1)));  ---> 121
```

QUAD() therefore calculates the square of an expression, regardless of the data type of that expression.

You can see from the last QUAD expression why each part of the expression for substitution should be in brackets in the definition of this macro. Because if you had defined:

```
# define QUAD(x) x * x
```

the last printf() call would have been converted to:

```
printf ("%d\n", i + 1 * i + 1);    ---> 21
```

with disastrous and certainly unintended results.

For practice, just be sure you understand what the following macros do:

```
# define SUM(x, y) ((x) + (y))
# define PRINTI(x) printf ("%d\n", (x))
# define PRINTI2(x, y) printf ("%d, %d\n", (x), (y))
# define INIT(x, y, z) ((x) = (y) = (z) = 1)
```

While SUM() speaks for itself, PRINTI() and PRINTI2() have surely only been defined to save writing time. (But then that is actually the point of macros).

The last macro INIT() is interesting in that it assigns a value to three parameters. In the following application:

```
int i = 13,
    j = 24,
    k = 68;
....
INIT (i, j, k);
/* i, j and k now have the value: 1 */
```

no-one looking at it would think that the value 1 is being assigned to the variables i, j and k by the INIT() "call", unless they knew that INIT() is not a C function but a macro.

With the longer macros it can happen that the macro definition extends for more than one program line. Unlike the C compiler, which has no problem with that, the pre-processor must be told by a special line continuation character that the pre-processor instruction continues on the next line. This continuation character is the sign \. So our INIT() definition for example could look like this:

```
# define INIT(x, y, z) \
            ((x) = (y) = (z) = 1)
```

You have to be particularly careful when using macros with expressions which produce side-effects within the substitution expression. For example in the following instructions

```
int x = 4;
printf ("%d\n", QUAD (++x));
```

the result is not 25, as the programmer perhaps thought, but 30. The expression QUAD (++x) is resolved into:

```
((++x) * (++x))
```

The variable x is thus incremented twice, which you cannot see from the call.

Pre-processor macros also allow some other conversions:

```
a. # define SHOW(x) printf (#x ": %d\n", x)
```

In the substitution expression #x is used to convert the parameter x into a string constant. From the calls

```
int i = 13,
    k = 8;
SHOW (i);
SHOW (k);
```

the pre-processor does:

```
printf ("i" ": %d\n", i);
printf ("k" ": %d\n", k);
```

and the compiler:

```
printf ("i: %d\n", i);   ---> i: 13
printf ("k: %d\n", k);   ---> k: 8
```

```
b. # define VAR(z) x_##z
```

Here x_##z is used to make a new token composed of x_ and the substitution value for z. In the following program extract

```
int x_a = 4,
    x_b = 17,
    x_123 = -9;
printf ("%d\n", VAR (a));
printf ("%d\n", VAR (b));
```

```
printf ("%d\n", VAR (123));
```

the pre-processor substitutes:

```
printf ("%d\n", x_a);    ---> 4

printf ("%d\n", x_b);    ---> 17

printf ("%d\n", x_123); ---> -9
```

But the variables could also have been defined using this macro:

```
int VAR (a) = 4,

    VAR (b) = 17,

    VAR (123) = -9;
```

Before we finish with macros, some thoughts on their use. When do you use pre-processor macros instead of C functions?

Apart from our special case INIT(), where a solution as a C function is not possible, macros are used to avoid function calls. We know that function calls always take a certain amount of time (Call by Value, return of the return value), which, if they are repeated very frequently, can have an impact on the running time of a program. It should be understood that the whole idea of stack overhead disappears if an operation is carried out by a macro. The pre-processor has more work to do, but the program runs faster. However, there is one criterion: the operation should not be too complex.

There are a number of "standard functions" which in reality are not functions but macros defined in header files. We are already familiar with the macros getchar() and putchar(). The way they can be defined using #define can be seen in stdio.h. (see also Chapter 14.)

10.4 # undef

#undef is used to undo an earlier definition of a constant or macro. In the following program extract

```
# define NUM 100
....
printf ("%d\n", NUM);
....
# undef NUM
....
printf ("%d\n", NUM); /* Compiler error!!! */
....
```

the second `printf()` call causes a compiler error, because the symbol NUM is not defined there, while the first NUM was replaced by the pre-processor with 100.

The directive #undef has its practical uses in redefining constants. It is then no problem at all to define a constant in the same way twice:

```
# define MAX 100
# define MAX 100
```

However, where the values are different there is a warning:

```
# define MAX 100
....
# define MAX 550    /* warning from the pre-processor */
```

This warning can be prevented by:

```
# define MAX 100
....
# undef MAX
# define MAX 550
```

10.5 # if...

The pre-processor directives to be dealt with here are connected with the subject of "conditional compiling". Whereas the C instruction if (...) controls which part of a program should be carried out while it is running , the various #if... directives of the pre-processor determine which part of a source program is to be translated by the compiler at all and become part of the executable program.

An example shows one version of this conditional compiling:

```
# define _MS_DOS_
# ifdef _MS_DOS_
#    define WORDLEN 2
# else
#    define WORDLEN 4
# endif
```

In the first instruction, the constant _MS_DOS_ is defined. But as what? As nothing. A subsequent C instruction such as:

```
int x = _MS_DOS_;
```

would cause an error message from the compiler, because the pre-processor then sent it the instruction:

```
int x = ;
```

In this constant definition, the only thing that matters is that the constant of that name is defined, not as what. But it is this very existence of the constant _MS_DOS_ which is checked by the following instruction # ifdef _MS_DOS_. Because in this case this check proves positive, the instruction:

```
#     define WORDLEN 2
```

is now transferred to the program to be translated. However, if the first instruction had been:

```
# define _VMS_
```

the instruction:

```
#     define WORDLEN 4
```

would have been transferred to the program.

The #else plays the same role in relation to #ifdef as else in relation to if. However, unlike with the C compiler, with the pre-processor each branch must be closed with the instruction #endif, even where there is no #else branch.

Whereas # ifdef symbol checks whether symbol is defined, the directive # if symbol checks whether symbol is unequal to 0. It assumes that symbol is defined as something, otherwise this instruction will cause a pre-processor error message.

The following example, which uses #if, also uses #elif to introduce a "multiple branching":

```
# include <stdio.h>
# define Z1 0
# define Z2 123
# define Z3 1
int main (void)
{
# if Z1
   printf ("Z1: %d\n", Z1);
# elif Z2
   printf ("Z2: %d\n", Z2);
# elif Z3
   printf ("Z3: %d\n", Z3);
# else
   printf ("None of those \n");
# endif
   return 0;
}
```

Because Z1 is defined as 0, the first `printf()` call is not transferred to the program. The following instruction `# elif Z2` must be seen as nesting:

```
# else
#     if Z2
```

As the check on this condition proves positive, the second `printf()` call is therefore transferred into the program to be translated. All further `#elif` and `#else` branches are therefore not needed. All that the pre-processor finally sends to the compiler is the following program:

```
int main (void)
{
   printf ("Z2: %d\n", 123);
   return 0;
}
```

The above program could also have been formulated in an explicitly nested way:

```
# include <stdio.h>
# define Z1 0
# define Z2 123
# define Z3 1
int main (void)
{
# if Z1
   printf ("Z1: %d\n", Z1);
# else
#     if Z2
         printf ("Z2: %d\n", Z2);
#     else
#         if Z3
             printf ("Z3: %d\n", Z3);
#         else
             printf ("None of those \n");
#         endif Z3
#     endif Z2
# endif Z1
   return 0;
}
```

You just have to ensure that each plain `#if` – unlike `#elif` – is closed by a `#endif`.

At the same time the above program demonstrates that #endif can also be followed by a comment which will be ignored by the pre-processor and serves only to make the nested branching easier for the programmer to read.

The #if directive is even more flexible than is shown above. There can be constant expressions after #if such as:

```
# if Z1 == 0 && Z2!= 0
```

The pre-processor "operator" defined(symbol) checks whether symbol has been defined. If so, the expression is evaluated with 1, otherwise with 0. In this way the operator is ideally suited for use after #if and #elif, and it is only there that it can be used. Let's use it by rewriting our first #ifdef example and expanding it:

```
# define _UNIX_
# if defined(_MS_DOS_)
#     define WORDLEN 2
# elif defined(_VMS_)
#     define WORDLEN 4
# elif defined(_UNIX_)
#     define WORDLEN 4
# else
#     define WORDLEN 2
# endif
```

It should be clear that, because of # define _UNIX_ the instruction # define WORDLEN 4 will be transferred into the program text.

It is also possible to have a negative form of defined():

```
# if! defined (...)
```

What is missing now is the directive #ifndef. That is the counterpart to #ifdef and checks whether a symbol is not defined.

Having explained the language elements of conditional compiling, let's show its practical explanation in three examples:

(a) Instructions for test purposes:

If you want to test the logic of a program when it is running, you can, for example, build specific screen outputs into your program for this purpose, which show the programmer during the rest run what the content is of certain variables at certain points in the program, or which show whether a loop is going to run or how often. Of course these instructions should be removed again after the test has been successful. Instead of giving yourself the job of removing all the screen outputs which you have inserted during the test runs, it is a good idea to insert each test instruction in the following way from the start:

```
# define _TEST_
....
# ifdef _TEST_
   printf (....);
# endif
....
```

If the test was successful, you only need to delete the instruction #define _TEST_ or remove it with a comment and retranslate the program. The executable program created in this way then no longer generates the test messages, which would only irritate the user.

(The procedure described here represents a simpler alternative to using debug programs. A debugger is a program which can control the running of a program being tested step by step (instruction for instruction) or up to certain so-called "breakpoints" in the source code, to show the content of all the variables.

In this way the running of a program can be followed in detail. A professional C development system always includes a debugger).

(b) Preventing multiple binding of header files:

For example, if a module prog.c contains the two pre-processor instructions:

```
# include "prog.h"
# include "my.h"
```

and the header file prog.h again contains the instruction:

```
# include "my.h"
```

then the content of my.h is bound twice into prog.c.

So long as there are only external declarations of global variables and function prototypes in my.h, that does not matter. The C compiler does not mind if it sees the prototypes of a function twice, provided that both prototypes for the function are the same. However, it is different if a self-defined data type – to be discussed later (see Chapter 11) – is defined in my.h. The double data type definition produced by the double binding of my.h would lead to an error message from the compiler.

That is the reason why you should ensure that a header file is definitely only bound once. We'll show you using my.h how that is done:

```
/* my.h */
# ifndef _MY_H_
# define _MY_H_
   int getline (char *, int);
   int get_int (void);
```

```
      double get_double (void);
# endif _MY_H_
```

So you check whether a symbol which, as above, is formed from the file name, does not exist. If that is the case, you define it and let the whole content of the header file follow. Then if the same section comes again, because my.h was bound again, the symbol _MY_H_ now exists and the whole #ifndef branch is omitted.

A good C programmer should get into the habit of packing the content of all his header files into a #ifndef branch like that. The standard header files of a C compiler also include this security against multiple binding.

(c) Modification of define constants:

Let us assume that our program file prog.c includes the following lines:

```
# define NUM 80
...
char textline[NUM];
...
```

However, a really definite version of this program, in the form of an executable program to be published, should contain a vector textline of 132 elements. The source program does not need to be changed for this, because C compilers allow #define constants to be defined when they are called to translate the program. In a UNIX C compiler such a call would look like this:

```
cc -DNUM=132 prog.c -oprog
```

Here the option -D is used to define NUM as 132. Unfortunately this compiler call leads to a warning, because NUM is now defined twice, and the pre-processor takes for NUM the value 80 which is also defined in the program, and not 132.

Only the following content for the program file gives the necessary flexibility:

```
# ifndef NUM
#     define NUM 80
# endif
...
char textline[NUM];
...
```

In the above compiler call, NUM already exists because of the compiler option -D, so that the #ifndef branch is not bound. The vector textline is then defined with 132 elements. But if you call:

```
cc prog.c -oprog
```

then NUM is not predefined, the #ifndef branch is transferred to the program and the vector textline becomes 80 characters long.

10.6 # line

This directive has the following syntax:

```
# line znr ["filename"]
```

Its effect is that the int constant znr is assigned to the next program line as the line number and the following lines are continued from znr.

This directive is used when one part of a program is copied from another file and you want to keep the line numbering from the other file. You also have the option of entering filename to transfer the other filename. If this is not specified, the original filename is used.

There are two ways of making use of this directive:

1 The C compiler refers to this information with its error messages;

2 The programmer can insert screen outputs into his program which use the predefined macros __LINE__ and __FILE__ (see below) to display the values specified by #line.

An example:

```
/* line2.c */
# include <stdio.h>
# define A "Otto"
# define B Anna
# define C() "Emma"
# line 1000 "prog2.c"
int main (void)
{
   printf (A "\n";
   printf ("B\n");
   printf (C() "\n");
   printf ("%s: text-line %d\n", __FILE__, __LINE__);
# line 15
   printf ("%s: text-line %d\n", __FILE__, __LINE__);
   return 0;
}
```

The first printf() call contains a syntax error. The C compiler then sends the following error message:

```
Error prog2.c 1002: Function call missing ) in function main
```

When the syntax error is corrected, the program produces:

```
Otto
B
Emma
prog2.c: text-line 1005
prog2.c: text-line 15
```

The last line of output demonstrates that a filename which has been "set" using #line has been retained. Only with the directive # line 15 "line2.c" would you have been able to see the original name of the file again:

```
line2.c: text-line 15
```

10.7 Predefined macros

The pre-processor of a C compiler generally has a series of predefined #define constants or macros, of which we have just seen two, namely __FILE__ and __LINE__. What predefined macros there are depends very much on the compiler. There are usually macros to control the translation process, i.e. containing information about the C standard being used, the operating system, the memory model etc. They either exist as int or string constants, or they only exist to be used for conditional translation.

The proud owner of a C compiler may like to inform himself about which predefined macros his preprocessor possesses. He could for example look out for macros such as __DATE__ and __TIME__, which mean you can first display the current "compiling status" of a program when you start it.

10.8 # error

Some pre-processors have this directive, which mean that the pre-translation by the pre-processor (and thus also the compiler called subsequently) can be terminated with an error message.

For example:

```
# if Z1!= 0 || Z2 == 0
#    error Z1 must and Z2 must not be 0!
# endif
```

would, in the right circumstances, send the above message and terminate the pre-processor.

10.9 # pragma

This directive enables the manufacturers of C compilers to invent new directives for their pre-processors. What new directives these are of course depends on the compiler. So if the pre-processor of a C compiler, in a C program which was originally written for a different C compiler, comes up against a #pragma instruction with a directive which it does not recognize, then the whole #pragma instruction is simply ignored.

Take the following examples for the BORLAND C compiler:

```
# pragma warn -sus
```

Suppresses the compiler warning: "Suspicious pointer conversion". (sus is the abbreviation for this message.)

```
# pragma option -C
```

Switches on permission for nested comments. (Yes, there are such things!)

The directive option allow some options to be specified in the source code which could also have been specified when calling the compiler. Instead of writing the above #pragma line into the source program, you could have called the compiler like this:

```
bcc -C ...
```

10.10 Exercises

1 Define a macro LEAPYEAR(y), which, for a given year y checks whether it is a leap year (evaluate with 1) or not (evaluate with 0).

   For the definition of a leap year, see Chapter 3, Exercise 1.

2 What is the result of the following program extract?

```
# define TEXT1 0
# define TEXT3 5
# ifdef TEXT1
#     if TEXT1
#         define TEXT2 0
#     else
#         define TEXT2 1
#     endif
# else
#     define TEXT3 0
# endif
```

```
# if TEXT2
    printf ("TEXT2 lives and is: %d\n", TEXT2);
# elif defined(TEXT3)
    printf ("TEXT3 lives\n");
#    if TEXT3
        printf (" and is: %d\n", TEXT3);
#    endif
# else
    printf ("TEXT2???\n");
# endif
```

3 Put the content of the file `srmem.h` (Chapter 8) in a `#ifndef` framework, so that multiple binding is prevented.

4 Modify the program from Exercise 3/4 in Chapter 9, so that with a new compiler call it can be created with any value DBNUM for the vector size of `dbvec`.

5 Build a screen output into the `main()` function of the program `lotto.c` (Chapter 6, Exercise 6), which shows the date of the last time the program was translated.

You can perform the same operation with any other program which you have written.

Data aggregates

As with other programming languages, with C you can combine various memory areas of different data types into data aggregates, which then as self-defined data types can be used to define corresponding variables or vectors and pointers.

We will now explain in order structures, variants, enumerations and bit fields, and finally we shall see how you can use `typedef` to make these self-defined data types appear as "true" data types.

11.1 Structures

Just as an object possesses certain attributes of reality, so a structure allows various variables of different data types to be strung together and combined into a whole. For example, a book (from a library) could be characterized by its signature, the name of the author and the title.

To simplify matters, let's assume that the signature just consists of a whole digit book number, and then the structure type in C is declared as follows:

```
struct book
{
    int bookno;
    char author[21];
    char title[50];
};
```

The C keyword shown here for the declaration of structure types is `struct`, while `book` is a randomly selected name. The components making up a structure have to be specified in the block following the `struct book` as a series of normal variable definitions. The following format is also possible:

```
struct book
{
    int bookno;
    char name[21],
         title[50];
};
```

Note that this `struct` instruction only determines what should be meant by a structure of the type `book`. No variable has yet been defined, and so no memory space reserved.

If you want to define variables of the type `struct book`, that could be done afterwards by means of the following instruction:

```
struct book book1,
             book2;
```

Only now will memory space be reserved for the two variables `book1` and `book2`. For `book1`, for example, the memory allocation will look a bit like that shown in Figure 11.1.

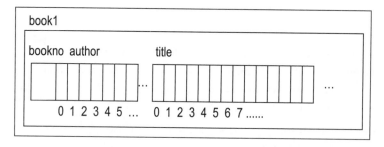

Figure 11.1 *Memory assignment by the structure variable book1*

(The indices of the vector elements are only shown without [] brackets for technical printing reasons.)

If you are interested in how long such a variable of the `book` type is, you may have the idea of adding together the length of the individual components, thus:

```
                            (MS/DOS)      (UNIX)
bookno (int):                 2 Byte      4 Byte
author (char-vector):+ 21 Byte + 21 Byte
title (char-vector): + 50 Byte + 50 Byte
-----------------------------------------------
Total length:                73 Byte     75 Byte
```

This result is usually only correct if the C compiler packs the components of the structure really "densely", i.e. not leaving any gaps between the components.

However, with the right compiler option, you can make the compiler align the starting addresses of certain structure components by word boundary, that is those main memory addresses which are divsble by the length of the machine word without a remainder. In MS/DOS that is all even-numbered addresses, in UNIX all addresses divisible by 4.

With word boundary alignment in MS/DOS, there would therefore have to be a lack-byte between the author and title components which remains unused. The total length would then be 74.

Because of this variability between operating systems and compilers, you should never try to calculate the length of structures yourself "by hand", but can safely let the operator sizeof() work it out.

The expression sizeof(book1) or sizeof(struct book) reliably works out the actual length. (Incidentally, it is not only while the program is running that a sizeof() expression is evaluated, but even while the program is being translated by the compiler it is converted into the relevant numerical value.)

To access the individual components of a structure variable, you have to use the primary operator '.' (level 1). With the instruction

```
book1.bookno = 137;
```

the component bookno of the structure variable book1 is assigned its value. As the other two components are char vectors, you cannot use assignments here but you have to use the standard function strcpy():

```
strcpy (book1.author, "Goethe");
strcpy (book1.title, "Faust, Part 1");
```

Note: the expression book1.author also represents the starting address of the char vector author of the structure variable book1. After these three instructions, the core image of book1 looks as in Figure 11.2.

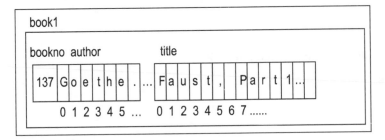

Figure 11.2 *Contents of the components of book1*

If you now want `book2` to have the same content as `book1`, the following instructions are possible:

```
book2.bookno = book1.bookno;
strcpy (book2.author, book1.author);
strcpy (book2.title, book1.title);
```

and the instruction:

```
printf ("Signature: %d\t%s, \"%s\"\n", book2.bookno,
        book2.author, book2.title);
```

produces the following standard output:

```
Signature: 137    Goethe, "Faust, Part 1"
```

Transferring the contents of one structure variable into another, as we did above, by transferring the individual components, dates from the times of the old K&R standard, where this was the only way of doing it (or by using a standard function such as `memcpy()` (see Chapter 12)).

Fortunately with the ANSI standard it is now possible to transfer one structure variable into another as a whole, using assignment. The three instructions above can therefore be replaced by:

```
book2 = book1;
```

Nevertheless, transferring component by component is still allowed and is sometimes even necessary if you only want to transfer some and not all of the components.

It is also possible to declare a structure type and at the same time define variables of this type. So we could have written:

```
struct book
{
    int bookno;
    char author[21];
    char title[50];
} book1,
  book2;
```

All further variables can then be defined with:

```
struct book book3;
```

In a third alternative, the structure type name can be omitted:

```
struct
{
    int bookno;
    char author[21];
    char title[50];
} book1,
  book2;
```

But then it is no longer possible to define other variables of this structure type at a later stage.

11.1.1   Vectors of structures

Of course it is not only simple variables which can be defined by the type of a structure, but also for example vectors. With the instruction:

```
struct book books[100];
```

a vector of 100 elements would be defined, each representing a structure variable of the type book (see Figure 11.3).

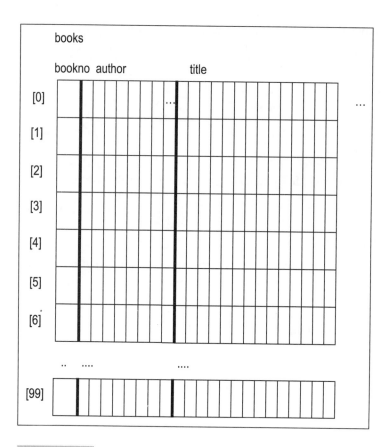

Figure 11.3 *The vector books*

If we wanted to transfer our Goethe into the fifth element of the vector, the following instructions would be needed:

```
books[4].bookno = 137;
strcpy (books[4].author, "Goethe");
strcpy (books[4].title, "Faust, Part 1");
```

Note the evaluation sequence. In the expression `books[4].bookno` both the index operator `[]` and the components operator '.' are on level 1 of the operator hierarchy, so will be processed from left to right. So `books[4]` is evaluated first as a variable of the `struct book` type. When `.bookno` is subsequently evaluated, you then obtain these components of the structure variables evaluated previously.

If you wanted to read in a maximum of 100 book titles into this vector, you could
write:

```
struct book books[100];
int i,
    b,
    n;
printf ("Signature: ");
for (i = 0 ; i < 100 && (b = get_int ()) != 0 ; ++i)
{
    books[i].bookno = b;
    printf ("Author: ");
    getline (books[i].author, 21);
    printf ("Title: ");
    getline (books[i].title, 50);
    printf ("Signature: ");
}
n = i;
```

And with the following loop you could display all the books which have been
entered:

```
for (i = 0 ; i < n ; ++i)
    printf ("Signature: %5.5d\tAuthor: %s, Title: \"%s\"\n",
            books[i].bookno, books[i].author,
            books[i].title);
```

11.1.2   Pointers to structures

Of course, there are also pointers to structures. We will add a pointer variable to
our vector definition:

```
struct book books[100];
struct book * bp = books;       /* or:
struct book * bp = &books[0];                */
```

With ++bp the pointer content would be increased incrementally by the length
of a structure variable, as if you had assigned to bp:

```
bp = &books[1];
```

It gets a bit more complicated if you want to access a component of a structure
variable by means of a pointer. With:

```
printf ("%d\n", (*bp).bookno);
```

you would see the signature of the second book. The brackets are necessary, because the component operator '.' takes priority over the reference operator '*'.

bp is evaluated using the starting address of a structure variable (data type: `struct book *`)

(`*bp`) is evaluated using the structure variable itself (data type: `struct book`)

(`*bp`).`bookno` is evaluated using its `int` component: `bookno`

If by mistake you had written:

```
printf ("%d\n", *bp.bookno);     /* Wrong!!! */
```

what would have been evaluated first would be:

```
bp.bookno
```

which would have generated an error message from the compiler. That is because there has to be a structure variable before the component operator '.' and not a pointer to a structure variable.

Because it is tedious having to pay attention to the brackets needed with structure pointers, the inventor of C introduced an alternative way of writing which does not need brackets. Thus, you can write:

```
printf ("%d\n", bp->bookno);
```

The component operator '->' for structure pointers is also on level 1 of the operator hierarchy. From now on we will always use it when using pointers, even though (`*bp`). is still valid.

Generally, the two expressions can be noted as follows:

→ structure variable . component
→ pointer variable -> component

Of course, pointers to structures are of great importance in transferring to functions. Whole structure variables can even be passed to functions as arguments, as shown in the following example:

```
void print_book (struct book b)
{
    printf ("Signature: %5.5d\tAuthor: %s, Title: \"%s\"\n",
            b.bookno, b.author, b.title);
}
```

But anyone passing such a – possibly very large – structure variable by "Call by Value" would thereby overload the stack. Instead, it is quicker and saves more space on the stack to pass the starting address of a structure variable to a pointer, even if you have no intention of having write access to the structure variable in the function. So our function would be better defined:

```
void print_book (struct book * bp)
{
    printf ("Signature: %5.5d\tAuthor: %s, Title: \"%s\"\n",
            bp->bookno, bp->author, bp->title);
}
```

And a book input function could not be defined in any other way:

```
int get_book (struct book * bp)
{
    printf ("Signature: ");
    if ((bp->bookno = get_int ()) == 0)
        return 0;
    printf ("Author: ");
    getline (bp->author, 21);
    printf ("Title: ");
    getline (bp->title, 50);
    return 1;
}
```

Our example above about inputting a maximum of 100 books and then displaying them could then be programmed using both functions in a `main()` function as follows:

```
# include <stdio.h>
# include "book.h"
struct book books[100];        /* global, so as not to over-
load the stack
                                                   */

int main (void)
{
    int i,
        n;
    for (i = 0 ; i < 100 && get_book (&books[i]) ; ++i)
        ;
    n = i;
    for (i = 0 ; i < n ; ++i)
        print_book (&books[i]);
    return 0;
}
```

and with the following content in the header file `book.h`:

```
struct book
{
    int bookno;
    char author[21];
    char title[50];
};
void print_book (struct book * bp); /* prototypes */
int get_book (struct book * bp);
```

It is assumed here that the definitions of the two functions used are in their own program file, where of course the same header file must be bound.

11.1.3 Structure variables as components of structures

A structure can contain components of any data type, so why not also those of the type of another structure? As every book is printed and marketed by a publishing house, one could imagine the following, simplified publisher structure type:

```
struct publisher
{
    int publisherno;
    char name[21];
    char address[50];
};
```

If you assume that every book can be attributed to a publishing house, then the book structure has to be significantly extended:

```
struct book
{
    int bookno;
    char author[21];
    char title[50];
    struct publisher publisher;
};
```

One of the components of the book structure is again a structure variable, and of the type `struct publisher`.

Another possibility would be to nest the structure type declarations:

```
struct book
{
    int bookno;
    char author[21];
    char title[50];
    struct publisher
    {
        int publisherno;
        char name[21];
        char address[50];
    } publisher;
};
```

Here the component `publisher` is defined with a data type which is itself only defined when the variables are defined. The structure `book` has four components, each has its data type, and the last has the data type `struct publisher`.

However, it is possible to define variables of the type of both structures, e.g.:

```
struct book b;
struct publisher p;
```

Access to the components now becomes somewhat more complicated:

```
b.publisher.publisherno = 101;
strcpy (b.publisher.name, "Routledge");
strcpy (b.publisher.address, "New York");
```

If we assume the following input function for a publisher structure:

```
int get_publisher (struct publisher * pp)
{
    printf ("Publisher no.: ");
    if ((pp->publisherno = get_int ()) == 0)
        return 0;
    printf ("Publisher name: ");
    getline (pp->name, 21);
    printf ("Address: ");
    getline (pp->address, 50);
    return 1;
}
```

then our book input function would have to be extended by calling: `get_publisher()`:

```
int get_book (struct book * bp)
{
```

```
    printf ("Signature: ");
    if ((bp->bookno = get_int ()) == 0)
        return 0;
    printf ("Author: ");
    getline (bp->author, 21);
    printf ("Title: ");
    getline (bp->title, 50);
    get_publisher (&bp->publisher); /* NEW!!! */
    return 1;
}
```

When `get_publisher (&bp->publisher);` is called, the starting address of the component `publisher` is passed to the `book` structure variable to which `bp` is pointing. Note here also the sequence of evaluation:

➔ `bp` is evaluated with the starting address of the `book` structure variable (data type: `struct book *`);

➔ `bp->publisher` is evaluated with its component `publisher` (data type: `struct publisher`);

➔ `&bp->publisher` is evaluated with its starting address (data type: `struct publisher *`).

A corresponding output function could then look like this:

```
void print_publisher (struct publisher * pp)
{
    printf ("Publisher No.: %5.5d\tPublisher: %s, %s\n",
            pp->publisherno, pp->name, pp->address);
}
```

And the function `print_book()` could then be expanded:

```
void print_book (struct book * bp)
{
    printf ("Signature: %5.5d\tAuthor: %s, Title: \"%s\"\n",
            bp->bookno, bp->author, bp->title);

    print_publisher (&bp->publisher);  /* NEW!!! */
}
```

11.1.4   Pointers as components of structures

Our book/publisher combination could in some cases turn out to be too close a link. Each publishing house appears as a component of a book. In reality there are definitely more books than publishing houses and simply for reasons of data modeling you would not want to store all the data about a publishing house with each book title. This can be solved by reconstructing our structures, by using pointers to structures as components:

```
struct publisher
{
    int publisherno;
    char name[21];
    char address[50];
};

struct book
{
    int bookno;
    char author[21];
    char title[50];
    struct publisher * pp;   /* NEW: only a pointer!!! */
};
```

If you now want to handle 1000 book titles from 40 different publishers, you would have to define:

```
struct book b[1000];
struct publisher p[40];
```

The 25th publisher would be defined by the following data:

```
p[24].publisherno = 1024;
strcpy (p[24].name, "Macmillan");
strcpy (p[24].address, "Basingstoke");
```

and the 798th book title by:

```
b[797].bookno = 472;
strcpy (b[797].author, "Other, A.N");
strcpy (b[797].title, "True Stories ");
b[797].pp = &p[24];
```

The connection between a book title and a publishing house is achieved here just by assigning a pointer. There will probably be other elements of the vector b which point with their pp component to the same publishing house. The data for that publisher though is only stored once, namely in p[24].

Our book output function would only have to be slightly modified:

```
void print_book (struct book * bp)
{
    printf ("Signature: %5.5d\tAuthor: %s, Title: \"%s\"\n",
            bp->bookno, bp->author, bp->title);
```

```
        print_publisher (bp->pp);   /* bp->pp instead of &bp->pub-
lisher!!! */
}
```

Modifying the book input function is rather more complicated. When the user inputs a book title he must be shown a list of all the publishing houses, or he must know the publisher number, for example. The starting address of the corresponding element of the p vector must then be identified using a special search function, to establish the pointer between the book and the publishing house. We will not go further into this issue now.

However, it should now be clear that using structure pointers as components of structures can be applied to great effect to avoid storing redundant data.

We will only be able to appreciate the full force of this procedure when we come to programming concatenated lists and tree structures using dynamic memory requests (see Chapter 13).

11.2 Variants

In their outward form, variants are very similar to structures. They differ from them in two ways:

1 by having the keyword `union` instead of `struct`;

2 in that the components of a variant are filed in the memory not one after the other but overlapping.

With

```
union var
{
    long z;
    unsigned char s[7];
};
```

a variant of the type `union var` is defined, which consists of the two components z and s.

Here too, with this type declaration no memory space is yet reserved. That only happens later when the variable is defined:

```
union var v;
```

The variable v then occupies the memory space shown in Figure 11.4:

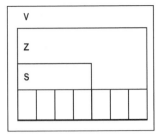

Figure 11.4 *Memory allocation of the union var variable v*

It is 7 bytes long, i.e. as long as its longest component. Both components occupy memory from the same starting address. In other words, it is not possible to store different data in the two components z and s at the same time. So if you assign the string "ABCDEF" to the component s, that means the component z has also been given a value which interprets the first 4 bytes of s as a long number.

The core image is shown in Figure 11.5.

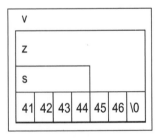

Figure 11.5 *Component allocation of v*

The assignment of the string was achieved as follows:

```
strcpy (v.s, "ABCDEF");
```

and the following instructions:

```
printf ("%s\n", v.s);
printf ("%8.8lX\n", v.z);
```

would generate the output:

```
ABCDEF
44434241
```

The last output line should be no mystery, if you assume that the above program code was running on a computer with INTEL processor. The INTEL convention was of course at work again here. On a computer with, for example, a Motorola processor, you would of course have got:

```
ABCDEF
41424344
```

This example shows how using variants can be extremely hardware-dependent. It is then of no practical importance if you definitely decide which components you want to use. So either:

```
strcpy (v.s, "Otto");
printf ("%s\n", v.s); ---> Otto
```

or:

```
v.z = 100239L;
printf ("%ld\n", v.z); ---> 100239
```

Variants are useful when you want to store very varied data in a variable, for example different record types of files. The above variant var could be used for data records consisting either of a long number or a max. six character-long string.

In order to make this selection in a particular case, you could extend the variant var by a type field into a structure:

```
struct rec
{
   int type;              /* data record type field */
   union var record;      /* actual data record */
};
```

An input function could then be defined like this:

```
int get_rec (struct rec * rp)
{
   if (rp->type == 0)
   {
      printf "Integer: ");
      scanf ("%ld", &rp->record.z);
   }
   else if (rp->type == 1)
   {
      printf "String: ");
      getline (rp->record.s, 7);
   }
   else
   {
      fprintf (stderr, "%d:Wrong record type!\n", rp->type);
      return 0;
```

```
   }
   return 1;
}
```

This also demonstrates how components of a structure can consist of variant variables, and that the same operators are used to access components with both structures and variants.

Equally, a variant can consist of several structure variables. The BORLAND C compiler, for example, provides the following data types in the header file dos.h for interrupt programming:

```
struct  WORDREGS
{
   unsigned int  ax, bx, cx, dx;
   unsigned int  si, di, cflag, flags;
};
struct  BYTEREGS
{
   unsigned char  al, ah, bl, bh;
   unsigned char  cl, ch, dl, dh;
};
union REGS
{
   struct   WORDREGS  x;
   struct   BYTEREGS  h;
};
```

The structure WORDREGS represents a main memory image of some important registers of the INTEL processor. For the first four registers there is another memory image in the BYTEREGS structure, in the form of 8 half-registers. The variant REGS causes the two images to overlap.

If we now define a variable:

```
union REGS r;
```

then r.x.ax gives you access to the AX register (or to be precise to its core image), while r.h.al allows access to the low-value byte of the AX register, the so-called AL half-register.

We will not discuss here the ways in which this variant REGS can be used for system programming.

While variant variables can be treated like structure variables in terms of form, they do have one particular feature which must be remembered when initializing variables:

A variable of the variant type can only be initialized during definition by initializing the first component. This initialization must, though, be done in the same way as for structures, i.e. using { } brackets. The following would therefore be possible:

```
var a = { 13L };          /* a.z is initialized with 13L */
```

while the following is prohibited:

```
var a = { "Otto" };
```

11.3 Enumerations

An enumeration (keyword enum) is a conglomerate of int constants, each one having a symbolic name.

A well-known demonstration example is an enumeration colors involving the storage of int constants for colors:

```
enum colors
{
    red,          /* = 0 */
    green,        /* = 1 */
    blue,         /* = 2 */
    cyan,         /* = 3 */
    yellow        /* = 4 */
};
```

This type declaration is outwardly similar to that of structures and variants, but with two main formal differences:

1   The components consist only of a name with no data type specified;

2   The components are separated by commas and not finished with a semi-colon.

Each component designates an int constant, with the first components having the value 0 as standard, and all the other components having a value 1 higher than the one before.

After a variable of this type has been defined:

```
enum colors col;
```

the following operations are then possible:

```
col = green;
col++;                    /* col is now: blue */
printf ("%d\n", col); /* output: 2 */
if (col == red)

    ....
col = 4;                  /* or: col = yellow; */
```

These examples show that an enum variable is actually nothing more than an int variable. The only special feature is that only one int value should be assigned to an enum variable from a specific number of digits. And it is this specific number of digits which was defined by the type declaration.

The above variable col of the type enum colors thus serves to store one of the five numbers: 0, 1, 2, 3, or 4, which function in response to their names red, green, blue, cyan or yellow.

The last instruction col = 4; shows that you can also assign simple int constants, but you should not do this.

(Note: in the language extension C++ an instruction like that causes a warning from the compiler, because in C++ an enumeration is an independent data type, and not simply an int value.)

It can turn out to be necessary to assign an int number to an enum variable, if, for example, you want to read a value into the variable col from the user. Of course scanf() knows no special format designator for enum variables, because they are after all a self-defined data type.

You therefore have no alternative but to proceed as follows:

```
printf ("Enter a color value:\n");
printf ("0 for red\n");
printf ("1 for green\n");
printf ("2 for blue\n");
printf ("3 for cyan\n");
printf ("4 for yellow\n");
scanf ("%d", &col);
```

So here the color value is read in using %d as the int number and stored in col. If the user enters the value 3, that has the same effect as the instruction col = cyan;

But what if the user enters the value 7? There is no enum colors component for this value. Nevertheless the number is stored.

So there is no control as to whether only one of the intended numerical values is being stored in an enum variable. It is up to the programmer to check that, for example by writing the following input function for our problem:

```
int get_col (enum colors * cp)
{
    int c;
    printf ("input of a color value:\n");
    printf ("0 for red\n");
    printf ("1 for green\n");
    printf ("2 for blue\n");
    printf ("3 for cyan\n");
    printf ("4 for yellow\n");
    scanf ("%d", &c);
    switch (c)
    {
        case 0:
            * cp = red;
            break;
        case 1:
            * cp = green;
            break;
        case 2:
            * cp = blue;
            break;
        case 3:
            * cp = cyan;
            break;
        case 4:
            * cp = yellow;
            break;
        default:
            fprintf (stderr, "%d: Wrong color value!\n", c);
            return 0;
    }
    return 1;
}
```

Incidentally, the sequence of numbers: 0, 1, 2, etc for the components which was used in our type declaration of enum colors is not compulsory. The components can be defined in a different sequence simply by initialization. In that case our declaration could have been:

```
enum colors
{
    red,                    /* = 0 */
    green,                  /* = 1 */
    blue = 5,               /* = 5 */
    cyan,                   /* = 6 */
    yellow = 12             /* = 12 */
};
```

So here there are the five color names for the int constants: 0, 1, 5, 6 and 12.
However, it remains the case that a component which has not been explicitly initialized, receives a value 1 higher than the one before.

In practice, the following enum data types are very popular:

(a)

```
enum bool
{
    false,        /* = 0 */
    true          /* = 1 */
};
.....
enum bool result;
.....
if (result == true)
    .....
```

(b)

```
enum switch
{
    off,          /* = 0 */
    on            /* = 1 */
};
```

Of course functions can have an enum data type as a return value. So our function
get_col() above, by using the data type enum bool could also have been defined:

```
enum bool get_col (enum colors * cp)
{
    int c;
    printf ("input of a color value:\n");
    printf ("0 for red\n");
    ......
    scanf ("%d", &c);
    switch (c)
```

```
    {
        case 0:
            * cp = red;
            break;
        case 1:
            . . . . . .
        . . . . . .
        default:
            fprintf (stderr, "%d:Wrong color value!\n", c);
            return false;
    }
    return true;
}
```

And a `main()` function could make use of it like this:

```
int main (void)
{
    enum colors col;
    while (get_col (&col) == false)
        fprintf (stderr, "Repeat input!\n");
    . . . . . .
}
```

Finally, we must point out one more important thing: the names of the `enum` components have – as shown in the above examples – global validity. So anywhere where for example the data type `enum colors` is recognized, it would be a mistake to define the variable double blue; or a function `char * yellow (int x)`;. No compiler will let such a mistake pass.

11.4 Bit-fields

Now we come to a particular type of structure. A structure has so far consisted of components of any data type. However, you can also define components of a structure as a variable, consisting only of a specific number of bits. Such a component is then called a bit-field.

In terms of syntax, such a bit-field should be defined as an `unsigned int` component, followed by a colon and an `int` constant for the number of bits. For example:

```
struct mask
{
    unsigned int x : 11;
    unsigned int y : 4;
```

```
    unsigned int z : 8;
};
struct mask mymask;
mymask.x = 3;
mymask.y = 10;
mymask.z = 0xffff;
printf ("%X:%X:%X\n", mymask.x, mymask.y, mymask.z);
```

In this example the bit-field x consists of 11 bits, y of 4 and z of 8. In the assignments which follow, each individual bit-field is treated as an `unsigned int` variable. It should be obvious that the value `0xffff` assigned to z does not fit there. So in the assignment process the excess leading bit-places are cut off, so that calling `printf()` produces the following output:

```
3:A:FF
```

Each bit-field cannot be longer than a machine word (`int` memory space), so 16 bits in MS/DOS, 32 bits in UNIX. Smaller bit-fields are, however, accommodated in a machine word where possible. If a bit-field no longer fits in an already partly occupied machine word, then it is placed at the start of the next machine word.

The sequence in which the bit-fields of a structure are added to the memory depends on the computer. Taking an example of assigning from left to right, then in a 16 bit operating system the core image of our variable `mymask` would appear as shown in Figure 11.6.

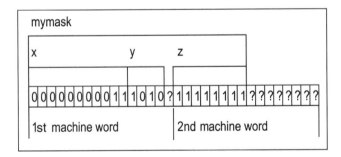

Figure 11.6 *The bit interpretation of mymask*

As you can see, between the bit-fields y and z is an unused bit, because z is aligned with the next word boundary.

There are now two additional ways of influencing the alignment of the bit-fields:

(a) With an unnamed bit-field, unused areas can be explicitly defined. If our structure declaration was:

```
struct mask
{
```

```
    unsigned int   : 8;
    unsigned int x : 3;
    unsigned int y : 4;
    unsigned int z : 8;
};
```

then we would have the core image shown in Figure 11.7:

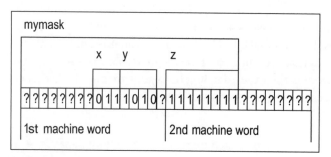

Figure 11.7 *Alignment with unnamed bit-field*

The first eight bits of the variable `mymask` would then not be usable, they make what a COBOL programmer would call a "filler".

(b) With the bit-field length 0 it is inevitable that the next bit field is in any case aligned with the word boundary. A corresponding structure declaration is:

```
struct mask
{
    unsigned int x : 11;
    unsigned int   : 0;
    unsigned int y : 4;
    unsigned int z : 8;
};
```

This declaration is shown in the memory assignment in Figure 11.8.

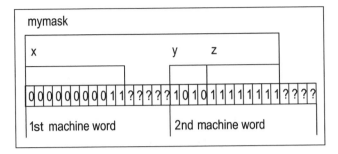

Figure 11.8 *Alignment with bit-field length 0*

In general you should bear in mind the following limitations with bit-fields:

(a) The address operator & cannot be used on bit-fields, nor can any pointers to bit-fields be used. So the expression &mymask.x leads to an error message from the compiler. On the other hand of course, it is still possible to define a pointer to the whole bit-field structure:

```
struct mask mymask,
              * mp = &mymask;
mp->x = 3;
.....
```

(b) Bit-fields are in principle of the type int resp. unsigned int. Even where int is being used, bit-fields are always unsigned.

(c) There are no vectors of bit-fields.

The practical applications of bit-fields are of course mainly in the area of system programming, where information often has to be stored in bits. Bit-fields are then often a simpler alternative to using bit manipulation operators. This should be explained by using the previously mentioned "attribute-byte" of a directory entry for a file under MS/DOS.

Look again at Chapter 3, at how bit manipulation operators were used there to check whether an attribute-byte was displaying a "hidden file".

Using bit-fields the same problem could be solved like this:

```
struct attrib
{
    unsigned int : 2;
    unsigned int archive : 1;
    unsigned int directory : 1;
    unsigned int label : 1;
    unsigned int system : 1;
```

```
        unsigned int hidden : 1;
        unsigned int readonly : 1;
};
struct attrib attr;
getfattrib (&attr); /* This is where the attribute byte is
involved */
if (attr.hidden)
    printf ("Hidden file\n");
if (attr.readonly && attr.hidden && attr.system)
    printf ("Hidden, read-only system file\n");
.....
attr.hidden = 0;     /* Make hidden file visible  */
changefattrib (&attr); /* Transfer attribute byte into
directory
    */
```

The functions `getfattrib()` and `changefattrib()` would of course still have to be defined, but that comes under system programming and is not dealt with in this book.

The advantage of a solution like that is obvious: you don't need to use bit operators, but can just access the relevant information using the names of the bit-fields as components of a structure.

11.5 typedef

The C instruction `typedef` allows you to introduce new data type names. Of course, you can't invent new data types, but only new names – additional alias names, so to speak – for existing data types.

So for example FORTRAN programmers could express their nostalgia for that good old programming language with the following instructions:

```
typedef int INTEGER;
typedef float REAL;
```

In this way the C data types `int` and `float` are given the additional names IN-TEGER and REAL. Then it doesn't matter if they define:

```
INTEGER x[5];
REAL z,
     * rp = &z;
or
int x[5];
float z,
      * rp = &z;
```

Of course you could also mix the type names:

```
int x[5];
float z;
REAL * rp = &z;
```

The syntax of the `typedef` instruction is:

```
typedef previous-data-type-name new-data-type-name
```

One way it can be used is to shorten unnecessarily long type names:

```
typedef unsigned char UCHAR;
UCHAR uc,
      uv[100],
      * ucp = uv;
```

By the way, it is conventional to write data type names which are newly introduced in this way using `typedef` with capitals.

In many header files supplied with a C compiler, `typedef` is often used to overcome hardware, operating system or compiler-dependent features. The following simplifying sequence of instructions would therefore be possible:

```
# ifdef _MS_DOS_
   typedef int WORD;
# elif defined(_UNIX_)
   typedef long WORD;
# else
   typedef long WORD;
# endif
```

A function using the prototype:

```
void func (WORD * wp);
```

would then use its `wp` parameter to access either an `int` or a `long` variable, depending on the operating system being used.

But C programmers find out about the best application of `typedef` if they apply this instruction to the self-defined data types which we have dealt with in this chapter.

Our book structure would then appear as a new data type BOOK:

```
typedef struct
        {
            int bookno;
            char author[21];
            char title[50];
        } BOOK;
```

Here the original structure type name book would be omitted after the keyword `struct`. It is no longer necessary.

Now the following:

```
struct book book1,
            book2;
```

becomes:

```
BOOK book1,
     book2;
```

Instead of using `sizeof(struct book)` we can now find out the length of our structure using `sizeof(BOOK)`.

The function `get_book()` now has the following prototypes:

```
int get_book (BOOK * bp);
```

But the following type derivation is also possible:

```
typedef BOOK * BOOKP;
```

Then you could define:

```
BOOK b[100];
BOOKP bp = b;
```

This last example in particular shows that you cannot tell from data types defined in this way whether they are masking a structure or, as in the case of BOOKP, a pointer to a structure.

In any case programmers have to have some idea about what is behind a name like that. In the case of our data type BOOK, of course, they really have to know the components of this structure, otherwise they could not do very much with variables of this type. However, in Chapter 14 we'll find out about a data type FILE defined in `stdio.h` using `typedef`, for which you don't necessarily have to know the structure components. All you need to know is that you have to define a pointer to FILE if you want to process a file.

Finally, here are a few more examples of the other self-defined data types:

```
typedef union                 instead of:    union var
{                                            {
   long z;                                      long z;
   unsigned char s[7];                          unsigned char s[7];
} VAR;                                        };
VAR v;                                        union var v;
```

and:

```
typedef enum              instead of:   enum bool
{                                       {
   false,                                  false,
   true                                    true
} BOOL;                                 };
BOOL result;              enum bool result;
```

and:

```
typedef struct            instead of:   struct attrib
{                                       {
 unsigned int : 2;                       unsigned int : 2;
 unsigned int archive : 1;               unsigned int archive : 1;
 unsigned int directory : 1;             unsigned int directory : 1;
 unsigned int label : 1;                 unsigned int label : 1;
 unsigned int system : 1;                unsigned int system : 1;
 unsigned int hidden : 1;                unsigned int hidden : 1;
 unsigned int readonly : 1;              unsigned int readonly : 1;
}ATTRIB;                                };
ATTRIB attr;                             struct attrib attr;
```

11.6 Exercises

1(a) Transfer the macro LEAPYEAR() from Exercise 1, Chapter 10 into the
header file date.h.

In the same header file use typedef to declare the data type
DATE for a structure which can store information about the date.
Components:

→ day (data type: char)
→ mon (data type: char)
→ year (data type: int)

Tip Warning! Information about days and months is in small numbers which fit in char variables.
So these char components are not storing characters but numbers.

(b) In the module `date.c` create the function `get_date()`, which reads date information from standard input into a variable of the type `DATE`. It should be assumed that the date is entered in the format DD.MM.YYYY.

No dialogue message should be sent before the date is read in.

Parameter: Pointer to a DATE variable

Return value:

→   1, if a complete date was entered

→   0 otherwise

Advice: define a sufficiently large char vector, into which you first read the date as a string (e.g. using `getline()` for example). If nothing was entered, the function is to be exited immediately with 0.

Otherwise the date components of the string are to be converted into numerical values and stored in the components of the DATE variable. The standard function `sscanf()` is available for that. This function works in principle exactly like the related function `scanf()`, but with the difference that `sscanf()` reads not from standard input but from a char vector.

Its effect is demonstrated here in the case of simple variables:

```
char sdat[] = "23.4.1999";
char t,
     m;
int j;
sscanf (sdat, "%d.%d.%d", &t, &m, &j);
```

The return value of `sscanf()` is the number of successfully converted and stored values. In this case it must be 3, if the date information contains three items of numerical information separated by full stops.

Transfer this demonstration example to the exercise and ensure that instead of the three variables you then have three components of a DATE structure.

If the user enters an incomplete date, for example "23.4", then the error message "23.4: Incomplete date" should be generated and the function exited with 0.

Enter the prototype of this function in `date.h`.

(c) In the `date.c` module, create the function `put_date()`, which displays date information in standard output, in the format: "DD.MM.YYYY".

Only the bare date – without final new-line – should be produced. (You can never know whether more text is to be displayed on the same line, after this function has been called.)

Parameter: Pointer to the `DATE` variable to be produced

Return value: none

Enter the prototype of this function in `date.h`!

(d) In the `date.c` module, create the function `datplaus()`, which checks whether a date is plausible.

Parameter: Pointer to the `DATE` variable to be checked

Return value:

➜ 1, if the date is plausible
➜ 0 otherwise

Tip: the plausibility rules for a date apply to the Gregorian calendar. Years < 1583 (or 1752) are therefore not valid.

Tip: Use the macro `LEAPYEAR()`!

Enter the prototype of this function in `date.h`!

(e) In the `tdate.c` module, create a `main()` function to test the date functions. Date information should be read in as often as you like into a `DATE` variable using `get_date()`.

If the date which has been entered is not plausible, (call `datplaus()`), an error message should be generated accordingly. Otherwise the date entered should be outputted again using `put_date()`, followed by a new-line.

The input loop is terminated if an incomplete date is entered.

Create a project file and test the program!

Use your test data to test as fully as possible all data on the boundary between plausible and implausible date information.

2 Similarly to in Exercise 1, create a program to manage time information. To do that the data type `TIME` is to be defined in `time.h` using `typedef`, for a structure which has the following components for hours and minutes:
```
char hrs;
char min;
```

The functions to be defined, corresponding to Exercise 1, are to be called `get_time()`, `put_timet()` and `timeplaus()` and be defined in the module `time.c`.

Define in `ttime.c` a `main()` function to test the time functions.

3 In the header file `appt.h` use `typedef` to define the data type `APPT` for a structure to store information about appointments.

Components of the `APPT` structure:

→ `dat` (Data type: `DATE`)
→ `time` (Data type: `TIME`)
→ `text` (Data type: `char` vector with 80 elements)

Don't forget to bind in `date.h` and `time.h` because without their content the data types `DATE` and `TIME` would not be recognized.

In the `appt.c` module, create – similarly to Exercises 1 and 2 – the functions: **(a)** `get_appt()` and **(b)** `put_appt()`.

As regards **(a)**: Here `get_date()`, `get_time()` and `getline()` are to be used to enter the three pieces of information for an appointment. The function is exited with return value 0 if no date (or an incomplete one) is entered, or if no appointment text is entered.

If the user enters no time information, the function is not to be exited prematurely, but the value –1 is to be stored in the component `hrs` of `time`, an indication as it were that there is no time information. (Think for example of the appointment: "29.8.1999 Marion's birthday! Phone her!". Why would you need a time here?)

At the end the function is to be exited with 1.

Parameter: Pointer to an APPT variable

As regards **(b)**: Use `put_date()`, `put_time()` and `printf()` to output all appointment information, but the time information only if the hours component `hrs` does not contain the value –1.

Parameter: Pointer to an `APPT` variable.

Return value: none

In the `ttermin.c` module, a `main()` function is then to be defined which reads any number of appointments up to max. 100 using `get_appt()` into a correspondingly large `APPT` vector.

Then the appointments which have been read in are to be displayed again in reverse order using `put_appt()`.

Standard functions

This chapter does not aim to give a complete account of all the functions in the standard library. A user of a C compiler generally has a reference manual available which offers a description of all the standard functions. Alternatively you can extract the prototypes of all the functions from the standard header files of the include directory, to get an overall idea, and use the online Help to display a description of any particular function.

The purpose of this chapter is to discuss the way some of the main standard functions work which are part of the day-to-day programming tool-kit of the C programmer. We will also show for some functions how they could have been written. That makes for a greater understanding of how these functions operate and also gives suggestions for how you could create your own functions for elementary tools.

The prototypes of the standard functions are distributed between different header files, depending on their functionality.

We will now look in some important header files for a few key functions, although, as we have said, the list by no means claims to be complete.

12.1 Functions for input/output: stdio.h

Most of these functions for input/output are actually dealt with in later chapters as they need treating separately. These are:

1   The functions for high-level data processing (see Chapter 14).

2   A few functions for data manipulation at operating system level (not discussed in this book).

3   `scanf()`/`printf()`, which are given special attention as functions with a variable number of parameters (see Chapter 19).

4 sscanf()/sprintf(), which will be dealt with further on in this chapter with the stdlib functions, although their prototypes are to be found in stdio.h.

What should just be mentioned in this section is the fact that stdio.h contains the "functions" getchar() and putchar() twice, once as function prototypes:

```
int getchar (void);
int putchar (int c);
```

but also as pre-processor macros (see Chapter 14).

It is fairly easy to understand that in normal usage actually only the macros are used, because it is always the pre-processor which is called as the first program, which ruthlessly replaces each getchar() or putchar() call by the corresponding macro expression. In other words, the compiler never gets to see a function call like that and so the linkage editor never has to look for the corresponding standard functions.

However, if you still want to work with the standard functions instead of with the macros, all you have to do is undo the macro definitions, as the following program does:

```
# include <stdio.h>
# undef getchar
# undef putchar
int main (void)
{
   int c;
   while ((c = getchar ()) != EOF)
      putchar (c);
   return 0;
}
```

In this case the getchar() and putchar() call is not triggered by the pre-processor, and the linkage editor has to extract the object code for the standard functions getchar() and putchar() from the standard library and bind it to this program.

Functions for the input/output of strings:

```
char * gets (char * s);
int    puts (const char  * s);
```

were already discussed in Chapter 5. Remember:

I   gets() reads a string from standard input into a char vector to which s is pointing. The programmer is responsible for ensuring that the vector to which s is pointing is large enough to store the string which has been entered. Otherwise it is stored beyond the end of the vector. (That was why we wrote our own function `getline()`.) A new-line which is entered is not stored, but replaced by a '\0';

2   `puts()` sends the content of a char vector ending in '\0' to which s is pointing, to standard output and attaches a new-line;

3   `gets()` sends as a return value the pointer s, and for EOF sends the value NULL;

4   `puts()` sends a positive value, or EOF in the event of an error.

It is worth noting that `gets()` also sends a return value for normal input, namely the pointer s which was passed. This fact can be used for the following program lines:

```
char s[100];
printf ("Input a string:\n");
printf ("Input was: %s\n", gets (s));
```

The last of these three lines replaces the more complicated formulation with two instructions:

```
gets (s);
printf ("Input was: %s\n", s);
```

12.2   The string functions: string.h

Here there are functions for almost everything you can do with strings:

12.2.1   size_t strlen (const char * s);

> **Tip** The data type `size_t` is usually defined with `typedef unsigned int size_t;`

`strlen()` provides the number of characters in the string ending in '\0' to which s is pointing.

This function could be written like this:

```
size_t strlen (const char * s)
{
    size_t n;
    for (n = 0 ; s[n] ; ++n)
        ;
    return n;
}
```

12.2.2   char * strcpy (char * t, const char * s);

This function copies the string ending in '\0' to which s is pointing, into the char vector to which t is pointing. The character '\0' is copied with it.

The char vector to which t is pointing must be large enough to take the string s.

The return value is the pointer t.

The same applies here as was said above for gets(), so the following call is possible:

```
printf ("Copied: %s\n", strcpy (t, s));
```

The definition of this function is also strikingly compact and clever:

```
char * strcpy (char * t, const char * s)
{
    char * temp = t;
    while (*t++ = *s++)
        ;
    return temp;
}
```

12.2.3   char * strcat (char * t, const char * s);

The function strcat() attaches the string s to the vector t (abbreviation taken from "catenate").

The return value is again t.

Here it is particularly important to note that the vector to which t is pointing is large enough to take the string, extended by s.

Here is one possible definition:

```c
char * strcat (char * t, const char * s)
{
    char * temp = t;
    for ( ; *t ; ++t)      /* Search for string end from t */
        ;
    while (*t++ = *s++)    /* Copy from s */
        ;
    return temp;
}
```

By using `strlen()` and `strcpy()`, this could have been written more concisely as:

```c
char * strcat (char * t, const char * s)
{
    char * temp = t;
    t += strlen (t);
    strcpy (t, s);
    return temp;
}
```

The last variant demonstrates the tool-kit concept, the programming philosophy of the C/UNIX world, which could be expressed thus: make yourself little tools (called "functions") for basic operations. Then make more powerful tools by combining your existing tools. That is the underlying idea of the programming language C and – in a more general way – also of the operating system UNIX, which Kernighan and Pike have described in their book [9].

A little application demonstration of `strcat()`:

```c
# include <string.h>
...
char str[100];
strcpy (str, "Otto ");
printf ("%s\n", strcat (str, "Morris")); ---> Otto Morris
```

12.2.4   int strcmp (const char * s1, const char * s2);

`strcmp()` compares two strings s1 and s2 "lexicographically", i.e. based on the alphabetical sorting of strings, as you find in any telephone directory. The characters are compared in pairs, starting with their starting address, for identical ones, or until '\0' is reached.

The return value is a number > 0, if s1 is "greater" than s2, it is < 0, if s1 is "smaller" than s2 and it is 0 if both strings are identical. The function simply returns the difference between the first differing characters of the two strings.

This principle is best understood using the following definition:

```
int strcmp (const char * s1, const char * s2)
{
    for ( ; *s1 && *s1 == *s2 ; s1++, s2++)
        ;
    return (int)(*s1 - *s2);
}
```

Note the end of the loop: the loop is exited if the character from s1 is '\0', or if it is no longer the same as the corresponding character from s2. The difference between the two characters is always returned.

This definition can be tested with the following data examples (Table 12.1):

	s1	s2	Return value	Interpretation
a.	"AbC"	"ABC"	32, so > 0	"AbC" is greater than "ABC"
b.	"ABC"	"AbC"	-32, so < 0	"ABC" is smaller than "AbC"
c.	"ABC"	"ABC"	0	"ABC" is the same as "ABC"
d.	"AB"	"ABC"	-67, so < 0	"AB" is smaller than "ABC"
e.	"ABC"	"AB"	67, so > 0	"ABC" is greater than "AB"

Table 12.1 *Testing the standard function strcmp()*

The following examples are typical applications of the strcmp() function:

(a)
```
# include <string.h>
...
char name[25];
...
printf ("Name: ");
getline (name, 25);
if (strcmp (name, "Morris") == 0)
    ...
else if (strcmp (name, "Smith") == 0)
    ...
```

(b)
```
# include <string.h>
...
```

```
char * name1 = "Smith",
     * name2 = "Morris",
     * hp;
...
if (strcmp (name1, name2) > 0) /* If name1 > name2 ... */
{
    hp = name1;              /* ... swap */
    name1 = name2;
    name2 = hp;
}
```

The second application example contains a basic swapping operation, such as there can be when sorting strings.

For `strcpy()`, `strcat()` and `strcmp()` there are related functions which mean that the operation in question is only applied to a certain number n of characters. Accordingly, these functions always have an 'n' in their name.

It should first be pointed out that working with these functions is rather more complicated, because you may have to deal in a particular way with a '\0' to finish the string.

12.2.5   char * strncpy (char * t, const char * s, size_t n);

This function copies a maximum of n characters from the string to which s is pointing into the vector to which t is pointing. The return value is again t.

The following special cases should be noted:

1 If the string s contains more than n characters, only the first n characters are copied from s, and not the '\0' which finishes the string s. In this case the programmer must, if that is his intention, insert a '\0' as the (n+1). character in t, unless the string s was longer than n characters, and the rest of t is supposed to remain after the first characters to exceed n.

2 If the string s contains fewer than n characters, then s is copied and the rest, up to the length of n is filled up with '\0' in the string t.

These effects are demonstrated in the following program:

```
# include <stdio.h>
# include <string.h>
int main (void)
{
    char str[100] = "Abracadabra";
    int i;
    strcpy (str, "ABC");
```

```
    printf ("%s\n", strncpy (str, "XYZUVW", 2));
    printf ("%s\n", strncpy (str, "XYZUVW", 4));
    strncpy (str, "123456", 4);
    str[4] = '\0';
    printf ("%s\n", str);
    strncpy (str, "x", 4);
    printf ("%s\n", str);
    for (i = 0 ; i < 5 ; ++i)
        printf ("%2.2X ", str[i]);
    putchar ('\n');
    return 0;
}
/* Program run:
XYC
XYZUcadabra
1234
x
78 00 00 00 00
*/
```

The way this function works can be explained by the following function:

```
char * strncpy (char * t, const char * s, size_t n)
{
    char * temp = t;
    while (n > 0 && *s && (*t++ = *s++))
        --n;
    while (n-- > 0)
        *t++ = '\0';
    return temp;
}
```

12.2.6   char * strncat (char * t, const char * s, size_t n);

Unlike strncpy(), strncat() attaches a maximum of n characters of the string s to the string t.

Here too, if n is smaller than the length of the string s, then the users of this function must see for themselves that there is a final '\0'.

The function could be defined as follows:

```
char * strncat (char * t, const char * s, size_t n)
{
   char * temp = t;
   t += strlen (t);
   strncpy (t, s, n);
   return temp;
}
```

12.2.7   int strncmp (const char * s1, const char * s2, size_t n);

The two strings are compared here as for `strcmp()`, the only difference being that a maximum of n characters are compared.

The following program shows what this function does:

```
# include <stdio.h>
# include <string.h>
int main (void)
{
   char s1[] = "ABCDEFGHIJ",
        s2[] = "ABCDeFGHIJ";
   if (strncmp (s1, s2, 4))
      printf ("%s different %s to 4 characters\n", s1, s2);
   else
      printf ("%s same %s to 4 characters\n", s1, s2);
   if (strncmp (s1, s2, 6))
      printf ("%s different %s to 6 characters\n", s1, s2);
   else
      printf ("%s same %s to 6 characters\n", s1, s2);
   s1[1] = '\0';
   if (strncmp (s1, s2, 4))
      printf ("%s different %s to 4 characters\n", s1, s2);
   else
      printf ("%s same %s to 4 characters\n", s1, s2);
   s2[1] = '\0';
   s1[2] = 'X';
   if (strncmp (s1, s2, 4))
      printf ("%s different %s to 4 characters\n", s1, s2);
   else
      printf ("%s same %s to 4 characters\n", s1, s2);
   return 0;
}
/* Program run:
```

```
ABCDEFGHIJ same as ABCDeFGHIJ to 4 characters
ABCDEFGHIJ different from ABCDeFGHIJ to 6 characters
A different from ABCDeFGHIJ to 4 characters
A same as A to 4 characters
*/
```

The last comparison shows that, where strings are the same length, `strncmp()` only compares as far as the '\0' and not necessarily n characters. That is also clear from the following definition:

```
int strncmp (const char * s1, const char * s2, size_t n)
{
    for ( ; n && *s1 && *s1 == *s2 ; s1++, s2++)
        if (--n == 0)
            break;
    return (int)(*s1 - *s2);
}
```

As well as the ANSI standard, some manufacturers of C compilers offer functions such as `strcmpi()` or `strncmpi()`, which ignore the difference between upper and lower case letters when comparing the strings ("i" stands for: ignore case).

Also not included in the ANSI standard are the functions `strset()` and `strnset()`, which replace all elements of a string by a given character. The substitution ends when '\0' is found or when n characters have been substituted (for `strnset()`).

12.2.8   char * strset (char * s, int c);

```
char * strset (char * s, int c)
{
    char * temp = s;
    while (*s)
        *s++ = (char)c;
    return temp;
}
```

12.2.9 char * strnset (char * s, int c, size_t n);

```
char * strnset (char * s, int c, size_t n)
{
   char * temp = s;
   while (n-- && *s)
      *s++ = (char)c;
   return temp;
}
```

And here is a possible application:

```
# include <stdio.h>
# include <string.h>
int main (void)
{
   char s[] = "ABCDEFGHIJ";
   puts (s);
   strset (s, '*');
   puts (s);
   strnset (s, '+', 5);
   puts (s);
   strnset (s, '-', 100);
   puts (s);
   return 0;
}
/* Program run:
ABCDEFGHIJ
*********
+++++*****
----------
*/
```

12.2.10 char * strchr (const char * s, int c);

This function searches in a string s for a character c. The search begins at the start of the string and ends with '\0', which is included in the search. That means you can also use strchr() to search for '\0'.

The return value is the starting address of the first character c to be found, or NULL, if the character being looked for is not found.

Possible definition:

```
char * strchr (const char * s, int c)
{
```

```
for ( ; *s ; ++s)
    if (*s == c)
        return s;
if (*s == c)
    return s;
return NULL;
}
```

12.2.11 char * strrchr (const char * s, int c);

Here the last character c to occur in the string s is being looked for. So the search begins at the end of the string and ends at the beginning. Here, too, the final '\0' is included in the search.

Possible definition:

```
char * strrchr (const char * s, int c)
{
    char * p = s + strlen (s);
    for ( ; p >= s ; --p)
        if (*p == c)
            return p;
    return NULL;
}
```

12.2.12 char * strstr (const char * s1, const char * s2);

This looks for a string s2 as a partial string in a string s1. The return value is the position within s1, at which s2 occurs for the first time, or NULL, if s2 is not found.

Possible definition:

```
char * strstr (const char * s1, const char * s2)
{
    int len1 = strlen (s1),
        len2 = strlen (s2);
    for ( ; len1 - len2 >= 0 ; ++len1, ++s1)
        if (strncmp (s1, s2, len2) == 0)
            return s1;
    return NULL;
}
```

The following program demonstrates the last three functions:

```
# include <stdio.h>
```

```
# include <string.h>
int main (void)
{
    char s [] = "The rain in Spain falls mainly on the plain";
    char * p;
    if (p = strchr (s, 'i'))
        puts (p);
    if (p = strrchr (s, 'i'))
        puts (p);
    if (p = strstr (s, "ain"))
        puts (p);
    return 0;
}
/* Program run:
in in Spain falls mainly on the plain
in
ain in Spain falls mainly on the plain
*/
```

12.2.13   char * strtok (char * s1, const char * s2);

This standard function has the job of breaking up a string, consisting of words
separated by separators, into individual "tokens", one token per word. The way
it works can be explained by the following program:

```
# include <stdio.h>
# include <string.h>
int main(void)
{
    char string[] = "abc,d:123";
    char *p;
    p = strtok (string, ",");
    if (p)
        printf ("1.: %s\n", p);
    p = strtok (NULL, ":");
    if (p)
        printf ("2.: %s\n", p);
    p = strtok (NULL, ":");
    if (p)
        printf ("3.: %s\n", p);
    printf ("4.: %s\n", string);
    return 0;
}
```

```
/* Program run:
1.: abc
2.: d
3.: 123
4.: abc
*/
```

What is important is that this function can be called several times in a row for any string. For each call it retrieves the next token.

With the first call, the starting address of the string to be analyzed must be passed to s1, and the starting address of the string with the separator(s) must be passed to s2.

For each time the same string is called, NULL must be passed to s1 and another string with separators (possibly different from the first time) passed to s2.

The return value is the starting address of the first or each subsequent token, or NULL, if the string contains no more tokens.

Let's go through the program. To start with we have the core image of the string shown in Figure 12.1.

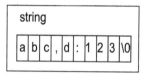

Figure 12.1   *Before the first strtok() call*

The first `strtok()` call, to which the starting address of `string` is passed, leaves the image shown in Figure 12.2.

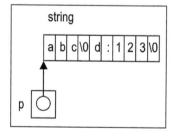

Figure 12.2   *First strtok() call*

The first separator to appear, a comma, was overwritten with '\0' and the starting address of the word before this '\0' was returned to p.

The second call should – because it has NULL as the first argument – look for the next token in the same string, but now a " : " is sent as the separator. That leads to Figure 12.3.

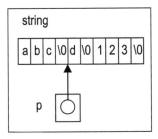

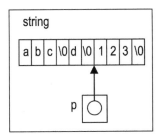

Figure 12.3 *Second strtok() call*

The third call, which this time looks for a third token with a colon as the separator, retrieves Figure 12.4.

Figure 12.4 *Third strtok() call*

Although the separator was not found, the final '\0' serves as the separator.

All further calls of strtok() would retrieve NULL. With the memory assignment shown here of the vector string, the last screen output of the program is explained.

Before we worry about how these standard functions could have been defined, two general features should be pointed out:

1 You can specify more than one separator in the second parameter. A first call:

```
p = strtok (string, ":,");
```

would not have changed the way the program ran.

2 If the search begins with leading separators, these are skipped. So if string had been initialized as follows:

```
char input [16] = ",,abc,,,d:123";
```

then the program would have run thus:

```
1.: abc
2.: ,,d
3.: 123
4.: ,,abc
```

With this information we can now define the function strtok(). First, two auxiliary functions:

```
char * strjmp (char * s, const char * delims)
{
    int found;
    const char * hp;
    for ( ; *s ; ++s)
    {
        for (hp = delims, found = 0 ; * hp ; ++hp)
            if (* s == * hp)
            {
                found++;
                break;
            }
        if (! found)
            break;
    }
    if (* s)
        return s;
    return NULL;
}
```

This function looks in the string s for the first character which is not one of the separators included in the string delims. In other words it skips all the specified separators and returns with the address of the first character which is not a separator. NULL is sent if there are only separators from delims.

The operation is performed the other way round by the following function:

```
char * strcjmp (char * s, const char * delims)
{
    int found = 0;
    const char * hp;
    for ( ; *s ; s++)
    {
        for (hp = delims ; * hp ; ++hp)
```

```
        if (* s == * hp)
        {
            found++;
            break;
        }
        if (found)
            break;
    }
    if (* s)
        return s;
    return NULL;
}
```

That skips all characters which are not included in `delims` and returns the starting address of the first character which corresponds to any of the characters from `delims`. NULL is sent if none of the specified separators occurs.

> **Tip** The function `strcjmp ()` which is shown here essentially equates to the standard function `strpbrk ()`, which will not be discussed further here. The reader can learn more from one of the reference works.

This means that `strtok ()` can be defined as follows:

```
char * strtok (char * sp, const char * delim)
{
    static char * p = NULL;        /* static variable!!! */
    char * hp;

    /* If by mistake the first call of all is called
       strtok (NULL, ...);  ...                          */
    if (sp == NULL && p == NULL)
        return NULL;
    if (sp!= NULL)         /* Initial call */
    {
        /* Skip all separators between words */
        if ((hp = strjmp (sp, delim)) == NULL) /* If string
end... */
        {
            p = NULL;
            return NULL;
```

```
        }
        if (p = strcjmp (hp, delim))
            * p++ = '\0';
        else
            p = NULL;
        return hp;
    }
    /* Each subsequent call: */
    /* Skip word */
    /* Skip all separators between words */
    if ((hp = strjmp (p, delim)) == NULL) /* If string end
... */
    {
        p = NULL;
        return NULL;
    }
    if (p = strcjmp (hp, delim))
        * p++ = '\0';
    else
        p = NULL;
    return hp;
}
```

Only a static variable such as the char pointer p can use a function call to observe where the last search for a separator ended and where the search is to continue after a new call with NULL as the first argument.

You are recommended to use the above main() function to work through this version of strtok() in a dry run.

An example of an application for strtok() would be the job of writing a command interpreter for an operating system. Generally a command line is read into a larger char vector. The separation of the individual command components, which are generally separated by blanks or tab signs, can then be done using strtok() as, for example, Marc J. Rochkind shows in his book [10] about UNIX system programming.

As a suggestion, although the function strtok() does not itself need to be defined, because it is a standard function, the auxiliary functions strjmp() and strcjmp() shown here are perhaps candidates for a private string library!?!

12.3 The memory functions: mem.h

As well as the actual string functions, there are in `string.h`, as well as in the header file `mem.h`, a small number of memory functions which in their names and effects are very similar to the corresponding string functions. Their main difference is that

1 any memory area (including structure variables or vectors) can be processed;

2 the string-end identifier '\0' therefore plays no role and a number of bytes always has to be specified which are to be processed;

3 all addresses are of the data type (void *), because any memory areas are to be processed.

12.3.1 *void * memcpy (void * dest, const void * src, size_t n);*

This function copies n bytes from `src` to `dest`. If the areas to be copied from and to overlap, the result is undefined. (You might wonder why, if you are assuming character-by-character transfer).

The return value is `dest`.

An application example:

```
BOOK books_1[100] =
{
    { 137, "Goethe", "Faust" },
    { 138, "Gorki", "My universities" },
    . . . .
    . . . .
};
BOOK books_2[30];
. . . .
. . . .
memcpy (books_2, books_1, 30 * sizeof(BOOK));
```

Here the first thirty books from the vector books_1 are copied into the vector books_2.

12.3.2 *void * memmove (void * dest, const void * src, size_t n);*

The only difference from `memcpy()` is that here the memory areas to be copied into and out of can overlap.

12.3.3   int memcmp (const void * s1, const void * s2, size_t n);

Both memory areas s1 and s2 are compared byte by byte for n bytes, with each byte being considered as an unsigned char. The comparison ends with the first byte which has a different value in s1 and s2, or when n bytes have been compared.

The return value is determined exactly as for strncmp().

An application example:

```
if (memcmp (&books_1[1], &books_2[1], sizeof(BOOK)) == 0)
    printf ("The 2nd book is the same for both vectors\n");
else
    printf ("The 2nd book is different in the two vec-
tors\n");
```

12.3.4   void * memset (void * s, int c, size_t n);

This function sets the first n bytes of the vector s to the value of c. The value of c is thereby reduced to the lowest value byte.

Return value is s.

An application example:

```
printf ("%s\n", memset (books_2[1].title, '*', 5));
Output: ***** Universities
```

12.3.5   void * memchr (const void * s, int c, size_t n);

Searches in n bytes from s for a byte with the content of c.

Return value:

1   The address of the first byte where the value c is found.
2   NULL, if the value of c was not found in all n bytes from s.

12.4 The classification functions: ctype.h

This header file contains a collection of useful tools for classifying or converting individual characters. They are available both as prototypes of standard functions and as macros. Here too it is always the macros which are used unless their definition is undone using #undef.

All the following classification functions or macros return a value not equal to 0, if the classification applies, otherwise the value is 0.

According to the ANSI standard the following applies:

1   **int isalnum (int c);**
    ➜ Is true (not equal to 0), if `isalpha(c)` or `isdigit(c)` is true.

2   **int isalpha (int c);**
    ➜ Is true, if the character c is an alphabetical character (A–Z or a-z).

3   **int iscntrl (int c);**
    ➜ Is true if the character c is a control character (ASCII-Code: 0X00–0X1F or 0X7F).

4   **int isdigit (int c);**
    ➜ Is true if the character c is a digit (0–9).

5   **int isgraph (int c);**
    ➜ Is true if `isprint(c)` is true, without the blank.

6   **int islower (int c);**
    ➜ Is true, if the character c is a lower case letter (a–z).

7   **int isprint (int c);**
    ➜ Is true if the character c is a printable character (ASCII-Code: 0X20–0X7E).

8   **int ispunct (int c);**
    ➜ Is true if the character c is a punctuation character, so if `iscntrl(c)` or `isspace(c)` is true.

9   **int isspace (int c);**
    ➜ Is true if the character c is a space character (ASCII-Code: 0X09–0X0D or 0X20).

10   **int isupper (int c);**
    ➜ Is true if the character c is a capital letter (A–Z).

11   **int isxdigit (int c);**
    ➜ Is true if the character c is a hexadecimal figure (0–9, A–F or a–f).

C compilers on UNIX systems offer in addition to the ANSI standard:

1   **int isascii (int c);**
    ➜ Is true if the character c is a character in the standardized 7-bit ASCII code (0X00–0X7F).
    ➜ The classification routine `isascii()` has a special significance, because on a few older UNIX systems you can only work with the 7-bit ASCII code. Its general importance is that `isascii(c)` is assumed to be valid so that the other classification routines can be true. Thus in a German character set, for example, the expressions `islower ('ä')` or `isalpha ('ß')` come back as untrue, i.e. 0, because the characters 'ä' and 'ß' belong to the extended 8-bit ASCII code.

In principle a vector is predefined for the classification routines which contains a classification code for every character in the 7-bit ASCII code. In the BORLAND C compiler for example these codes are defined in ctype.h like this:

```
# define _IS_SP  1        /* is space */
# define _IS_DIG 2        /* is digit indicator */
# define _IS_UPP 4        /* is upper case */
# define _IS_LOW 8        /* is lower case */
# define _IS_HEX 16       /* [0..9] or [A-F] or [a-f] */
# define _IS_CTL 32       /* Control */
# define _IS_PUN 64       /* punctuation */
```

The pre-defined char vector is also declared there:

```
extern  char _ctype[];    /* Character type array */
```

If you use the following program:

```
# include <stdio.h>
# include <ctype.h>
int main (void)
{
    int i;
    for (i = 0 ; i < 128 ; ++i)
        printf ("%2.2X:%2.2X\n", i, _ctype[i + 1]);
    return 0;
}
```

to display all the entries of the vector, you get:

00:20	01:20	02:20	03:20	04:20	05:20
06:20	07:20	08:20	09:21	0A:21	0B:21
0C:21	0D:21	0E:20	0F:20	10:20	11:20
12:20	13:20	14:20	15:20	16:20	17:20
18:20	19:20	1A:20	1B:20	1C:20	1D:20
1E:20	1F:20	20:01	21:40	22:40	23:40
24:40	25:40	26:40	27:40	28:40	29:40
2A:40	2B:40	2C:40	2D:40	2E:40	2F:40
30:02	31:02	32:02	33:02	34:02	35:02
36:02	37:02	38:02	39:02	3A:40	3B:40
3C:40	3D:40	3E:40	3F:40	40:40	41:14
42:14	43:14	44:14	45:14	46:14	47:04
48:04	49:04	4A:04	4B:04	4C:04	4D:04
4E:04	4F:04	50:04	51:04	52:04	53:04
54:04	55:04	56:04	57:04	58:04	59:04
5A:04	5B:40	5C:40	5D:40	5E:40	5F:40

```
60:40    61:18    62:18    63:18    64:18    65:18
66:18    67:08    68:08    69:08    6A:08    6B:08
6C:08    6D:08    6E:08    6F:08    70:08    71:08
72:08    73:08    74:08    75:08    76:08    77:08
78:08    79:08    7A:08    7B:40    7C:40    7D:40
7E:40    7F:20
```

Remarks:

1 The line-by-line representation is not to do with the program but was generated by the command call ctype |pr -6. (Any attentive reader should be able to write the filter program pr, which equates to the UNIX command of the same name, for themselves.)

2 The character with the ASCII code 0 has its entry in _ctype[1], the one with ASCII code 1 in _ctype[2] etc.

For the character 0X41 (i.e. 'A') for example we find as a classification code the hexadecimal value 0X14. It should be understood that this value is the same as the bit expression: 0x10 | 0X04, or the decimal: 16 | 4. But that is the same as: _IS_HEX | _IS_UPP. That contains the information: the character 'A' is a hexadecimal figure or a capital letter.

The macro for isupper() is defined in ctype.h for example as follows:

```
# define isupper(c)  (_ctype[(c) + 1] & _IS_UPP)
```

and the expression isupper ('A') is then evaluated with:

```
(_ctype[('A') + 1] & _IS_UPP) ---> 0x14 & 0X4 ---> 0X4 --->
true
```

The same for isxdigit():

```
# define isxdigit(c) (_ctype[(c) + 1] & (_IS_DIG | _IS_HEX))
```

the expression isxdigit ('A') is then evaluated with:

```
(_ctype[('A') + 1] & (_IS_DIG | _IS_HEX)) ---> 0x14 & (0X2 |
0X10)
     ---> 0x14 | 0X12 ---> 0X10 ---> true
```

Here to show how classification routines can be applied is a small program, whose effect the careful reader will be able to work out:

```
/* stripcnt.c */
# include <stdio.h>
# include <ctype.h>
int main (void)
```

```
{
    int c;
    while ((c = getchar ())!= EOF)
        if (isprint (c))
            putchar (c);
        else
            putchar ('.');
    return 0;
}
```

You can have this program translated and then call it for example like this:

```
stripcnt <stripcnt.exe
```

(For MS/DOS users it should be mentioned that with this call you do not unfortunately get to see all the content of `stripcnt.exe`, because the first occurrence of a character with ASCII-Code 26 of `getchar()` is interpreted as an EOF character. To overcome this problem see Chapters 14/15.)

For the sake of completeness we should also mention the functions:

```
int tolower (int c);
int toupper (int c);
```

which convert upper case to lower case letters and vice versa.

12.5 The conversion functions: stdlib.h

We are already familiar with some of the standard functions which have their prototypes in `stdlib.h`. These are `qsort()` and `bsearch()` (see Chapter 9). We also dealt in Chapter 5 with the function `asctoint()`, in connection with which the standard functions `atoi()` and `atof()` were referred to.

Another group of the standard functions in `stdlib.h` will again not be discussed here, because they are explained in more detail in the next chapter. They include:

→ the functions for dynamic memory allocation (see Chapter 13);
→ some system routines which are not dealt with in this book;
→ a few mathematical functions which are also declared in `math.h`.

The string conversion functions:

12.5.1   int atoi (const char *s);

This function converts figures in the string to which s is pointing into an int value and sends this int value as the return value. The following are allowed in the string, in the order specified:

→ Any number of space characters;
→ An optional prefix operator;
→ A sequence of decimal numbers (0–9).

If there is an invalid character the conversion is terminated and the value added up so far is returned. There is no check as to whether there has been an overflow.

For a closer look at how this function works, look back at the function ascto-int() in Chapter 5.

12.5.2   long atol (const char *s);

The only difference between this function and atoi() is that the string of digits is converted into a long value.

12.5.3   double atof (const char *s);

This function converts a string of digits into a double number, where the structure of the string can be more complex than with atoi(). The following very general example is used to demonstrate all the valid character types:

```
# include <stdlib.h>
...
double x;
char s[] = "\t\t    -9.056e-24";
x = atof (s);
```

This function behaves in exactly the same way in relation to invalid characters and a possible overflow as does atoi().

As well as atoi() and atol(), however, atof() also recognizes the special strings "+INF", "-INF" (infinite), and "+NAN" and "-NAN" (not a number).

```
double x;
x = atof ("+NAN");
printf ("%lf\n", x); ---> +NAN
x = atof ("-INF");
printf ("%lf\n", x); ---> -INF
```

Note that output with the notation %lf produces these strings. It follows that printf() must also be involved in producing the output which is displayed. Also, which numerical value was stored in x so that printf() produces this string?

With the following test program you can have the individual bytes of the double variable displayed:

```c
# include <stdio.h>
# include <stdlib.h>
# include <math.h>
void printbytes (double x)
{
    unsigned char * ucp;
    printf ("%lf\n", x);
    /* Warning: because of the INTEL convention, the bytes */
    /* are displayed in reverse order! */
    ucp = ((unsigned char *) &x) + sizeof(double) - 1;
    for ( ; ucp >= (unsigned char *) &x ; --ucp)
        printf ("%2.2X ", *ucp);
    putchar ('\n');
}
int main (void)
{
    double x;
    x = HUGE_VAL;
    printbytes (x);
    x = atof ("+INF");
    printbytes (x);
    x = atof ("-INF");
    printbytes (x);
    x = atof ("+NAN");
    printbytes (x);
    x = atof ("-NAN");
    printbytes (x);
    return 0;
}
/* Program run: (In MS/DOS / BORLAND-C)
1.79769313486231571000000000000000000000e+308
7F EF FF FF FF FF FF FF
+INF
7F F0 00 00 00 00 00 00
-INF
```

```
FF F0 00 00 00 00 00 00
+NAN
7F F8 00 00 00 00 00 00
-NAN
FF F8 00 00 00 00 00 00
*/
```

First the largest memorable `double` number is displayed, for which there is the `define` constant `HUGE_VAL` in the header file `math.h`.

When individual bytes are displayed hexadecimally, you have to remember the structure of a floating point number according to the IEEE standard (see Chapter 2). The first bit is the prefix operator, then follow 11 bits for the exponents, making 1 1/2 bytes or 3 half bytes. Next comes the mantissa.

The binary interpretation then looks as in Figure 12.5.

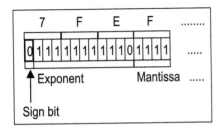

Figure 12.5 *The floating point value HUGE_VAL*

The value `0X7FE` is the hexadecimal pattern for the exponent of the largest memorable `double` number. (It is incidentally the complicated binary coding for the maximum decimal exponent 308 according to the IEEE standard, described above.)

You may be wondering, why not `0X7FF`? But it is this value which has been reserved for representing `+INF` (+infinite) and `-INF` (-infinite) or `+NAN` and `-NAN` (no number).

Because the exponent `0X7FF`, being a reserved value, cannot occur with normal `double` values, you can use the mantissa to distinguish `INF` from `NAN`.

To summarize, it can be said that `printf()` only produces a `double` number with the format notation `%lf` in its usual form if the exponent does not have the value `0x7FF`.

`INF` and `NAN` can not only be string arguments for `atof()`, but some mathematical functions send these values in the event of singularities or invalid arguments (see Section 12.6).

For `atol()` and `atof()` the ANSI standard has more modern alternatives which deal with errors better and in the long term should replace the previous functions, so we will introduce them now.

12.5.4   double strtod (const char * s, char ** endptr);

Just like `atof()` `strtod()` converts the number string to which s is pointing into a `double` value and sends it as the return value. The validity rules for the numbers are the same as for `atof()`. In addition, however, `strtod()` stores the address of the first invalid character in the `char` pointer to which `endptr` is pointing. That means errors can be handled as shown in the following program extract:

```
# include <stdlib.h>
...
char s[100];
char * end;
double x;
...
printf ("Decimal number: ");
getline (s, 100);
x = strtod (s, &end);
while (* end)
{
    fprintf (stderr, "%s: Invalid input area!\n", end);
    printf ("Stored value: %lf\n", x);
    printf ("Decimal number: ");
    getline (s, 100);
    x = strtod (s, &end);
}
printf ("Valid input: %lf\n", x);
...
```

Program run:

```
Decimal number: 2.3a4
a4: Invalid input area!
Stored value: 2.300000
Decimal number: 2.3 e4
 e4: Invalid input area!
Stored value: 2.300000
Decimal number: 2.3e4
Valid input: 23000.000000
```

Note that a pointer to `char` (end) must be defined of which the starting address will be passed to `endptr`.

With the first input (2.3a4), the conversion terminates at the character 'a'. So only the value 2.3 is returned and the starting address of the invalid character is stored in the pointer end. The error messages therefore always show the rest of the string from the invalid character.

With the second input the blank is invalid. (Only leading blanks are allowed.)

It is important to understand that in a valid input the final '\0' ending the string is the "invalid" character. In other words with a valid input end always points to '\0', and only then is the error loop exited.

If NULL is passed to `endptr`, the storing of the invalid character stops and `strtod()` then behaves like `atof()`.

In the event of an overflow, `HUGE_VAL` is sent as the return value (declared in `math.h`).

Like `atof()`, `strtod()` also recognizes the string arguments `"+INF"`, `"-INF"`, `"+NAN"` and `"-NAN"`.

12.5.5   *long strtol (const char *s, char ** endptr, int radix);*

Like `atol()`, `strtol()` changes the number string to which s is pointing into a `long` number and sends it as the return value. The `endptr` mechanism functions exactly as for `strtod()`. In addition the basis of a number system is to be passed to `radix`, according to which the number sequence is to be interpreted.

If `radix` = 0, then the numbers are interpreted as octal, hexadecimal or decimal numbers, depending on whether the number string begins with 0, 0X or a number 1–9.

As well as 0, the values 2 to 36 are allowed as the basis of a number system. The total of valid number characters is then sorted on this basis.

A few examples are shown in Table 12.2.

radix	Valid numbers
5	0 to 4
8	0 to 7
20	0 to 9 and A to J (or a to j)

Table 12.2 *Valid numbers for selected values of radix*

In the event of an overflow 0L is returned as the return value (declared in `math.h`).

```
unsigned long strtoul (const char *s, char ** endptr, int
```

```
radix);
```

`strtoul()` works exactly like `strtol()`, with the difference that the return value is always of the type `unsigned long`. There must therefore be no negative prefix operator in the number string. The negative prefix operator is not in fact recognized as an invalid character but the negative `long` number is interpreted as an `unsigned-long` number.

The functions so far were all to solve the problem of converting a number string into a numerical value.

For the opposite problem, converting a numerical value into a number string, most C compiler producers offer the following functions in addition to the ANSI standard:

```
char * itoa(int value, char * string, int radix);
char * ltoa(long value, char * string, int radix);
char * ultoa(unsigned long value, char * string, int radix);
```

Unfortunately there is no `ftoa()` function as the reverse of `atof()`.

However, for the whole problem of converting number strings <–> numerical value there is a much more elegant solution, so we will say no more about the three functions above. This solution reverts to functions from `stdio.h`.

Even in the following call:

```
printf ("%6.2lf\n", 123.4);      ---> 123.40
```

there is a conversion from numerical to string, only the string is on the screen and not in a `char` vector. It is the other way round for:

```
double x;
scanf ("%lf", &x); <--- 123.4
```

Here a string is entered via the keypad which is converted into a numerical value.

Now if the output area of the screen or the key sequence could be replaced by a `char` vector, they you would have conversion options using all the capabilities of the format notation of `printf()` or `scanf()`.

That is exactly what `sprintf()` and `sscanf()` do. We have already used the latter in Chapter 11. The starting address of a `char` vector is passed to an additional first parameter, otherwise these functions have the same parameters as `printf()` or `scanf()`.

Our `atof()` example:

```
# include <stdlib.h>
...
```

```
double x;
char s[] = "\t\t   -9.056e-24";
x = atof (s);
```

would be solved like this with `sscanf()`:

```
# include <stdio.h>
...
double x;
char s[] = "\t\t   -9.056e-24";
sscanf (s, "%le", &x);
```

The process in reverse uses `sprintf()`:

```
x *= 2.;
sprintf (s, "%le", x);
puts (s);
```

The advantage of these two functions is that you can use the most complicated format expressions, such as `printf()` and `scanf()` can understand.

The functions `rand()` and `srand()` for generating random numbers were introduced in Exercise 6 of Chapter 6.

12.6 The mathematical functions: math.h

These are functions from the mathematical functions library. Readers who don't get on very well with maths and think they are entitled to the view that as programmers they can avoid all mathematical problems may safely skip this section.

For the reader who is interested in maths, however, there is just a list of prototypes, to give you an idea about the mathematical operations for which there are standard functions available (Table 12.3).

Prototype	Mathematical function
`int abs (int x);`	Absolute value
`double acos (double x);`	ArcusCosinus
`double asin (double x);`	ArcusSinus
`double atan (double x);`	ArcusTangens
`double atan2 (double y, double x);`	ArcusTangens (y / x)
`double ceil (double x);`	Rounding up to integer
`double cos (double x);`	Cosinus
`double cosh (double x);`	CosinusHyperbolicus
`double exp (double x);`	Exponential function (Basis: e)
`double fabs (double x);`	Absolute value

Prototype	Mathematical function
`double floor (double x);`	Rounding down to integer
`double fmod (double x, double y);`	Modulo function
`double frexp (double x, int *exponent);`	Decat into a 2nd potency
`long labs (long x);`	Absolute value
`double ldexp (double x, int exponent);`	x * 2nd high exponent
`double log (double x);`	Natural logarithm
`double log10 (double x);`	Common logarithm
`double modf (double x, double *ipart);`	Break down into mantissa and exponent
`double pow (double x, double y);`	Potency function: x high y
`double sin (double x);`	Sinus
`double sinh (double x);`	SinusHyperbolicus
`double sqrt (double x);`	Square root
`double tan (double x);`	Tangent
`double tanh (double x);`	TangensHyperbolicus

Table 12.3 *The mathematical functions*

There is also the macro `cabs()`, which calculates the absolute value of a complex number z. To present the complex numbers it uses the structure defined in `math.h`

```
struct complex
{
   double x,     /* Real part */
          y;     /* Imaginary part */
};
```

and can be defined like this:

```
# define cabs(z) (sqrt ((z).x * (z).x + (z).y * (z).y))
```

As well as this ANSI macro `cabs()`, some producers of C compilers also offer complex versions of all trigonometry and hyperbolic standard functions as well as for the logarithm, exponential, potency and square root functions. They are connected to the structure declaration given above.

In `math.h` a series of mathematical constants can be defined. Thus the BOR-LAND –C compiler offers:

```
/* Euler's number e */
# define M_E          2.71828182845904523536
/* Logarithm (e) on base 2 */
# define M_LOG2E      1.44269504088896340736
/* Logarithm (e) on base 10 */
# define M_LOG10E     0.434294481903251827651
/* Natural logarithm (2) */
# define M_LN2        0.693147180559945309417
/* Natural logarithm (10) */
# define M_LN10       2.30258509299404568402
/* Number Pi */
# define M_PI         3.14159265358979323846
/* Pi / 2 */
# define M_PI_2       1.57079632679489661923
/* Pi / 4 */
# define M_PI_4       0.785398163397448309616
/* 1 / Pi */
# define M_1_PI       0.318309886183790671538
/* 2 / Pi */
# define M_2_PI       0.636619772367581343076
/* 1 / sqrt (Pi) */
# define M_1_SQRTPI   0.564189583547756286948
/* 2 / sqrt (Pi) */
# define M_2_SQRTPI   1.12837916709551257390
/* sqrt (2) */
# define M_SQRT2      1.41421356237309504880
/* sqrt (2) / 2 */
# define M_SQRT_2     0.707106781186547524401
```

Any mathematically experienced reader will know which function he can use for which problems. For each function he can refer to a reference work or the online Help on his computer to find out how to use it.

> **Tip** The trigonometry functions expect their argument in `rad`, and not in `grad`. The arc functions also retrieve `rad` values. (rad = M_PI / 180. * grad)

In Chapter 15 we will discuss the options for error handling, with reference to the BORLAND C compiler, because there is no ANSI standard for it.

12.7 Exercises

I In the `strsort.c` module create a program which reads a maximum of 100 strings into a two-dimensional `char` array with 81-character long lines and then displays them sorted (a) in ascending and (b) in descending order and (c) in the original order.

A vector is to be sorted of 100 `char` pointers which must be pointed at the start with the 100 lines of the array. To sort you should use `qsort()` (see Chapter 9).

The main job will be to define the `qsort`-comparison functions for the two sort processes. Think about whether you could use string functions for this.

A program could look like this:

```
Input of strings:
1.: Max
2.: Anna
3.: Emily
4.: Xavier
5.: Bert
6.: <Return>
Sorted in ascending order:
Anna
Bert
Emil
Max
Xavier
Unsorted:
Max
Anna
Emil
Xavier
Bert
```

2 In the module `telnr.c` create a program which reads any number of strings from standard input into a `char` vector with the record structure: "Telephone no. Name".

Each string which is read in is only to be displayed if the telephone number contains a foreign dialing code (beginning with 00) and this dialing code is not that of the United States (00 1).

For example with the following input file `telnr.inp`:

```
0231/123456 Otto Morris
0031/18320/5318 Ann Harris
0431/918273 Carl Smith
001212/657483 John Pretender
0400/182736 Henry Mills
0090/564738 Celim Onur
001/716/42285721 Eileen Edwards
002163/765490 Mustafa Habas
```

when `telnr < telnr.inp` is called, the program runs as follows:

```
0031/18320/5318 Ann Harris
001212/657483 John Pretender
0090/564738 Celim Onur
002163/765490 Mustafa Habas
```

Use the correct string functions.

3   In the module `uniq.c` create a program which reads any quantity of text from standard input and only displays all adjacent and identical lines of text once.

UNIX users already know this filter program `uniq`. To avoid any conflict of names, they should call their program `unique`.

For example with the following input file `uniq.inp`:

```
AAAAA
AAAAA
11111111
++++
AAAAA
AAAAA
AAAAA
********
11111111
11111111
AAAAA
```

when `uniq < uniq.inp` is called, the program runs as follows:

```
AAAAA
11111111
++++
AAAAA
********
11111111
AAAAA
```

You have guessed right if you think that string functions are involved here too.

Tip: define two char vectors, because you always have to compare two records which have been read in.

4   The following program `mulchar`:

```
# include <stdio.h>
# include <string.h>
/* Definition of mulchar() needed here*/
int main (void)
{
    static char str[100] = "abbbc    deffffg";
    char * mp;
    puts (str);
    if ((mp = mulchar (str)) == NULL)
        return 1;
    puts (mp);
    while (mp = mulchar (NULL))
        puts (mp);
    strcpy (str, "111 22    99999934567");
    puts (str);
    if ((mp = mulchar (str)) == NULL)
        return 1;
    puts (mp);
    while (mp = mulchar (NULL))
        puts (mp);
    return 0;
}
```

gives the following output when it runs:

```
abbbc    deffffg
bbbc    deffffg
    deffffg
ffffg
111 22    99999934567
111 22    99999934567
22    99999934567
    99999934567
9999934567
```

It demonstrates the effect of the function `mulchar()`, which for any string provides a pointer to the start of a sequence of identical characters. Like `strtok()`, this function is called the first time with a string and retrieves the starting address of the first sequence of identical characters. For each subsequent call with NULL as the argument, the next sequence is retrieved.

If no (more) sequences of that kind are retrieved, then NULL is returned. It is the same if NULL is sent at the first call.

Define the function mulchar().

Tip: look again at how strtok() was defined (see above).

5 In the module hex.c create a filter program which reads any number of characters from standard input up to EOF and displays the characters it has read in the following format:

```
$ hex <hex (in UNIX) or: C:\> hex <hex.exe (in
MS/DOS)
000000   4D 5A C4 00 10 00 0D 00 20 00 15 00 FF
FF D9 01  MZ...... .......
000016   80 00 00 00 00 00 00 00 3E 00 00 00 01
00 FB 50  ........>......P
000032   6A 72 00 00 00 00 00 00 00 00 00 00 00
00 00 00  jr..............
000048   00 00 00 00 00 00 00 00 00 00 00 00 00
00 01 00  ................
000064   00 00 5B 01 00 00 DB 00 88 01 D0 00 88
01 B5 00  ..[.............
000080   88 01 95 00 88 01 68 00 88 01 2E 00 88
01 14 00  ......h.........
...      ...
...      ...
007792   14 14 14 14 14 14 14 00 70 72 69 6E 74
20 73 63  .......print sc
007808   61 6E 66 20 3A 20 66 6C 6F 61 74 69 6E
67 20 70  anf : floating p
007824   6F 69 6E 74 20 66 6F 72 6D 61 74 73 20
6E 6F 74  oint formats not
007840   20 6C 69 6E 6B 65 64 0D 0A 00 00 00 00
00 00 00  linked..........
007856   0D 00 00 00 00 00 B3 0A B8 0A B8 0A B8
0A 00 02  ................
007872   D4 04 00 00
....
```

STANDARD FUNCTIONS **305**

The output is always 16 characters to a line. Each line is made up of the following three areas:

1 a 6-digit character number beginning at 0 for the 1st character of each line (equates to the "offset" of the character in the file);

2 the hexadecimal codes for a maximum of 16 characters;

3 a display of a maximum of 16 characters as characters, if the character is a printable one, or as a full-stop ("."), if not. Note the appearance of the last line, which can contain less than 16 characters.

Tips for MS/DOS users:

1 Perhaps the appearance of the hex output seems familiar to you, if you have ever worked with the DOS program DEBUG, because that is what its display format was based on. (With DEBUG the offset is displayed hexadecimally in the form of a memory address.)

2 In MS/DOS the standard input is opened as a text file. So that when getchar() reads a character with ASCII code 26 it does not interpret it as EOF, you should convert the standard input into a binary file. With a BORLAND C compiler that is done with the function setmode(), which should be called at the start of the main() function thus:

```
# include <io.h>        /* for setmode() */
# include <fcntl.h>     /* for O_BINARY  */
...
int main (void)
{
    setmode (0, O_BINARY); ...
}
```

Dynamic memory management

13.1 The problem

The programming problem which creates the requirement for dynamic memory can be seen from the following program:

```c
int main (void)
{
   int n,
       i;
   printf ("How many numbers? ");
   scanf ("%d", &n);
   {
      double number[n];
      printf ("Input of numbers:\n");
      printf ("1. ");
      for (i = 0 ; i < n ; ++i)
      {
         scanf ("%lf", &number[i]);
         if (i < n - 1)
            printf ("%d. ", i + 2);
      }
      ...
   }
   ...
}
```

It should be clear what the programmer was thinking: users are allowed to specify the number of decimal numbers which they intend to enter and process while the program is running. After this number has been read in, a double vector is defined at the start of an inner block with this number n of elements, and the reading in of n decimal numbers can begin.

The programmer's thinking was very sophisticated, but unfortunately the C compiler won't play along. The instruction double number[n]; causes an error message. The careful reader will remember Chapter 5, where it was explained in relation to the syntax of a vector definition that the number of vector elements can only be a constant expression, and never a variable.

So the intention of the programmer to define a vector, the size of which is only determined when the program is running, cannot be realized. At least not like that.

Of course there is a way of doing it, by sending a request to the operating system when the program is running, to make a certain number of bytes available to the program from the area of free main memory which has not yet been used by the program (or in UNIX: which is out of the address area allocated to the program). The allocation of the main memory when carrying out a binary program looks – disregarding the particular features of the operating systems – approximately as shown in Figure 13.1.

TEXT SEGMENT	DATA SEGMENT	HEAP	STACK
		→	←

Figure 13.1 *Allocation of the address area of a program*

A program (or a process in UNIX) first occupies the three main memory areas:

1. text segment: the program code, i.e. the machine instructions making up the program;

2. data segment: the global and `static` variables. (To be precise, this area is divided into initialized and uninitialized variables);

3. stack: the area for all automatic variables.

Between the data segment and the stack there is free memory which is called the heap, and a program can ask the operating system for any portions of this at any time.

For this purpose there are two alternative system calls: `brk()` and `sbrk()`. These system calls carry out the corresponding memory requests, by simply moving the upper limit of the data segment towards the stack.

13.2 Standard functions for dynamic memory allocation

We do not need to concern ourselves further with these system calls, because there are C standard functions which can easily satisfy our memory requirements. These standard functions use `brk()` or `sbrk()` to acquire whole blocks of free memory in which the requested memory areas are reserved. Anyone interested in how these standard functions manage their dynamic memory should refer to Kernighan and Ritchie (1983) [2] where a possible implementation of these standard functions is demonstrated.

The most important C standard function for acquiring dynamic memory is `malloc()`, and its prototype is this:

```
# include <stdlib.h>
void * malloc (size_t size);
```

The number of bytes one wants to acquire is passed to `size`. It is very important that every time `malloc()` is called, a contiguous memory area of size bytes is acquired from the heap. The return value for `malloc()` is the starting address of this memory area, or if there is no free memory of the required size left, the address value NULL.

It is worth noting that the data type of the function: `malloc()` retrieves the starting address as a value of the type `void *`. That is of course because the author of this function cannot know the purpose for which you want to use the dynamically acquired memory space, whether as an `int` vector, a `double` vector or a vector of book structures. The information which this function receives as an argument is after all only the number of bytes.

By using `malloc()` the above program can be converted into one which will run:

```
# include <stdio.h>
# include <stdlib.h>

int main (void)
{
    int n,
        i;
    double * dp;
    printf ("How many numbers? ");
    scanf ("%d", &n);
    if ((dp = malloc (n * sizeof(double))) == NULL)
    {
        fprintf (stderr, "Short of memory! Program
            terminated!\n");
        exit (1);
    }
    printf ("Input of numbers:\n");
    printf ("1. ");
    for (i = 0 ; i < n ; ++i)
    {
```

```
        scanf ("%lf", &dp[i]);
        if (i < n - 1)
            printf ("%d. ", i + 2);
    }
    ...
}
```

Four things must be noted:

→ As memory is being requested for a `double` vector, a pointer to `double` must be defined to which the return value from `malloc()` is assigned.

→ As memory space is required for n `double` elements, `malloc()` must be passed the expression `n * sizeof(double)` as an argument, because `malloc()` needs to know the number of bytes to be reserved, not the number of double elements!

→ There is no need for a cast operator to be used in the assignment to the `double` pointer. We know from Chapter 6 that a pointer to `void` can be assigned to any other pointer without cast operator.

→ This tip is important for historical reasons. In the old K&R style of C there was not yet any data type `void *`. The function `malloc()` had the data type `char *`, and an address like that had to be assigned to another pointer using casting.

With the K&R standard, the corresponding instruction looked like this:

```
if ((dp = (double *)malloc (n * sizeof(double))) == NULL)
```

The query to NULL should never be forgotten, because it may be that there is no more free memory. That also means of course that you have to consider straightaway how the program should react at this point to an error of this type.

Another example: if it was not a vector of n `double` elements which you wanted to acquire dynamically, but a 3 x 4 matrix of `BOOK` structures (see Chapter 11), then you would program:

```
/* pointer to a vector of 4 BOOK structures */
BOOK (* bp) [4];

if ((bp = malloc (3 * 4 * sizeof(BOOK))) == NULL)
....
```

After `malloc()`, let's now meet its twin, `calloc()`. The difference lies mainly in just a small external characteristic, as shown in the prototype:

```
# include <stdlib.h>
void * calloc (size_t nitems, size_t size);
```

Now two arguments have to be passed here, for `calloc()` insists on a differentiated specification of the size of the memory: `nitems` is the number of elements of the dynamic vector, while size specifies the length of an element. The above `malloc()` call would look like this with `calloc()`:

```
if ((dp = calloc (n, sizeof(double))) == NULL)
{
    fprintf (stderr, "Short of memory! Program termi-
nated!\n");
    exit (1);
}
```

Here it can be left to `calloc()` to work out for itself from the parameters `nitems` and `size` the number of bytes, namely `nitems * size`.

As well as this external characteristic there is however an important internal difference: `calloc()` initializes each byte of the dynamic memory space which has been acquired with 00 (hexadecimal), whereas you cannot assume that memory acquired with `malloc()` has been automatically initialized, so each element can contain a random value.

Each dynamic memory area which was acquired with `malloc()` or `calloc()` can be released again if it is no longer needed. For this there is the function `free ()`:

```
# include <stdlib.h>
void free (void * block);
```

A starting address retrieved from `malloc()` or `calloc()` (or `realloc()`, see below) must always be passed to the pointer `block`. The memory space which was originally reserved will then be released, and so can be reserved again by subsequent `malloc()` or `calloc()` calls.

If a memory address which does not comply with this rule is passed to `free()`, it is impossible to predict the possibly disastrous results!

A call to release our dynamic vector of n `double` elements would simply look like this:

```
free (dp);
```

Because the function has the data type `void`, no return value can be asked for.

Tip Note the following programming tip: any dynamic memory which is no longer required should be released using `free()`, by the end of the `main()` function at the latest. If you forget it there, it does not matter because at the end of a program all the memory occupied by a program is released, including the dynamic memory.

However, there are programs which repeatedly read in data to be stored dynamically and where you have to ensure that there is enough free memory available for the running of the program. In that case it should be obvious that each individual memory area which is no longer needed should be released immediately, so that it is available for new memory requirements. So, for example, when a text editor which stores its text lines in dynamic char vectors deletes lines, it should not only no longer display them but also release the relevant memory space, because more new text lines may be entered subsequently which must be stored dynamically.

13.3 Modifying dynamic memory space

We stated above that each individual `malloc()` or `calloc()` call acquires a contiguous memory space, which because it is contiguous can be interpreted as a vector (or as a high-dimensional array). But what if it turns out when the program runs that a dynamically acquired vector is too small and has to be expanded later?

We will first attempt it in a rather naïve way:

```
int i;
double * dp;
dp = malloc (4 * sizeof(double));  /* First 4 elements */
for (i = 0 ; i < 4 ; ++i)
{
    scanf ("%lf", &dp[i]);           /* Index: 0 to 3 */
    ...
}
...
malloc (3 * sizeof(double));        /* Another 3 ... */
for (i = 4 ; i < 7 ; ++i)
{
    scanf ("%lf", &dp[i]);           /* Index: 4 to 6 */
    ...
}
```

For the sake of shortness, the NULL queries which are actually needed were omitted.

The programmer obviously wanted to retrospectively increase by three a dynamic vector of four `double` elements. To do this he or she called `malloc()` a second time, without assigning the return value to dp, because dp should still point to the beginning of the vector, now seven elements in size. He or she is therefore banking on the memory space acquired by the second `malloc()` call being directly connected to that from the first call, so that dp can be safely used to access the new elements with dp[4] to dp[6].

And that is exactly what he cannot bank on. Two `malloc()` or `calloc()` calls, even if they follow straight after one another, will not necessarily mean that the two memory spaces will form a contiguous space.

The problem becomes obvious in the following case:

```
int i;
int * ip;
double * dp;
dp = malloc (4 * sizeof(double)); /* 4 double elements */
...
ip = malloc (8 * sizeof(int));    /* Now 8 int elements */
...
malloc (3 * sizeof(double));      /* Another 3 double ele-
ments */
...
```

Here there is an `int` vector between two `double` vectors, and there can be no connection between the first and the last `double` vector.

If you try to find the right solution to the problem of retrospective expansion of a dynamic vector, you realize that – in our case – you need to acquire a vector of seven `double` elements, the four elements of the first vector have to be copied into the first four elements of the second vector, the first vector must be freed and the pointer set to the starting address of the second vector.

For this complex job there is the standard function `realloc()`. Its prototype is:

```
# include <stdlib.h>
void * realloc (void * block, size_t size);
```

The previous starting address of the dynamic vector to be extended (or reduced) is passed to `block`, and to `size` the total size (again in bytes) of the new changed vector.

The return value is the starting address of the new, enlarged (or reduced) vector.

So an unthinking application of `realloc()` to the problem we had above could look like this:

```
int i;
int * ip;
double * dp;
dp = malloc (4 * sizeof(double)); /* 4 double elements */
...
ip = malloc (8 * sizeof(int));    /* Now 8 int elements */
...
dp = realloc (dp, 7 * sizeof(double));
/* 4 double elements expanded by 3 to 7 */
...
```

It should be clear that in this example of `realloc()`, a different address is assigned to the pointer dp from the one originally stored in dp and passed to `realloc()` as the first argument.

And therein lies the "unthinking" aspect of this program example. `realloc()` also returns NULL as the return value if no sufficiently large contiguous memory space can be found in the heap when enlarging a dynamic vector. But in this case even the old vector which could not be expanded was not released, so that you could at least carry on working with the old vector. Unfortunately, through the "unthinking" assignment to dp we have overwritten the starting address of the old vector by NULL and no longer have any access to the data stored there.

In order to avoid this problem, you should always first assign the return value from `realloc()` to a separate auxiliary pointer and only if it is not NULL pass it to the actual pointer variable. After this correction our program would look like this:

```
int i;
int n = 4;
int * ip;
double * dp;
double * hp;                                 /* auxiliary pointer */

dp = malloc (n * sizeof(double)); /* 4 double elements */
...
ip = malloc (8 * sizeof(int));    /* Now 8 int elements */
...
/* Increase 4 double elements by three to 7 */
if ((hp = realloc (dp, (n + 3) * sizeof(double))) == NULL)
{    /* If it has not worked... */
   fprintf (stderr, "Short of memory!\n");
```

```
    fprintf (stderr, "No more numbers!\n");
}
else /* If it has worked... */
{
    n += 3;         /* n is adjusted */
    dp = hp;        /* dp is pointed to the new address */
    ...
}
...
for (i = 0 ; i < n ; ++i) /* n is 4 or 7, depending ... */
    ... dp[i] ...
...
```

In this corrected version, an `int` variable n was introduced for the number of elements, which is only increased by three if the expansion has worked. The last `for` loop, which somehow processes all the elements, then functions correctly regardless of which branch was taken.

The same applies to the pointer dp: in the last loop dp points to the old vector, if the expansion has not worked, otherwise it points to the new, enlarged vector.

For the sake of completeness it should be mentioned that the above problem cannot occur if a dynamic vector is decreased using `realloc()`. If you are sure that a vector is to be reduced and not enlarged using a `realloc()` call, then, and only then, you can do without the auxiliary pointer.

File processing

14.1 Basic principles

This chapter deals with processing data which is, or is intended to be, permanently stored on peripheral data carriers. Unlike these data carriers, the main memory of a computer is a temporary memory, i.e. all data stored in it (in the form of variables, vectors, etc.) is lost as soon as the program in question is finished or the computer is switched off.

The main peripheral data carriers are hard disks, but the remarks which follow about file processing can – with few exceptions – also be applied to other data carriers such as diskettes, CD-ROM, magnetic tape storage, etc.

In principle it is the job of an operating system to manage external data carriers and provide access to them. A data stock stored in a hard disk area is known to the operating system as a file and is generally identified by a unique name (or access path). An operating system offers several commands for accessing these files. In addition, though, it provides a programming interface for the various file accesses, which can be used by the compilers of various programming languages.

The basic operations defined by this programming interface consist of:

1. Opening a file: preparing a file for access. That includes reserving operating system buffers, where data is temporarily stored while being transferred between the main memory and a file. Generally the opened file is also assigned a program-internal name which the opened file then functions in response to in the program.

2. Reading a file: transferring data from the file to the main memory.

3. Writing to a file: transferring data from the main memory to a file.

4. Closing a file: canceling the allocation between file and program-internal file name. Possible release of the memory reserved for managing the file access.

5 Positioning in a file: in order to have direct access to specific data in a file, it can be positioned on any byte to which subsequent read or write operations refer. (This option is however connected to the hardware specifications of the data carrier. It is not available for magnetic tape or terminals.)

All these basic operations are carried out by sub-routines of the operating system. The interfaces to these sub-routines consist in the C compiler of system calls which – where they are to do with file access – are called low-level system calls for file processing.

As well as these low-level system calls, the C standard library also offers high-level standard functions for file processing, which are at a higher level in that they buffer the data transfer between the file and the main memory in special memory areas and offer easy, portable file access.

We will discuss the connection between the low-level and the high-level routines later. We will just say here that the high-level functions obviously make use of the low-level system calls. But you do not need to know how they are connected in order to write programs for file processing. So we shall begin with the high-level functions, which are themselves sufficient for this purpose.

14.2 The high-level functions

These functions – as already mentioned – transfer data between the file and the main memory through the intermediary of a buffer memory. This buffering means that if, for example, one character is to be read from a file, then a whole buffer's worth of data is read from the file and the first character retrieved from the buffer. For each subsequent reading of a character, each character is retrieved from the buffer. Only when the buffer has all been read and a new character is requested is the buffer refilled with data by accessing the file again. This obviously considerably reduces the number of times the file has to be accessed.

So the users of a function reading individual characters do not know for each individual call whether only one character has been retrieved from the buffer or whether the file has been accessed. Nor do they need to know, and so that this internal working of the buffer management is kept hidden from them, a structure is defined in the header file `stdio.h` using `typedef`, the components of which are used by all high-level standard functions for their buffered file access.

This structure has the type name `FILE`, and for every high-level file access to a program the following two criteria must be met:

1 The header file `stdio.h` must be bound (partly because `FILE` is defined there).

2 A pointer to FILE must be defined for each file to be opened.

To demonstrate the use of a FILE pointer, let's look at a first real programming example, which also uses high-level standard functions. The program is to copy a file original character-by-character into a file copy:

```c
# include <stdio.h>
int main (void)
{
    int c;
    FILE * fpin,
          * fpout;
    if ((fpin = fopen ("original", "r")) == NULL)
    {
        fprintf (stderr, "original: file does not exist!\n");
        return 2;
    }
    if ((fpout = fopen ("copy", "w")) == NULL)
    {
        fprintf (stderr, "copy: cannot open!\n");
        fclose (fpin);
        return 1;
    }
    while ((c = fgetc (fpin)) != EOF)
        if (fputc (c, fpout) == EOF)
        {
            fprintf (stderr, "Write error!\n");
            fclose (fpin);
            fclose (fpout);
            return 3;
        }
    fclose (fpin);
    fclose (fpout);
    printf ("'original' copied to 'copy'\n");
    return 0;
}
```

Because there are two files, two pointers to FILE must be defined: fpin and fpout. The instruction:

```c
if ((fpin = fopen ("original", "r")) == NULL)
{
    fprintf (stderr, "original: file does not exist!\n");
    return 2;
}
```

uses the standard function `fopen()` to open the file `original` to be read. The prototype of this function is:

```
FILE * fopen (const char * filename, const char * mode);
```

The first parameter `filename` is a pointer to the operating system name of the file to be opened, the second parameter `mode` points to a string containing information on "opening mode". In this case the passing of "r" to `mode` means that the file is to be opened to read (r = read). Note that the second argument, passed to `mode` must be a string even if the string only consists of one character.

What is important about a `fopen()` call is the return value: a pointer to a `FILE` structure, which has been set up for the successfully opened file. This return value of `fopen()` must definitely be assigned to a `FILE` pointer, because it must be specified for all subsequent operations relating to this file. This is so to speak the program-internal file name while the operating system name is only specified once, when calling `fopen()`, and then never again.

If it was not possible to open the file, `fopen()` returns the pointer value NULL. There must always be a query for this error, in the above program it is acknowledged with the error message:

```
"original: file does not exist!"
```

That is a bold assertion which only applies to an operating system like MS/DOS. In UNIX or when accessing files in a local network, the `fopen()` call could also fail if the file does exist but the program (or the process) does not have the read rights to this file. In this case the error message should perhaps be:

```
"original: file does not exist, or no read rights!"
```

With the second `fopen()` call the opening mode "w" (w = write) is used for the file `copy`, to open the file for write access. If in this case it cannot be opened, it may be that either the file already exists but there are no write rights to the file or there are no write rights to the directory in which the file must have been newly created.

Opening for write access must mean that the file has been newly created, if it did not exist before or that an existing file has been shortened to file length 0, i.e. its old content is to be rewritten by subsequent write operations.

The error message has been formulated in an appropriately sibylline way. In our program the first successfully opened file `original` was to be closed again in the event of this error. That happens with the call:

```
fclose (fpin);
```

Here too the operating system name of the file must not be used, but the `FILE` pointer `fpin` originating from `fopen()`.

The prototype for `fclose()`:

```
int fclose (FILE * stream);
```

The file is closed, i.e. the FILE structure to which `stream` is pointing is initialized for further use. If the file was previously opened for write access, data was written to the file and perhaps there is still data in the buffers, then the `fclose()` call empties these buffers into the file on the hard disk.

Often people are careless with closing files which have been opened. In fact it would not be so bad if, in the case of the above program, all the `fclose()` calls which occur there were omitted. Because at the end of a program (a process in UNIX), all files still open are automatically closed.

Nevertheless there are good reasons why a programmer should get into the habit of specifically using `fclose()` to close each file opened once its processing is finished. The reason why is that an `fopen()` call retrieves the starting address of a FILE structure which is not acquired dynamically but comes from an element of a static vector of FILE structures of finite size. The size of this vector is determined by the maximum number of simultaneously open files determined by the operating system.

In MS/DOS, for example, this number is 20. Each `fopen()` call retrieves the starting address of one element of this vector, which is not already being used for an open file. If you wanted to write a program which processed 50 files in succession, you could open each file using `fopen()` in a loop which will run 50 times and then process it. If you were to omit to close the file at the end of the loop, then the next time the loop ran, the `fopen()` call would open another FILE structure from the static vector. When all 20 FILE structures had been used, each further `fopen()` call would cause an error. The program can only correctly process all 50 files if at the end of the loop each previously opened file is closed again. And it is possible that each `fopen()` call will then retrieve the same element of the FILE vector, but it is initialized each time for a different file.

The function `fclose()` returns a return value of 0 if closing the file was successful and EOF otherwise. From the little that `fclose()` ever does, you may well ask for what reasons an `fclose()` call could ever not be successful. It can only really happen if `fclose()` is accidentally sent a random memory address or the starting address of a FILE structure which cannot be assigned to an open file. You can cause this error by for example closing a file twice:

```
fclose (fpin);
fclose (fpin);
```

The second `fclose()` call would count as an error. To identify an error like that, you have to code more accurately for each `fclose()` call:

```
if (fclose (fpin) == EOF)
{
    fprintf (stderr, "Error when closing!\n");
    exit (4); /* Terminating program */
}
```

Careful programmers do do that, though it must be said that such an error can really only arise from a logical program error. If you as a programmer have sufficient faith in your own program logic, i.e. you are sure that a file will now be closed if it was previously opened successfully, you can manage without evaluating the return value of `fclose()`.

If both files have been opened successfully,

```
c = fgetc (fpin)
```

can be used to read a character from the input file. The prototype for this function is:

```
int fgetc (FILE *);
```

A `FILE` pointer is to be sent as an argument which belongs to a file which has been opened to read. The function reads a character from this file and sends it as a return value. Here too, as with `getchar()`, the character is sent as an `int` value, because `fgetc()` also sends the int value EOF, when the file-end is reached during reading.

To write the character which has been read into the variable c in the output file, `fputc()` is used:

```
fputc (c, fpout);
```

with the following prototype:

```
int fputc (int, FILE *);
```

The character which is to be written (as an `int` value) and the `FILE` pointer linked to a file opened for write access have to be passed to `fputc()`. The return value is the successfully written character or EOF where there is a write error.

At the end of the program both files are closed with `fclose()`.

This program should have explained the procedure for processing files:

→ Opening files;
→ Processing files (read and/or write);
→ Closing files.

What this first program example has not yet shown is:

→ The different opening modes of `fopen()`;
→ The different ways of reading and writing;
→ Positioning in a file.

This will be explained by the following systematic account of the relevant standard functions.

14.3 Opening and closing files

14.3.1 FILE * fopen (const char * fn, const char * mode);

Opens the file with the operating system name `fn` in opening mode `mode`.

The return value is the starting address of a `FILE` structure for the successfully opened file, or `NULL`, if the file could not be opened.

A complete path of a file (absolute or relative) can be passed to the parameter `fn`, for example:

```
"/home/paul/myprogs/prog09.c"  (in UNIX)
"d:..\\texts\\letter.doc"      (in MS/DOS)
```

The following values can be passed to the parameter `mode`:

→ `"r"` = read access (the file must exist);
→ `"w"` = write access (if the file exists, its contents are deleted, if not, it is newly created);
→ `"a"` = Attached writing (all write access is at the end of the file. If the file does not exist, it is newly created);
→ `"r+"` = read + write access (the file must exist. Read and/or write begins at the start of the file);
→ `"w+"` = read + write access (if the file exists, its contents are deleted, if not it is newly created. Read and/or write begins at the start of the file);
→ `"a+"` = read + write access (all write access is at the end of the file. If the file does not exist, it is newly created. All parts of the file can be read).

Also, one of two characters: `"t"` (text file) or `"b"` (binary file) can be specified, but this only applies to operating systems which make such a distinction (e.g. MS/DOS, but not UNIX, where the `t` or `b` information is ignored).

Example for mode: `"r+b"` – opening to read and write as a binary file.

14.3.2　int fclose (FILE * fp);

Closes the file to which the FILE structure fp is assigned. If the file was open for write access, the buffer is first emptied into the file.

Return value: 0, or in the event of an error: EOF.

14.4 Character-by-character file processing

14.4.1　int fgetc (FILE * fp);

Reads a character from the file fp, converts it with no prefix operator into an int value and sends it as the return value. When reading at the end of the file or where there is a read error, EOF is returned.

14.4.2　int fputc (int c, FILE * fp);

Writes the character c in the file fp. The return value is the character which has been written, or EOF where there is a write error.

14.5 Line-by-line file processing

14.5.1　char * fgets (char * s, int n, FILE * fp);

Reads a number of characters into the char vector to which s is pointing, from the file fp. The read process is stopped when the n-1 character or the new-line character ('\n') are read. The new-line character is also stored. The string stored in s is completed with a '\0'.

The return value is s or NULL when reading at the end of the file.

The function fgets() is used for reading text files line-by-line.

14.5.2　int fputs (const char * s, FILE * fp);

Writes the string to which s is pointing into the file fp. The character '\0' which closes the string is not written to the file. Important: unlike puts(), fputs() does not attach a new-line character to the string which has been written.

The return value is the last character written. If there is a write error, fputs() returns EOF.

The two functions `fgets()` and `fputs()` are used for processing text files line-by-line. They are designed to work together in a complementary way. The above copy program which works character-by-character could also be converted into a line-by-line version:

```c
# include <stdio.h>
# define RECLEN (80 + 1)
int main (void)
{
   static char line[RECLEN];
   FILE * fpin,
        * fpout;
   if ((fpin = fopen ("original", "r")) == NULL)
   {
      fprintf (stderr,
               "original: File does not exist!\n");
      return 2;
   }
   if ((fpout = fopen ("copy", "w")) == NULL)
   {
      fprintf (stderr,
               "copy: Cannot open!\n");
      fclose (fpin);
      return 1;
   }
   while (fgets (line, RECLEN, fpin) != NULL)
      if (fputs (line, fpout) == EOF)
      {
         fprintf (stderr, "Write error!\n");
         fclose (fpin);
         fclose (fpout);
         return 3;
      }
   fclose (fpin);
   fclose (fpout);
   printf ("'original' copied to 'copy'\n");
   return 0;
}
```

Note that, even if a text line is too long to fit in the vector `sentence`, the whole line is still copied, albeit with several `fgets()` and `fputs()` calls in succession. `fputs()` only writes a new-line if it was previously read in with `fgets()`.

If you also wanted to output the number of text lines which had been copied, the program would have to be extended like this:

```
. . . . .
int main (void)
{
    . . . . .
    int c;
    long count = 0L;
    . . . . .
    while (fgets (line, RECLEN, fpin) != NULL)
    {
        if ((c = fputs (line, fpout)) == EOF)
        {
            fprintf (stderr, "Write error!\n");
            fclose (fpin);
            fclose (fpout);
            return 3;
        }
        if (c == '\n')
            count++;
    }
    . . . . .
    printf ("'original' copied to 'copy' (%ld lines)\n",
            count);
    return 0;
}
```

14.6 Formatted reading and writing

14.6.1   int fscanf (FILE * fp, const char * format, ...);

Reads from the file fp data which, because of the format string to which for-mat points, are interpreted, converted and stored in memory areas of which the starting addresses have to be passed as additional arguments. The ellipse ... is the ANSI format for displaying access to any number of further arguments. The function fscanf () works exactly like scanf (), but with the difference that the data can be read not only from standard input but from any file.

The return value is the number of those input fields which have been success-fully read, converted using format notation and stored. The return value is 0, if no input fields were stored. And it is EOF when reading at the end of the file.

14.6.2 *int fprintf (FILE * fp, const char * format, ...);*

This converts the additional arguments designated by ellipse into strings in accordance with the format notation specified in `format` and writes them to the file `fp`.

This function also works just like `printf()`, with the difference that the output is not only in standard output but to any file.

The return value is the number of bytes produced, or `EOF` if there is an error.

The interaction between `fscanf()` and `fprintf()` can be demonstrated by the following program:

```
# include <stdio.h>
int main (void)
{
    int x;
    double z;
    FILE * fpout;
    if ((fpout = fopen ("numbers.dat", "a")) == NULL)
    {
        fprintf (stderr, "Cannot open output file.\n");
        return 1;
    }
    printf ("Input: decimal integer: ");
    while (fscanf (stdin, "%d %lf", &x, &z) == 2)
    {
        fprintf (fpout, "%6d:%10.2lf", x, z);
        printf ("Input: decimal integer: ");
    }
    fclose (fpout);
    return 0;
}
```

The file `numbers.dat` is opened for attached writing. In the loop, an integer and a decimal number are read into the variables `x` and `z` using `fscanf()`. The FILE pointer which is specified as first argument is called `stdin`, is defined as a constant in `stdio.h` and designates the file: standard input. It does not need to be opened in advance, because it is opened automatically.

14.7 Redirecting standard files

Operating systems automatically open (in UNIX: for each process) at least three standard files. These standard files are linked to devices and in `stdio.h` a FILE pointer constant is defined for each of these files (see Table 14.1).

standard file	linked to device	FILE pointer
standard input	keypad	stdin
standard output	screen	stdout
standard error output	screen	stderr
(only in MS/DOS)	1st parallel interface (Printer)	stdprn
(only in MS/DOS)	1st serial interface	stdaux

Table 14.1 *Standard files*

In other words the devices keypad and screen function in response to files. That also happens with all functions which access the standard files, even if you can't see it. So the above call:

```
fscanf (stdin, "%d %lf", &x, &z)
```

is identical to:

```
scanf ("%d %lf", &x, &z)
```

Equally, `printf ("...", ...)` can be replaced by `fprintf (stdout, "...", ...)`. And in the output of error messages we have already used:

```
fprintf (stderr, "Error!\n");
```

The advantage of the concept of standard files is that these can also be linked with other files instead of with the devices: "redirecting of standard files". This redirection can take place at operating system level. If we assume that the above program was called `numbers`, then it could be called like this:

```
$ numbers <numbers.new    (Call in UNIX)
```

Here the command interpreter, which reads the command line which is entered, takes from the information: `<numbers.new` the request that the file `numbers.new` is to be opened for read access, standard input is to be linked to this file and then the command `numbers` is to be started. The program `numbers` uses `fscanf (stdin, ...)` to read from standard input, i.e. from the file `numbers.new`, and not from the keypad – without knowing it. The numbers read from `numbers.new` are then attached by the program to the file `numbers.dat`. At the end of the program the file `numbers.new` is closed again by the command interpreter.

The numbers are written to the output file `numbers.dat` following the call:

```
fprintf (fpout, "%6d:%10.2lf", x, z);
```

Here a different format is used from when reading the numbers from standard input. It is important to note that, if the numbers stored in this way – by a different program – are to be read from the file again, it is recommended that you use the same format. For example:

```
fscanf (fpin, "%6d:%10lf", &x, &z);
```

Note however that the `scanf()` functions – unlike the `printf()` functions – do not understand precision details in the format notation. So for read it must be: `"%10lf"` and not `"%10.2lf"`.

So the functions `fscanf()` and `fprintf()` are used for formatted reading from or writing to files. The file created in formatted writing is a text file, the content of which can be seen using the UNIX command `cat` or the MS/DOS command `type`. In this way you can create print files which can later be printed out on a printer and generate lists with numerical data which is ready to print.

14.8 Reading and writing binary data

Not every file in which numerical data is stored is to be used as a print file. Often the data is simply intended to remain stored for further processing later by other programs. In that case it is not necessary to convert the numerical data format into strings. You can write the numerical data just as it is in the memory directly to a file. This is done by the following functions `fread()` and `fwrite()`.

These functions work in a relatively basic way, i.e. they are similar to the low-level system calls `read()` and `write()` (see below). The result of that is that it is now only a matter of what size byte blocks are to be read or written. These functions do not recognize text lines ending with new-line nor do they do any kind of formatting. What has been read looks in the main memory exactly as it did when it was on the hard disk, and vice versa for writing. Files to be processed by these two functions should – with a few reasonable exceptions – be opened as binary files, so long as the relevant operating system does make this distinction from text files.

We will see that despite the basic nature of these functions, such a file can still be given a structure, that of data records of fixed length.

14.8.1 size_t fread (void * p, size_t size, size_t n, FILE * fp);

This reads from the file `fp` a maximum of `n` data blocks of length `size` into the main memory area to which `p` is pointing. (The data type `size_t` is defined in `stdio.h` by `typedef` generally as `unsigned int`.)

The return value is the number of data blocks which were actually read. This number can be smaller than `n`, if there is a read error or the end of the file is reached. A value < n or even 0 does not therefore necessarily mean there is an error, but can be caused by the end of the file.

14.8.2 size_t fwrite (void * p, size_t size, size_t n, FILE * fp);

Writes n data blocks of length `size` from the main memory starting from address `p` into the file `fp`.

The return value is the number of data blocks which were actually written. This number can be smaller than `n`, if a write error has occurred.

The following program is intended to demonstrate the use of `fread()` and `fwrite()`. The header file `date.h` should have the following content: (See also Exercise 1 from Chapter 11.)

```
# ifndef _DATE_H_
# define _DATE_H_
   typedef struct
   {
      char day;
      char mon;
      int year;
   } DATE;
   int get_date (DATE * dp);
   void put_date (DATE * dp);
# endif _DATE_H_
```

And here is the program:

```
# include <stdio.h>
# include "date.h"
int main (void)
{
   DATE date;
   int num;
   FILE * fpin;
   FILE * fpout;

   if ((fpout = fopen ("date.bin", "ab")) == NULL)
```

```
{
    fprintf (stderr,
            "Error in opening output file!\n");
    return 1;
}
for (num = 0 ; get_date (&date) ; ++num)
    if (fwrite (&date, sizeof(DATE), 1, fpout) < 1)
    {
        fprintf (stderr,
                "date.bin: Write error!\n");
        fclose (fpout);
        return 2;
    }
fclose (fpout);
if ((fpin = fopen ("date.bin", "rb")) == NULL)
{
    fprintf (stderr,
            "Error in opening input file!\n");
    return 1;
}
while (fread (&date, sizeof(DATE), 1, fpin) > 0)
{
    put_date (&date);
    putchar ('\n');
}
fclose (fpin);
return 0;
}
```

First the file date.bin is opened for attached writing. For operating systems such as MS/DOS it is important that the file is opened as a binary file.

With get_date() date information is repeatedly read from the standard input into the variable date and then written to the file using fwrite(). Note that there is only ever one structure variable written for each fwrite() call, so the return value should be 1. If not, there is a write error. When the user stops inputting data, the file is closed but at once reopened, this time to read.

In the read loop, fread() is used to read date information from the file into the variable date and then put_date() displays it on standard output. Here too the return value must be 1. If not, there is a read error or the end of the file has been reached, and 0 records were read. The loop control mechanism cannot distinguish between these two cases, read error or EOF, from the return value. You should really ask after the loop whether EOF has been reached or not. We will find out later how to do that (see below, functions feof() and ferror()).

14.9 Manipulating the internal file pointer

In order to keep control of all file accesses, all file functions use an internal file pointer, which always indicates the next byte in the file to be read or written. For each read or write access to a file, this internal file pointer is automatically updated by the number of bytes read or written. That applies to all the functions mentioned so far.

Now however it is also possible, disregarding automatic updating, to set the internal file pointer to any positions within an open file, or to calculate the current position of the internal file pointer. This is done by the following functions.

14.9.1   int fseek (FILE * fp, long offset, int whence);

Points the internal file pointer of the file fp to offset bytes from the reference point whence. For the latter, three define constants are defined in stdio.h (see Table 14.2).

Value for whence	Define constant	Meaning
0	SEEK_SET	Start of file
1	SEEK_CUR	Current position of internal file pointer
2	SEEK_END	End of file

Table 14.2 *Reference points for file positioning*

The value SEEK_CUR allows a relative movement of the internal file pointer, while the other two values allow an absolute positioning. The parameter offset is of the data type long, so that very large files can also be processed. offset can also be negative.

The return value is 0 where positioning was successful, not 0 if there was an error.

The following program extract

```
/* positioning at the start of the file */
fseek (fp, 0L, SEEK_SET);
/* Read the first record */
fread (&date, sizeof(DATE), 1, fp);
/* positioning at the start of the last record */
fseek (fp, -1L * sizeof(DATE), SEEK_END);
```

```
/* Write the record which was read */
fwrite (&date, sizeof(DATE), 1, fp);
```

overwrites the last record of the file date.bin with the first. To do this, the file date.bin must have been opened with read and write access (mode: "r+").

This program extract shows up a problem with files open for read and write access. Read and write calls can only alternate if they are separated by an fseek() call. If you wanted to read a record and then immediately afterwards write to it, you would have to program:

```
fread (&date, sizeof(DATE), 1, fp);
fseek (fp, 0L, SEEK_CUR);
fwrite (&date, sizeof(DATE), 1, fp);
```

You cannot use fseek() to position before the start of a file (error) but you can after the end of the file. If data is written in the latter case, there is a gap between the old and the new data which counts in the data stock of the file but of which the content is not defined.

14.9.2   void rewind (FILE * fp);

Points the data pointer to the start of the file. This function is (almost) the same in its effect as:

```
fseek (fp, 0L, SEEK_SET);
```

14.9.3   long ftell (FILE * fp);

It calculates the current position of the internal file pointer. The return value is the offset of the internal file pointer from the start of the file. In the event of an error ftell() sends the value -1L. Such an error can in fact only occur if fp is not bound to an open file.

The following application example demonstrates the interaction between fseek() and ftell():

```
# include <stdio.h>
# include <dir.h>
# include "my.h"
int main (void)
{
    long pos;
    static char fn[MAXPATH];
    FILE * fp;
    printf ("file name: ");
    if (getline (fn, MAXPATH) <= 0)
```

```
        return 1;
    if ((fp = fopen (fn, "r")) == NULL)
    {
        fprintf (stderr, "%s:File does not exist!\n", fn);
        return 2;
    }
    fseek (fp, 0L, SEEK_END);
    pos = ftell (fp);
    fclose (fp);
    printf ("File: %s - length: %ld Byte\n", fn, pos);
    return 0;
}
```

The file which has been read in with getline() is opened for read access, the internal file pointer is pointed using fseek() to the end of the file and ftell() is then used to calculate the position of the file pointer and store it in pos. This information is also the length of the file and is displayed together with the file name on standard output.

We should go into two problems connected with fseek() and ftell():

I In MS/DOS the return value of fseek() does not always indicate an error when it should. That is because the interrupt function which underlies the fseek() call does not always verify the positioning. (See Warning on Exercise 6.)

2 In some operating systems file formats are used which require a different data type from long for the offset. For this reason the ANSI standard has introduced two new functions instead of fseek() and ftell():
   → int fsetpos (FILE * fp, const fpos_t * pos);
   → int fgetpos (FILE * fp, fpos_t * pos);

There, pos always represents a pointer to an offset, calculated from the start of the file. The data type fpos_t can be defined by the producer of the compiler in stdio.h using typedef, in accordance with the requirements of the operating system.

14.10 Recognizing end of file

14.10.1 int feof (FILE * fp);

Checks whether the end of a file has been reached.

The return value is not 0 for EOF, otherwise 0.

You might think that this function is superfluous, because all read functions recognize EOF. However, one exception is reading structures using `fread()`. In our sample program on `fread()` / `fwrite()` it said:

```
while (fread (&date, sizeof(DATE), 1, fpin) > 0)
{
    put_date (&date);
    putchar ('\n');
}
```

We assumed that `fread()` normally returns with the return value 1, because it has read a data record of length `sizeof(DATE)`. Accordingly, the return value 0 must come back if EOF has been reached and there are no more data records to read. But what if, because of a file structure error in the last `fread()` call for example there are only three bytes left to read and not a whole DATE structure? In this case too `fread()` comes back with 0. To distinguish this error from EOF, you could add an `feof()` call to the above loop:

```
while (fread (&date, sizeof(DATE), 1, fpin) > 0)
{
    put_date (&date);
    putchar ('\n');
}
if (! feof (fp))
{
    fprintf (stderr,
             "Terminated because of file structure
error!\n");
    fclose (fp);
    return 2;
}
```

As well as this, `feof()` can be used generally to control read loops, for example:

```
c = fgetc (fp);
while (! feof (fp))
{
    putchar (c);
    c = fgetc (fp);
}
```

It should be possible to solve most file processing problems with the high-level functions described so far. Anything else will be mentioned after the discussion of low-level system calls.

So that you can solve the exercises which follow, one more function will be introduced here to help you.

Our ability to write programs for file processing are still suffering from the deficiency that we do not yet know how, when we call a program, to pass to it the names of the files which this program is to process.

For the time being we have to read in any file names after the start of the program in a dialog. As we cannot know whether the user is going to call the program by redirecting the standard files, but the dialog definitely must take place on a terminal (keypad/screen), we can use the following function `fdialog()`, which is stored in its own module `fdialog.c` and should be bound to every program.

First a header file:

```
/* ---- fdialog.h ---- */
# define F_INP_ 1
# define F_OUT_ 2
void fdialog (char * fn, int len, int mode);
```

Here is the program file:

```
/* ---- fdialog.c ---- */
# include <stdio.h>
# include <stdlib.h>
# include <string.h>
# include "fdialog.h"
# define _UNIX_ /* UNIX version */
/* # define _MS_DOS_ */ /* MS/DOS version */
# if defined (_MS_DOS_)
# include <io.h>
# endif
void fdialog (char * fn, int len, int mode)
{
   FILE * fp;
   FILE * fptemp = stdin;
   char * mesg = "Input file: ";
   char * fntty;
   if (mode == F_OUT_)
   {
      fptemp = stdout;
      mesg = "Output file: ";
   }
# if defined (_UNIX_)
   fntty = "/dev/tty";
# elif defined (_MS_DOS_)
   fntty = "CON";
# else
```

```
#  error No Operating System defined!
#  endif
    /* If fptemp is linked to a terminal... */
    if (isatty (fileno (fptemp)))  /* see Chapter 17 */
    {
        if ((fp = fopen (fntty, "r+")) == NULL)
        {
            fprintf (stderr, "%s: Failed to be opened!\n",
                     fntty);
            exit (1);
        }
        fprintf (fp, mesg);
      rewind (fp); /* because of changing from write to read
*/
        fgets (fn, len, fp);
        fn[strlen (fn) - 1] = '\0';
        fclose (fp);
    }
}
```

The call `isatty (fileno (fptemp))` used in the above function checks whether `fptemp` is linked to a terminal device file.

The way in which this function is operating system-dependent is in the name of the terminal file, which is controlled by pre-processor instructions.

The `FILE` pointer `fptemp` is initialized with `stdin` or `stdout`, depending on whether an input or an output file name is being read in. Only if `fptemp` is bound to a terminal (and is not diverted into a file when the program is called) is the name read in. To do this the terminal device file is opened for read and write access and the dialog takes place. This statement appears to be contradictory. Why must the terminal device file be open if the standard input or output is bound to the terminal in any case?

Let's assume that a program `prog` is reading from standard input, but the output is to go to a file of which the name is to be read in by a `fdialog()` call. This dialog only takes place if the standard output is bound to the terminal. If not, the users have to specify an output file name themselves using the call `prog >prog.out`.

But if the dialog takes place to define the output file, the users could still have called: `prog <prog.inp`.

While the output of the dialog message (`mesg`) could take place on `stdout`, under no circumstances must the file name now be read in by `stdin`, because it would then be read from the file `prog.inp`.

When reading in the name of an input file, the problem is the other way round. Because the function fdialog() is intended for both cases, for the sake of simplicity the dialog is generally conducted with a terminal file open for both read and write.

So the function fdialog() can be used like this:

```
# include "fdialog.h"
int main (void)
{
    static char fn[100];
    FILE * fp;
    dialog (fn, 100, F_OUT_);
    if (*fn == '\0')
        fp = stdout;
    else
        if ((fp = fopen (fn, "w")) == NULL)
        {
            fprintf (stderr, "... Error ...\n");
            exit (1);
        }
    ....
    .... (Output to fp)
    ....
    if (fp!= stdout)
        fclose (fp);
    return 0;
}
```

14.11 Exercises

1   Change the program fahr.c from Exercise 4, Chapter 1, so that its output is to a file, the name of which is read in using fdialog(). If the user does not enter a filename, stdout is to be used.

2   Change the program crypt.c from Exercise 3, Chapter 2, so that both an input and an output file are read in with fdialog(). If nothing is entered for one of the file names, the relevant standard file is to be used.

Test the program with the following call:

```
cat <file |crypt
```

and work out why only one output file name is requested.

3 Change the program `hex.c` from Exercise 3, Chapter 11, so that both an input and an output file are read in using `fdialog()`. If nothing is entered for one of the file names, use the relevant standard file.

In any case the input file should always be opened as a binary file (so long as you are working in MS/DOS).

Test the program again with the following call:

```
hex <hex |more        (in UNIX)
```

or

```
hex <hex.exe |more   (in MS/DOS)
```

and work out why no file name is then requested.

4 This exercise deals with storing appointments in a file. For this purpose we'll extend the program from Exercise 2 of Chapter 13:

→ In a new module `appfile.c` globally define a `FILE` pointer fp.

→ In `appfile.c` define the int function `read_appt()`, which uses `fread()` to read in an `APPT` data record from the file fp.
  → Parameter: pointer to the `APPT` structure which is to be read to.
  → Return value: the return value of `fread()`.

→ Define in `appfile.c` the int function `write_appt()`, which uses `fwrite()` to write an `APPT` data record into the file fp.
  → Parameter: pointer to the `APPT` structure which is to be written.
  → Return value: the return value of `fwrite()`.

→ Define in `appfile.c` the int function `readappfile()`, which opens an `APPT` file (binary) to read, uses `read_appt()` to read record by record from this file and uses `new_entry()` to store them in the concatenated list of appointments.
  → Parameter: the name of the `APPT` file. If the file cannot be opened, an error message is sent accordingly and the function is exited with return value: 0. If it is successful, 1 is returned. If an error occurs (`ferror()`), an error message is to be sent accordingly and the program to be exited with the `exit` code: 2.

→ Define in `appfile.c` the int function `writeappfile()`, which opens an `APPT` file (binary) for writing, uses `write_appt()` to acquire the list record by record using `get_entry()` and uses `write_appt()` to write to the file.

→ Parameter: the name of the APPT file. If the file cannot be opened, an error message is to be sent accordingly and the functions exited with return value 0. If it is successful, 1 is to be returned. If a write error occurs (ferror()), an error message is to be sent accordingly and the program exited with exit code: 1.

→ Define in the module tapptlf.c a main() function as a copy of tapptl.c from Exercise 2/Chapter 13. Extend this main() function:

→ Enter the prototypes of readapptfile() and writeapptfile() here (or in the header file apptl.h).

→ At the start of the main() function read in the name of an APPT file using fdialog(). Once the name is entered, use readapptfile() to read in all the appointments of this file into the concatenated list. If readapptfile() was not successful, a message is to be sent about the not (yet) existing file, but under no circumstances is the program to be terminated.

→ At the end of the main() function, all the appointments stored in the list are to be stored again in the APPT file by calling writeapptfile(), but of course only if a file name was specified at the start.

If writeapptfile() returns without success, the error message:

```
"Appointments could not be stored!"
```

is to be sent.

5 In the module ilc.c create a main() function which shows the number of lines of which each file consists, for any number of files whose names are read in in succession using fdialog(). Assume that the lines can be any length, but they should be read with fgets().

If no file name is entered at the first fdialog() call, data should be read from standard input.

Examples of a program call:

```
C:\> ilc
Input file: fdialog.c
fdialog.c: 50 lines
Input file: notinhere
hueppel: File does not exist!
Input file: iihex.c
iihex.c: 73 lines
Input file: <Strg>Z
C:\> ilc
```

```
Input file: <Return>
Line 1
Line 2
Line 3
<Strg>Z
stdin: 3 lines
C:\>
```

6 In the module `irevfile.c` create a `main()` function, which reads in a file name using `fdialog()` and outputs this file on standard output character by character backwards.

Warning This program runs in UNIX, but because of the well known `fseek()` limitations, not in MS/DOS. DOS programmers need not even attempt this exercise.

Part I

Take that!

Error handling for mathematical functions

This chapter will explain the options for error handling with mathematical functions, using the BORLAND C compiler, because there is no ANSI standard for it.

15.1 The function matherr()

Take as an example the function `log()`, described as follows:

double log (double x);
```
log calculates the natural logarithm of x.
Return value:
  if completed correctly:
    log returns the natural logarithm of  x.
  If there is the error: if x is 0, this function points
                  errno to ERANGE.
                  log returns the negative value HUGE_VAL.
  If there is the error: if x < 0, log points
                  errno to EDOM (domain error)
The error handling for log can be altered by matherr.
```

Firstly, we know that the logarithm function for $x = 0$ has a singularity, and that values $x < 0$ are invalid arguments. Or, as a mathematician would say: the (real) logarithm function is not defined for $x <= 0$.

The description mentions `errno`. That is a globally predefined variable, which is declared in `stdlib.h` using

```
external int errno;
```

It is there to apply an error number in the event of an incorrect system call, which identifies the specific error.

For all possible system error numbers there are `define` constants defined with mnemotechnical names. There is also a vector of `char` pointers defined in `stdlib.h` using:

```
external char * sys_errlist[];
```

the elements of which point to the original error messages from the operating system.

If the variable `errno` is pointed to a particular value, it can be used as an index in this vector, in order to have the official system error message displayed.

The connection to the mathematical standard functions is that at least two of the `errno` values are reserved for mathematical errors. In BORLAND-C they are:

```
# define EDOM     33      /* Invalid argument */
# define ERANGE   34      /* Result too big */
```

We can see from the description of `log()` that `errno` is pointed to `ERANGE` for the call `log(0.)` and to `EDOM` for an argument < 0. That equates to the mathematical results: -infinite and not defined.

The constant `HUGE_VAL` which was already mentioned under `atof()` is also specified for the largest memorable `double` number as the return value of `log(0.)` (to be precise, its negative value).

In this the BORLAND C compiler is different from the GNU-C compiler in Linux, which returns `-Inf` for this call.

Finally, we should mention the following mathematical error handling function:

```
int matherr (struct exception *e);
```

with the following structure type declaration (in `math.h`):

```
struct exception
{
  int     type;
  char    *name;
  double  arg1,
          arg2,
          retval;
};
```

This error handling routine is called by the mathematical standard functions if there is a mathematical error.

For the time being let's not worry about the function `matherr()` and the structure exception, but consider the effect of `matherr()` when certain mathematical functions are called. Take the following demonstration program:

```
# include <stdio.h>
# include <math.h>
# include <stdlib.h>
int main (void)
{
   printf ("log (0.): %lf\n", log (0.));
   if (errno)
   {
      perror ("log");
      errno = 0;
   }
   putchar ('\n');
   printf ("log (-1.): %lf\n", log (-1.));
   if (errno)
   {
      perror ("log");
      errno = 0;
   }
   putchar ('\n');
   printf ("exp (-1000.): %lf\n", exp (-1000.));
   if (errno)
   {
      perror ("exp");
      errno = 0;
   }
   putchar ('\n');
   printf ("sin (1e70): %lf\n", sin (1e70));
   if (errno)
   {
      perror ("sin");
      errno = 0;
   }
   putchar ('\n');
   return 0;
}
/* Program run:
log: SING error
log (0.): -1.7976931348623157100000000000000000000000e+308
log: 33 (Math argument)

log: DOMAIN error
log (-1.): -NAN
```

```
log: 33 (Math argument)

exp (-1000.): 0.000000

sin (1e70): +NAN

*/
```

In this program three mathematical functions are called rather unthinkingly a total of four times. The unthinking part relates to the sometimes invalid arguments.

For safety's sake, the global variable `errno` was scanned after each call. When each mathematical function was called, an error code could be stored there. If that is the case, the standard function `perror()` (a standard function for outputting system error messages) is called, which produces the string which has been passed, the value of `errno` and the string to which `sys_errlist[errno]` is pointing.

You can easily see that something must have gone wrong with the first two calls. It is not so easy to recognize that the last two calls are also not quite right, so here too `matherr()` was called.

Let's consider the first call:

```
printf ("log (0.): %lf\n", log (0.));
```

Remember that the arguments from `printf()` are evaluated from right to left before `printf()` is carried out (see Chapter 9).

So `log(0.)` must be carried out first, before `printf()` can carry out its job.

Now the argument `0.` represents a singularity for the logarithm function. So the error message is sent by `log()`:

```
log: SING error
```

and after `log()` has called the function `matherr()`. For the function `log()` only sends an error message if a `matherr()` call carried out previously sends the return value `0`. And only then does it point `errno` to an error message, in this case to `EDOM`, which is displayed by the `main()` function with the help of `perror()`.

Despite these error messages, `log()` still returns a return value which is displayed by `printf()` and which we can easily recognize as the value -`HUGE_VAL`. This value was intended by `log()` for this type of error. It is of course mathematically incorrect, but for many practical cases not so far from the truth, from the mathematical limit value -`infinite`. You could equally well have returned -`INF`, but the value -`HUGE_VAL` has the advantage that you can calculate with it.

With the second call:

```
printf ("log (-1.): %lf\n", log (-1.));
```

the argument for `log()` is outside the valid definition area of the function. While the `matherr()` call ends with the same result as above (return value: 0), `log()` now returns the value -NAN, sends the error message:

```
log: DOMAIN error
```

but again points errno to EDOM.

The third call:

```
printf ("exp (-1000.): %lf\n", exp (-1000.));
```

generates an output which appears quite sensible:

```
exp (-1000.): 0.000000
```

It should be obvious that in this case the deviation from 0 is so small that it can no longer be represented in the degree of precision of `double` values, so the function value 0.0 is to be considered as a precise function value in this context.

Nevertheless the function `exp()` has recognized this problem, that it considers as a loss of precision (underflow), and has therefore called `matherr()`. `matherr()` has, instructed by `exp()`, ensured that there is a return value of 0. from `exp()` and itself returned with the return value: 1. Where a return value is not 0, `exp()` does not send a message or point errno. The error loss of precision is now considered as corrected by `matherr()`.

With the fourth call,

```
printf ("sin (1e70): %lf\n", sin (1e70));
```

you may wonder why the result is:

```
sin (1e70): +NAN
```

Mathematically, there should be no problem here. But it must be remembered here that sine is a periodic function. It is sufficient to calculate the function values for the definition area from 0 to 2. * M_PI. For all larger arguments x the function value is calculated by:

```
sin (fmod (x, 2. * M_PI)) /* x modulo ( 2 * Pi) */
```

However the number Pi is an irrational number, so has infinite decimal places, and its value can only be represented approximately by the `define` constant `M_PI` (21 decimal places). But this small deviation leads in a modulo operation like this for large arguments to such large deviations that there can be no question of a correct result to the sine calculation. This error is referred to as a total loss of precision. It is only correct if `sin()` returns +NAN in this case.

Just as with the third call, in this case `matherr()` returns a return value which is not 0, so no error message is sent and `errno` is not pointed.

In the description so far it has remained very unclear how the relevant mathematical function calls `matherr()` and what that then does.

The producers of the BORLAND C standard library have made available for their compiler the source code of their `matherr()` function. By using this source code we can now have a look at the internal workings:

```c
int matherr (struct exception * e)
{
    if (e->type == UNDERFLOW)
    {
        /* flush underflow to 0 */
        e->retval = 0;
        return 1;
    }
    if (e->type == TLOSS)
    {
        /* total loss of precision, but ignore the problem */
        return 1;
    }
    /* all other errors are fatal */
    return 0;
}
```

To understand this function, the components of the structure `exception` (see below) must be explained:

type: is the type of error. For possible values, there are the components of the following enum type:

```c
typedef enum
{
    DOMAIN = 1,    /* argument domain error -- log (-1)
*/
    SING,          /* argument singularity  -- pow (0,-2))
*/
    OVERFLOW,      /* overflow range error  -- exp (1000)
*/
    UNDERFLOW,     /* underflow range error -- exp (-1000)
*/
    TLOSS,         /* total loss of significance -- sin(10e70)
*/
    PLOSS,         /* partial loss of signif. -- not used
```

```
*/
   STACKFAULT    /* floating point unit stack overflow
*/
} _mexcep;
```

`name`: is a pointer to the name of the function,

`arg1`: contains the first argument of the function,

`arg2`: may contain a second argument of the function,

`retval`: retrieves a return value to be returned by the mathematical function.

When `matherr()` is called from a mathematical function, the starting address of an `exception` variable must be passed after all components of this variable (with the possible exception of `retval`) have been initialized.

We can see that the function `matherr()` only gives the return value 1 in the event of UNDERFLOW and TLOSS, and otherwise 0. BORLAND justifies the fact that it is UNDERFLOW and TLOSS which are indicated by return value 1 as counting as identified errors by `matherr()`, while all others are declared as fatal errors with the return code 0, by the ANSI standard, which envisages it in this way.

(The UNIX version of `matherr()`, which is also given in the BORLAND source code, sends an error message for all errors and ends the program (or to be precise, the process). It is thus not ANSI compatible).

With BORLAND of course the function `matherr()` is available as an object function in the mathematical library. However, as soon as a programmer defines their own function with the same prototype, it is this, and not the standard `matherr()` function which is used in the program. The source code of the standard version was published so it could be used as a sample for changes and extensions to one's own `matherr()` version.

That is what we will do here. A new mathematical function `yarc()` is to be defined, which calculates the ordinates y of a circle with center xm / ym and radius r for any abscissas x. Because in a circle not all x values are valid, invalid arguments are to be dealt with by our own `matherr()` function, extended beyond the BORLAND standard. Here is the whole program:

```
# include <stdio.h>
# include <stdlib.h>
# include <string.h>
# include <math.h>
int matherr (struct exception * e)
{
   if (e->type == DOMAIN)    /* Start of the extension */
   {
      if (strcmp (e->name, "yarc") == 0)
```

```
                    {
                        e->retval = atof ("+NAN");
                        return 0;           /* Means: fatal error! */
                    }
            }                               /* End of the extension */
            if (e->type == UNDERFLOW)
            {
                    e->retval = 0;
                    return 1;
            }
            if (e->type == TLOSS)
            {
                    return 1;
            }
        return 0;
}
double yarc (double xm, double ym, double r, double x)
{
    struct exception e;
    /* If x is outside the definition range... */
    if (x < xm - r || x > xm + r)
    {
        e.name = "yarc";
        e.type = DOMAIN;
        e.arg1 = x;
        e.arg2 = 0.;        /* For safety's sake */
        if (! matherr (&e))
        {
            errno = EDOM;
            fprintf (stderr, "%s: DOMAIN error\n", e.name);
        }
        return e.retval;
    }
    return ym + sqrt (r * r - (x - xm) * (x - xm));
}
# define NUM 7
double val[NUM] = { -2., -1., 0., 1., 2., 3., 10. };
int main (void)
{
    double y;
    int i;
    for (i = 0 ; i < NUM ; ++i)
```

```
    {
        y = yarc (3., 0., 5., val[i]);
        printf ("y(%lg): %lf\n", val[i], y);
        if (errno)
        {
            perror ("yarc");
            errno = 0;
        }
    }
    return 0;
}
/* Program run:
y(-2): 0.000000
y(-1): 3.000000
y(0): 4.000000
y(1): 4.582576
y(2): 4.898979
y(3): 5.000000
yarc: DOMAIN error
y(10): +NAN
yarc: Math argument
*/
```

The extended part of `matherr()` can handle the DOMAIN error, but only for the special case of the `yarc()` function. As we can see, `matherr()` also makes a suggestion for the return value from `yarc()`, by storing +NAN in `retval`.

You can also see from the relevant instruction how the value +NAN or -NAN or +INF or -INF can be passed to a `double` variable, simply by:

```
e->retval = atof ("+NAN");
```

or:

```
e->retval = strtod ("+NAN", NULL);
```

The return value 0 signifies: fatal error, and `yarc()` takes account of that by sending an error message and pointing `errno`.

In the `main()` function, `yarc()` is called in a loop for a series of arguments, of which the last causes the DOMAIN error.

The DOMAIN branch of the `matherr()` function can easily be extended by other functions, distinguished by their return values. For example, if we were fully in control of the `log()` function, which we are not, we would have been able to extend this branch thus:

```
if (e->type == DOMAIN)
```

```
{
    if (strcmp (e->name, "yarc") == 0)
    {
        e->retval = atof ("+NAN");
        return 0;
    }
    if (strcmp (e->name, "log") == 0 && e->arg1 == 0.)
    {
        e->retval = atof ("-INF"); /* instead of: -HUGE_VAL */
        return 0;
    }
}
```

However, an extension of `matherr()` like that has no effect on the mathematical standard function `log()` from BORLAND. Borland's function apparently ignores the suggestion from `matherr()` and persistently returns `-HUGE_VAL` for `log (0.)`.

(General tip: the above error handling by `matherr()` relates to BORLAND-C, Version 3.1. From Version 4.0 this function was renamed: `_matherr()`.)

15.2 Exercises

Create in `xp1_xm1.c` a function `xp11_xmin1()`, which, for a `double` argument x, calculates and returns the function value of the mathematical function:

```
y(x)  =  (x + 1) / (x - 1)
```

The singularity of x = 1.0 should trigger the return value +NAN.

If you have a C compiler, which, like the BORLAND compiler, allows you to redefine a `matherr()` function, build into your function a `matherr()` call with the exception-type SING. Extend `matherr()` by a corresponding branch, which provides the return value +NAN – but only for this function (!) and then does *not* lead to the program terminating.

In the same module create a `main()` function, which displays the function values for the arguments: -10., -9., ... to +10.

Part III

Go ahead!

Appendix

16.1 The standard functions

The following overview is intended as a quick reference source for programmers. You can see the calling syntax at a glance in the form of the prototypes. Standard macros are not identified separately, but represented as if they were C functions (which they sometimes are).

This overview also includes system calls. They have been marked (NON ANSI!), like other C functions that are not included in the ANSI standard.

The header file that has to be included is given for each function, and the chapter in which it is described or mentioned.

This overview does not claim to be exhaustive; it merely lists the routines used in the book, and a few others of interest.

`math.h`	Chapter 12
int abs (int x);	
`math.h`	Chapter 12
double acos (double x);	
`math.h`	Chapter 12
double asin (double x);	
`math.h`	Chapter 12
double atan (double x);	
`math.h`	Chapter 12
double atan2 (double y, double x);	
`stdlib.h`	Chapter 5
double atof (const char * s);	
`stdlib.h`	Chapter 5
int atoi (const char * s);	
`stdlib.h`	Chapter 12
long atol (const char *s);	

```
stdlib.h
```
Chapter 9

void *bsearch (const void *key, const void *base, size_t nelem,

size_t width, int (*fcmp)(const void*, const void*));

```
math.h
```
Chapter 12

double cabs (struct complex z);

```
stdlib.h
```
Chapter 13

void * calloc (size_t nitems, size_t size);

```
math.h
```
Chapter 12

double ceil (double x);

```
stdio.h
```

int clearerr (FILE * fp);

```
sys/types.h, sys/stat.h, fcntl.h
```
(NON ANSI!)

int close (int fd);

```
math.h
```
Chapter 12

double cos (double x);

```
math.h
```
Chapter 12

double cosh (double x);

```
sys/types.h, sys/stat.h, fcntl.h
```
(NON ANSI!)

int creat (const char * fn, int mode);

```
math.h
```
Chapter 12

double exp (double x);

```
math.h
```
Chapter 12

double fabs (double x);

```
stdio.h
```
Chapter 14

int fclose (FILE * fp);

```
stdio.h
```
Chapter 14

int feof (FILE * fp);

```
stdio.h
```

int ferror (FILE * fp);

```
stdio.h
```

int fflush (FILE * fp);

```
stdio.h
```
Chapter 14

int fgetc (FILE * fp);

```
stdio.h
```
Chapter 12

int fgetpos (FILE * fp, fpos_t * pos);

`stdio.h`   Chapter 14
char * fgets (char * s, int n, FILE * fp);

`stdio.h`   (NON ANSI!)
int fileno (FILE * fp);

`math.h`   Chapter 12
double floor (double x);

`math.h`   Chapter 12
double fmod (double x, double y);

`stdio.h`   Chapter 14
FILE * fopen (const char * fn, const char * mode);

`stdio.h`   Chapter 14
int fprintf (FILE * fp, const char * format, ...);

`stdio.h`   Chapter 14
int fputc (int c, FILE * fp);

`stdio.h`   Chapter 14
int fputs (const char * s, FILE * fp);

`stdio.h`   Chapter 14
size_t fread (void * p, size_t size, size_t n, FILE * fp);

`stdlib.h`   Chapter 13
void free (void * block);

`stdio.h`
FILE * freopen (const char * fn, const char * mode, FILE * fp);

`math.h`   Chapter 12
double frexp (double x, int *exponent);

`stdio.h`   Chapter 12
int fscanf (FILE * fp, const char * format, ...);

`stdio.h`   Chapter 12
int fseek (FILE * fp, long offset, int whence);

`stdio.h`   Chapter 12
int fsetpos (FILE * fp, const fpos_t * pos);

`stdio.h`   Chapter 12
long ftell (FILE * fp);

`stdio.h`   Chapter 14
size_t fwrite (void * p, size_t size, size_t n, FILE * fp);

`stdio.h`
int getc (FILE * fp);

`stdio.h` **int getchar (void);**	Chapter 12
`stdlib.h` **char * getenv (const char * name);**	
`stdio.h` **char * gets (char * s);**	Chapter 12
`ctype.h` **int isalnum (int c);**	Chapter 12
`ctype.h` **int isalpha (int c);**	Chapter 12
`ctype.h` **int isascii (int c);**	Chapter 12 (NON ANSI!)
`Borland-C: io.h, UNIX: termios.h` **int isatty (int fd);**	(NON ANSI!)
`ctype.h` **int iscntrl (int c);**	Chapter 12
`ctype.h` **int isdigit (int c);**	Chapter 12
`ctype.h` **int isgraph (int c);**	Chapter 12
`ctype.h` **int islower (int c);**	Chapter 12
`ctype.h` **int isprint (int c);**	Chapter 12
`ctype.h` **int ispunct (int c);**	Chapter 12
`ctype.h` **int isspace (int c);**	Chapter 12
`ctype.h` **int isupper (int c);**	Chapter 12
`ctype.h` **int isxdigit (int c);**	Chapter 12
`stdlib.h` **char * itoa(int value, char * string, int radix);**	(NON ANSI!)
`math.h` **long labs (long x);**	Chapter 12

```
math.h                                    Chapter 12
double ldexp (double x, int exponent);

math.h                                    Chapter 12
double log (double x);

math.h                                    Chapter 12
double log10 (double x);

sys/types.h, sys/stat.h, fcntl.h          (NON ANSI!)
long lseek (int fd, long offset, int whence);

stdlib.h                                  Chapter 12 (NON ANSI!)
char * ltoa(long value, char * string, int radix);

stdlib.h                                  Chapter 13
void * malloc (size_t size);

math.h                                    Chapter 15
int matherr (struct exception *e);

mem.h                                     Chapter 12
void * memchr (const void * s, int c, size_t n);

mem.h                                     Chapter 12
int memcmp (const void * s1, const void * s2, size_t n);

mem.h                                     Chapter 12
void * memcpy (void * dest, const void * src, size_t n);

mem.h                                     Chapter 12
void * memmove (void * dest, const void * src, size_t n);

mem.h                                     Chapter 12
void * memset (void * s, int c, size_t n);

math.h                                    Chapter 12
double modf (double x, double  *ipart);

sys/types.h, sys/stat.h, fcntl.h          (NON ANSI!)
int open (const char * fn, int flag);

math.h                                    Chapter 12
double pow (double x, double y);

stdio.h
int putc (int c, FILE * fp);

stdio.h
int putchar (int c);

stdlib.h                                  (NON ANSI!)
int putenv (const char * vardef);
```

```
stdio.h
```
int puts (const char * s);

Chapter 12

```
stdlib.h
```
void qsort (void * base, size_t elem, size_t size,

int (*vf)(const void *, const void *));

Chapter 9

```
stdlib.h
```
int rand (void);

Chapter 6

```
sys/types.h, sys/stat.h, fcntl.h
```
int read (int fd, void * buf, unsigned int n);

(NON ANSI!)

```
stdlib.h
```
void * realloc (void * block, size_t size);

Chapter 13

```
stdio.h
```
void rewind (FILE * fp);

Chapter 14

```
stdio.h
```
void setbuf (FILE * fp, char * buf);

```
fcntl.h
```
int setmode (int fd, int mode);

Chapter 12 (NON ANSI!)

```
stdio.h
```
int setvbuf (FILE * fp, char * buf, int type, size_t size);

```
math.h
```
double sin (double x);

Chapter 12

```
math.h
```
double sinh (double x);

Chapter 12

```
stdio.h
```
int sprintf (char * s, const char * format, ...);

Chapter 9

```
math.h
```
double sqrt (double x);

Chapter 12

```
stdlib.h
```
void srand (unsigned seed);

Chapter 6

```
stdio.h
```
int sscanf (const char * s, const char * format, ...);

Chapter 9

```
string.h
```
char * strcat (char * t, const char * s);

Chapter 12

```
string.h
```
char * strchr (const char * s, int c);

Chapter 12

```
string.h
```
int strcmp (const char * s1, const char * s2);
Chapter 12

```
string.h
```
char * strcpy (char * t, const char * s);
Chapter 12

```
string.h
```
size_t strlen (const char * s);
Chapter 12

```
string.h
```
char * strncat (char * t, const char * s, size_t n);
Chapter 12

```
string.h
```
int strncmp (const char * s1, const char * s2, size_t n);
Chapter 12

```
string.h
```
char * strncpy (char * t, const char * s, size_t n);
Chapter 12

```
string.h
```
char * strnset (char * s, int c, size_t n);
Chapter 12

```
string.h
```
char * strrchr (const char * s, int c);
Chapter 12

```
string.h
```
char * strset (char * s, int c);
Chapter 12

```
string.h
```
char * strstr (const char * s1, const char * s2);
Chapter 12

```
stdlib.h
```
double strtod (const char * s, char ** endptr);
Chapter 12

```
string.h
```
char * strtok (char * s1, const char * s2);
Chapter 12

```
stdlib.h
```
long strtol (const char *s, char ** endptr, int radix);
Chapter 12

```
stdlib.h
```
unsigned long strtoul (const char *s, char ** endptr, int radix);
Chapter 12

```
math.h
```
double tan (double x);
Chapter 12

```
math.h
```
double tanh (double x);
Chapter 12

```
stdlib.h
```
char * ultoa (unsigned long value, char * string, int radix);
Chapter 12

```
stdio.h
```
int ungetc (int c, FILE * fp);

16

GO AHEAD! ■

```
stdarg.h
```
type va_arg (va_list ap, type);

```
stdarg.h
```
void va_end (va_list ap);

```
stdarg.h
```
void va_start (va_list ap, lastfix);

```
sys/types.h, sys/stat.h, fcntl.h        (NON ANSI!)
```
int write (int fd, void * buf, unsigned int n);

16.2 The format descriptors

16.2.1   Output with printf()

The simplest case of a format descriptor looks like this:

```
%<type>,
```

e.g. %d, to convert an int value to a decimal number and output it. But we have also met format descriptors such as %7.4d, which shows that other information can be given apart from the % sign and a type symbol.

In the most general case, a format descriptor consists of the following components:

%[switch][length][.precision][modifier]<type>

Where:

<type>	Value to be output	Outputs
d	Integer	Signed decimal integer
i	Integer	Signed decimal integer
u	Integer	Unsigned decimal integer
o	Integer	Unsigned octal integer
x	Integer	Unsigned hexadecimal integer (digits: 0–9, a–f)
X	Integer	Unsigned hexadecimal integer (digits: 0–9, A–F)
f	Floating point number	Decimal number with decimal places and sign
e	Floating point number	Decimal number with decimal places and sign in the form [-]9.99e[+|-]99
E	Floating point number	Decimal number with decimal places and sign in the form [-]9.99E[+|-]99
g	Floating point number	Decimal number in e or f format, depending on size or precision

<type>	Value to be output	Outputs
G	Floating point number	Decimal number in E or F format, depending on size or precision
c	Character	Individual character
s	char *	Character string
%	./.	The character %
p	Pointer	Hexadecimal memory address
n	int *	Stores the number of characters output so far in the int value to which the pointer is pointing

An example of %n and %%:

```
int no;
printf ("Hello%n, world!\n", &no);
printf ("%d\n was stored in %%n\n", no);
```

Outputs:

```
Hello, world!
5 was stored in %n
```

[length]: optional length information for an output field.

length	Effect
<n>	Output in an n character long output field (default is right justified)
0<n>	As <n>, but with leading blanks replaced by 0
*	The length information is in the argument list, comma-delimited, before the argument to be output

Examples:

```
int x = 24;
float z = 3.5f;
printf ("12345678901234567890\n");   --->
12345678901234567890
printf ("%15s\n", "Otto");           --->                 Otto
printf ("%6d\n", x);                 --->      24
printf ("%06d\n", x);                --->  000024
printf ("%12f\n", z);                --->     3.500000
printf ("%012f\n", z);               --->  00003.500000
printf ("%*f\n", 10, z);             --->     3.500000
printf ("%0*d\n", 10, x);            --->  0000000024
```

[.precision]: determines the minimum number of digits to be output (%d), or the maximum number of decimal places (%f) or characters (%s) to be output.

.precision	Effect
.<n>	At least n characters are output as digits (%d, %i, %o, %x, %X)
	A maximum of n decimal places are output (%f), rounded if necessary
	A maximum of n characters are output (%s), truncated if necessary
.*	The precision information is in the argument list, comma delimited, before the argument to be output

Examples:

```
int x = 37;
float f = 8.6f;
printf ("12345678901234567890\n");   --->
12345678901234567890
printf ("%7.5d\n", x);                       --->      00037
printf ("%7.3f\n", f);                       --->      8.600
printf ("%.5d\n", x);                        ---> 00037
printf ("%.3f\n", f);                        ---> 8.600
printf ("%.1d\n", x);                        ---> 37
printf ("%.0f\n", f);                        ---> 9
printf ("%15.6s\n", "Otto");                 --->                       Otto
printf ("%15.2s\n", "Otto");                 --->                         Ot
printf ("%.2s\n", "Otto");                   ---> Ot
printf ("%*.*d\n", 7, 5, x);                 --->      00037
printf ("%*.*f\n", 7, 3, f);                 --->      8.600
```

[switch]: determines sign or justification in an output field.

switch	Effect
-	Left justified output
+	Positive numerical values are output with sign (+)
Blank	Positive numerical values are output with leading blanks
#	Preceded by a leading 0 (in the case of %#o); preceded by an 0x or 0X (in the case of %#x or %#X)
	Output of a decimal point (in the case of %#.0f or %#.0e or %#.0E). Also trailing zeroes are not suppressed (in the case of %#g or %#G)

Examples:

```
int x = 25;
float f = 3.81f;
printf (">%6d<\n", x);            ---> >      25<
printf (">%-6d<\n", x);           ---> >25      <
printf (">%6.2f<\n", f);          ---> >  3.81<
printf (">%-6.2f<\n", f);         ---> >3.81   <
printf (">% 6d<\n", x);           ---> >      25<
```

```
printf (">%+6d\n", x);         ---> >    +25<
printf (">% 6d\n", -x);        ---> >    -25<
printf (">%15s\n", "Otto");    ---> >          Otto<
printf (">%-15s\n", "Otto");   ---> >Otto          <
```
Examples relating to %#:
```
int x = 13;
float f = 9.f;
printf ("%#o\n", x);           ---> 015
printf ("%#5o\n", x);          --->   015
printf ("%#X\n", x);           ---> 0XD
printf ("%#x\n", x);           ---> 0xd
printf ("%.0e\n", f);          ---> 9e+00
printf ("%#.0e\n", f);         ---> 9.e+00
printf ("%12.0f\n", f);        --->            9
printf ("%#12.0f\n", f);       --->           9.
f = 4e-22;
printf ("%G\n", f);            ---> 4E-22
printf ("%#G\n", f);           ---> 4.00000E-22
```

[modifier]: determines size information of the data types to be output.

modifier	Data type to be output
h	short (for %d, %o, %u, %x, %X)
l	long (for %d, %o, %u, %x, %X)
	double (for %f, %e, %E, %g, %G)
L	long double (for %f, %e, %E, %g, %G)

(The following modifiers only exist in C compilers in the 16 bit MS/DOS operating system:)

modifier	Data type to be output
F	far pointer (for %p, %s, %n)
N	near pointer (for %p, %s, %n)

16.2.2 Input with scanf()

The function scanf() reads characterwise from the standard input, splitting the data flow read in into input fields, interprets each input field on the basis of a format descriptor, converts it into the corresponding data type, and stores it in a variable whose starting address has to be passed to scanf() as a supplementary argument.

If the format string contains normal characters (apart from information for a format descriptor), then these characters must occur in the input.

Example:

```
int x;
double z;
scanf (%d:%lf", &x, &z);        /* Input: 123:45.678 */
printf ("%d - %lg\n", x, z);    /* Output: 123 - 45.678 */
```

In the most general case, a format descriptor consists of the following components:

%[*][length][modifier]<type>

It is striking that in contrast to printf(), there is no precision, and * is the only possible switch. Specifically:

<type>: determines the interpretation and conversion of the characters read, and must correspond with the data type of the parameter concerned.

<type>	Interpretation as	Data type of the parameter
d	Integer (decimal)	int *
D	Integer (decimal)	long *
o	Integer (octal)	int *
O	Integer (octal)	long *
x	Integer (hexadecimal)	unsigned int *
X	Integer (hexadecimal)	unsigned long *
i	Integer (decimal, octal or hexadecimal)	int *
I	Integer (decimal, octal or hexadecimal)	long *
u	Integer (decimal)	unsigned int *
U	Integer (decimal)	unsigned long *
f	Floating point number	float *
e	Floating point number	float *
E	Floating point number	float *
g	Floating point number	float *
G	Floating point number	float *
s	String	char * (points to char vector)
[...]	String (selected characters)	char * (points to char vector)
c	Character	char *
n	(No input)	int * (the number of characters read in so far is stored here)
p	Address (hexadecimal!)	type ** (any type)

In the case of `scanf()`, there is a difference between `%d` and `%i`. The latter format descriptor permits the input of octal numbers (with a leading 0) or a hexadecimal number (with a leading 0x or 0X).

Examples relating to `%[...]`:

```
char s[100];
scanf ("%[abcdefghij]", s);     /* Input: harmless */
puts (s);                       /* Output: ha */
scanf ("%[a-z]", s);            /* Input: asc2int */
puts (s);                       /* Output: asc */
scanf ("%[A-Z]", s);            /* Input: ASCtoint */
puts (s);                       /* Output: ASC */
scanf ("%[A-Za-z]", s);         /* Input: ASCtoint/long */
puts (s);                       /* Output: ASCtoint */
scanf ("%[0-9]", s);            /* Input: 104B5(hex) */
puts (s);                       /* Output: 104 */
scanf ("%[0-9A-F]", s);         /* Input: 104B5(hex) */
puts (s);                       /* Output: 104B5 */
/* No (!) character from the quantity... */
scanf ("%[^A-Z]", s);           /* Input: 104B5(hex) */
puts (s);                       /* Output: 104 */
```

[length]: Optional length information for the maximum number of characters to be read. If a character is read that is not valid for the format descriptor before a `length` character is read, the conversion is aborted and only the part so far read is stored in the corresponding variable. Invalid characters include the separators; blank, tabulator and new line.

An example:

```
int x;
scanf ("%4d", &x);       /* Input: 12AB */
printf ("%d\n", x);      /* Output: 12 */
```

`%c` has a peculiarity. More than one character can be read in with length information, but only into a vector. A separator does not then terminate the input.

An example:

```
char s[100];
scanf ("%6c", s);        /* Input: ab cdefg hij */
puts (s);                /* Output: ab cde */
/* but: ... */
scanf ("%6s", s);        /* Input: ab cdefg hij */
puts (s);                /* Output: ab */
```

[modifier]: The same modifiers apply as in the case of printf().

modifier	Data type of the parameter
h	short * (for %d, %i, %o, %u, %x, %X)
l	long * (for %d, %i, %o, %u, %x, %X)
	double * (for %f, %e, %E, %g, %G)
L	long double * (for %f, %e, %E, %g, %G)

(The following modifiers exist only in C compilers in the 16 bit MS/DOS operating system:)

modifier	Data type of the parameter
F	far pointer (for %p, %s, %n)
N	near pointer (for %p, %s, %n)

[*]: The switch %* permits characters to be read and interpreted, but not stored.

An example:

```
int x;
scanf (%*d:%d", &x);    /* Input: 123:45 */
printf ("%d\n", x);     /* Output: 45 */
```

16.3 The modifiers const and volatile

16.3.1   The modifier const

In addition to an optional memory class and a data type, a "modifier" const can be specified at the time of definition.

In the instruction:

```
const double pi = 3.141592;
```

the double variable pi is defined as a variable and initialized with the value 3.141592. The keyword const means merely that the content of this variable is constant. So it is not possible after this definition instruction to carry out for example the instruction:

```
pi /= 2.;        /* Invalid! */
```

Note that pi is not just a symbolic name for the double constant 3.141592 (as e.g. in FORTRAN), but pi is a constant variable, contradictory though this concept may appear. It is evident from the fact that one can determine its memory address by &pi, which is not possible for the constant 3.141592. Such a constant variable is therefore better described as a read-only variable.

It follows logically that such a `const` variable has to be initialized at the definition stage, if it is to contain a defined value at all. The following definition is therefore not meaningful:

```
const double pi; /* pi contains a random value! */
```

But the following is entirely possible:

```
const pi = 3.141592; /* ---> const double pi = 3.141592; */
const f = 134;       /* ---> const int f = 134; */
```

Here the compiler derives the data type of the variable from the constant with which the variable is initialized.

The modifier `const` can have a double meaning in the case of pointers. Either the pointer variable is constant, or the content of the memory location to which the pointer is pointing.

As an example:

```
char s[] = "ABCDEFGHIJ";
const char * pc; /* does not have to be initialized  */
char * const cp = s; /* has to be initialized */
```

Where `pc` is a pointer to `char` values regarded as constant when you access them using `pc`. On the other hand `cp` is a constant pointer that can only point to `s`.

The following expressions are accordingly permitted and not permitted respectively:

```
++pc;   /* Permitted */
putchar (*pc); /* Permitted. Output: B */
++*pc;   /* Not permitted! */
/* But: ... */
++s[1]; /* Permitted */
putchar (*pc); /* Permitted. Output: C */

++cp;   /* Not permitted! */
putchar (*cp); /* Permitted. Output: A */
/* But: ... */
putchar (*(cp + 3)); /* Permitted. Output: D */
/* ... but: ... */
putchar (*(cp += 3)); /* Not permitted! */
```

It is also possible to define constant pointers to constant values:

```
char s[] = "ABCDEFGHIJ";
const char * const cpc = s;
++cpc;   /* Not permitted! */
++*cpc; /* Not permitted! */
/* but: ... */
putchar (*(cpc + 3));     /* Permitted. Output: D */
putchar (*(cpc + 3) + 2); /* Permitted. Output: F */
```

A particular problem is the relationship with normal pointers. Whereas constant pointers can readily be assigned to normal pointers, the same does not apply to a pointer to const values:

```
char s[] = "ABCDEFGHIJ";
char * const cp = s;
const char * pc = s;
char * p;
p = cp;          /* No problems */
p = pc;          /* Compiler warning! */
```

The compiler warning is justified. By using pc you are forbidding yourself write access to the elements of the vector s. By assigning pc to p, this prohibition can be circumvented, because you can have write access to the elements of s using p. You reassure the C compiler by using a cast operator:

```
p = (char *)pc; /* No warning */
```

But such forced conversions should be avoided, because they are not permitted in C++. The C++ compiler uses a straightforward error message.

The reverse case, of assigning a normal pointer to a pointer to const values, is of course permitted. That is practically what you do in the case of the following function call:

```
char s[] = "ABCDEFGHIJ";
char str[11];
char * p = s;
strcpy (str, p);
```

Here the normal pointer p is transferred to a pointer to const char. (s. strcpy(), Chapter 12). strcpy() forbids itself write access to the elements of the vector s with its second parameter, whereas you could do exactly that with p.

16.3.2   The modifier volatile

Normally the content of a variable can only be manipulated by functions of a program in which the variable is defined. But if the content of a variable is to be changed from outside the program, the variable must be defined with the modifier volatile.

An example:

```
volatile unsigned int x = 1;
```

The variable x can be changed from outside both by the program and e.g. by interrupts. This is done by functions installed as interrupt routines accessing x.

If x is to be influenced only from outside, volatile can be combined with const:

```
volatile const unsigned int x = 1;
```

The keyword volatile basically only means that the C compiler makes no assumptions about the content of the variable at compile time. In the following program extract

```
unsigned int x = 1;
while (x > 0)
    ;
```

an optimizing compiler would remove the condition x > 0 from the loop, since x is not changed in the loop. The keyword volatile suppresses this optimization.

Since this book does not deal with interrupt programming, the practical use of volatile variables is not pursued further.

16.4 The old language standard of Kernighan and Ritchie

I am including the old K&R language standard because there are a lot of extremely good books from the early stages of C before the ANSI standard existed, and they are still worth reading (e.g. [4], [9], [10] and [11], see Appendix 16.5).

A C programmer should be able to read the programs written in the old style, and convert them to the ANSI form. It is not a big problem. The main differences are set out in the table below:

ANSI	K&R
Definition of a function	Definition of a function
	Parameters are listed in the function header and defined subsequently, but before the function block

ANSI	K&R

`int getline (char * s, int lim)`
`{`
`    ...`
`}`
	`int getline (s, lim)`
	`char * s;`
	`int lim;`
	`{`
	`    ...`
	`}`

Declaration of a function (Prototype)	Declaration of a function
	No information on parameters

`int getline (char * s, int lim);`
`or:`
`int getline (char *, int);`
	`int getline ();`

Function calls are the same in both language standards.

In the K&R standard, function definitions prefer to make use of the fact that there is a default data type, namely `int`. Kernighan and Ritchie defined their function `getline()`, for example, thus:

```
getline (s, lim)
char * s;
int lim;
{
    ...
    return i;
}
```

Here the C compiler assumes a data type with the function of the data type `int` if no data type is indicated.

It is also possible to define a function with the default data type `int` that does not return a value. Then a random value is returned by the function. For example, Kernighan and Ritchie's Hello world program in [2]:

```
main ()
{
    printf ("Hello, world!\n");
}
```

The default data type `int` also exists in the ANSI standard. (I have not used a default data type in my book. All functions have an explicit data type, and return a defined value except in the case of `void` functions.)

No.	Title
[1]	Dworatschek, Sebastian: Grundlagen der Datenverarbeitung Berlin, New York, Walter de Gruyter 1986 (German language only)
[2]	Kernighan, B. and Ritchie, D. (1978) *The C Programming Language*. Upper Saddle River, NJ: Prentice Hall PTR.
[3]	Axel T. Schreiner: Objektorientierte Programmierung mit ANSI-C Munich, Vienna, Carl Hanser Verlag 1994 (German language only)
[4]	Axel T. Schreiner: System-Programmierung in UNIX, Teil I Stuttgart, B.G. Teubner, 1984 (German language only)
[5]	Wirth, N. (1976) *Algorithms and Data Structures*. Englewood Cliffs, NJ: Prentice Hall.
[6]	Sedgewick, R. (1988) *Algorithms*, 2nd Edition. Reading, Mass. : Addison-Wesley.
[7]	Bentley, J. (2000) *Programming Pearls*, 2nd Edition. Reading, Mass. : Addison-Wesley.
[8]	Bach/Domann/Weng-Beckmann: UNIX. Handbuch zur Programmentwicklung Munich, Vienna, Carl Hanser Verlag 1987 (German language only)
[9]	Kernighan, B. and Pike, R. (1984) *The UNIX Programming Environment*. Upper Saddle River, NJ: Prentice Hall PTR.
[10]	Rochkind M. J. (1986) *Advanced UNIX Programming*. Upper Saddle River, NJ: Prentice Hall PTR.
[11]	Leendert Ammeraal: Programmdesign und Algorithmen in C Munich, Vienna, Carl Hanser Verlag 1989 (German language only)
[12]	Stevens, W. R. (1992) *Advanced Programming in the UNIX Environment*. Reading, Mass. : Addison Wesley.

16

GO AHEAD! ▪

Index